THE
PAYNE
STEWART
STORY

THE PAYNE STEWART STORY

Larry Guest

WOODFORD PRESS

Andrews McMeel
Publishing
Kansas City

02 03 04 05 06 RDH 10 9 8 7 6 5 4 3

A hardcover edition of this book was published in 2000
by Andrews McMeel Publishing and Woodford Press.

Book design by Holly Camerlinck

Cover design by Jim Santore

Cover photo: Payne Stewart at St. Andrews Old Course in Scotland,
wearing knickers made from his family's tartan during the British Open
Championship in 1995. Photo by Alex Jackson, AGJ—Golf Library.

ISBN: 0-7407-2221-2

Library of Congress Control Number: 00-101329

─────── **Attention: Schools and Businesses** ───────

Andrews McMeel books are available at quantity discounts with bulk
purchase for educational, business, or sales promotional use.
For information, please write to: Special Sales Department,
Andrews McMeel Publishing, 4520 Main Street, Kansas City, Missouri 64111.

To Christa, Dorrie, and Gina, who blossomed into successful and special young women, each in her own way, thanks mostly to the world's most loving and exemplary mother

c o n t e n t s

Acknowledgments

I'd like to offer my heartfelt gratitude to Woodford's Dave Burgin for being the feisty pit bull I've long admired; to Andrews McMeel Publishing's Allan Stark for taking a flier on a rumpled old sportswriter he didn't know from brushed truffles; to Woodford's Jim Santore for that inspired, traffic-stopping cover design; to the First Foundation's Randall James for his Christian spine and counsel; to Elaine Gallant, a volunteer research angel right out of the blue; to Payne's wonderful mother, Bee, and others of Springfield, Missouri's Stewart clan for their assistance and their faith in the pure intentions of this project; to my boss, Van McKenzie, and other *Orlando Sentinel* brass for their understanding and support during this demanding sprint; to CNN's Jim Huber for his research help; to Larry Rinker, Chuck Cook, Mark Lye, Peter Jacobsen, Phil Mickelson, Harvie Ward, the Reverend J. D. Collingsworth, Brian Bowen, Arvin Ginn, Perry Leslie, and others for their keen insights; to Scott Hoch for the courage to do what he knew was right; and to President George Bush, who in six paragraphs said what took me two hundred pages.

And, finally, to Payne himself, for becoming a compelling figure who inspired so many of us to strive to be better, giving persons.

Reflections on Payne Stewart

Former president George Bush is an avid golfer who keeps tabs on the PGA Tour. He knew Payne Stewart. Larry Guest asked President Bush for his thoughts about Stewart. These are the president's reflections.

Like all Americans who watch CNN, I followed the unfolding events of Payne's final flight with horror. Having had altitude training way back in my naval aviation days, I could understand how oxygen loss could be so devastating.

As the story unfolded, I vividly recalled that early training, when they would take new pilots up in a chamber, then have us remove our masks at altitude. We could see how fast we began to lose control of our minds and bodies.

I watched clips from the memorial services and wondered how Payne's family and friends could get through the emotion of it all. The bagpiper in Houston, at the Tour Championship, will always stand out in my memory. So will the great turnout of Payne's fellow players at the memorial—a true and heartfelt tribute.

I wrote a note of condolence. I knew Payne quite well, but not his family.

Barbara and I will always treasure a private little visit we had with Payne on day two of the Ryder Cup matches at Brookline. We were sitting "inside the ropes," up against a tree. Payne, following one of the matches, graciously stopped and had a good visit with us. We were again touched by his warmth and his humor.

Golf has lost a great competitor, but much more, one of its heroes. What a lovely man. Everyone who knew him, everyone who loves the game, will miss him for years to come.

Sincerely,

George Bush
Honorary Captain
1999 U.S. Ryder Cup Team

THE
PAYNE
STEWART
STORY

part one

THE END
OF A NEW
BEGINNING

Q&A

w i t h   T r a c e y   S t e w a r t

A significant part of the massive, bittersweet reaction to the charismatic life and tragic death of Payne Stewart was the uncommon strength displayed by his Australia-born wife, Tracey. Her willingness to appear as one of the speakers at Payne's globally televised memorial service, where she shared both tears and laughter in a sweet eulogy of her husband, served as compelling testimony to their strength and their love.

Insiders long knew that this mother of two was a force within the Stewart household. The long-standing joke was that Payne wore the knickers, but Tracey wore the pants. For most of their married life, she led and Payne followed. But the true insiders also knew and appreciated that when, in recent years, the flighty golf star matured and deepened his religious faith—when he became capable of leading—Tracey was wise enough to step aside and let him lead.

Although Payne and Tracey were deeply in love and devoted mates, in her first interview she demonstrated her uncommon ability to cope with his tragic and very public death, offering chilling details of their last hours together and the moments of uncertainty, then despair. This question-and-answer session came just thirty days after she and the rest of the world had watched on television as the chartered jet carrying the presumably dead and frozen bodies of her husband, two of his business representatives, a golf course architect, and two pilots streaked aimlessly on autopilot into oblivion.

Question: *You were such an obvious tower of strength in handling the shock of it all. How did you manage to get though those difficult first days?*

Tracey: I just knew it was what God wanted and it was in His plan. And that we were honored that He was using Payne to bring people closer to Him. And not only Payne, but also Robert Fraley and Van Ardan and the others who were on the plane. [The memorial service] made a huge impact all around the world.

Q: *When you first met Payne, nearly twenty years ago, what was he like?*
Tracey: He was always a person with strong beliefs in Christianity. From the beginning, that was one of the things that attracted me to him—what a wonderful and good person he was. You know—that he always tried to do the right thing.

Q: *When did you first notice that Payne's spirituality was growing significantly?*
Tracey: Probably when Paul [Azinger] was sick. He spent a lot of time with Paul right after Paul's cancer was discovered [in 1993] and he was really encouraged by Paul's faith. I think that triggered it. Then he started to go to a Bible study at First Baptist Church that was being led by [major-league pitcher] Orel Hershiser. Orel had been a friend for years. He was doing a Bible study at the church and he invited us to go. It's a couples' Sunday school class on Sunday morning. We started going often. And then after the U.S. Open loss in '98 [to neighbor and friend Lee Janzen, at San Francisco's Olympic Club], I think he realized there were more important things than just golf—his family, being a good person was pretty important, too. He kind of rededicated himself to his golf game as well as to everything else in his life.

Q: *You weren't at that '98 Open. Instead, he shared that Open week in the Bay Area with his mother, Bee.*
Tracey: Yes, the children and I stayed in Orlando. It was a wonderful time for Payne and his mother.

Q: *Others who knew Payne—competitors and the press—were stunned by the changes. In what ways did he change?*

Tracey: He just made a conscious effort to be a better person, basically, in everything he did. A better father, a better husband, a better friend, better son, better brother—everything he could possibly do.

Q: *What is your religious background?*
Tracey: I'm Catholic, born and raised. I went to Catholic schools all my life.

Q: *After you and your family became involved in the First Baptist Church of Orlando, with your two children attending the school there on the church campus, did you convert and join that church?*
Tracey: No, we're not actually members of the church. I'm still Catholic and Payne was Methodist and the kids go to a Baptist-supported school. So *(laughing)*, we're very well-rounded.

Q: *In the hours and days following Payne's tragic flight, did some aviation or other government official contact you with confirmations or developments?*
Tracey: No. Never have.

Q: *Never have?*
Tracey: No. All my information [about the resulting investigation] came out of the newspaper. Not a very good deal, I don't think.

Q: *When I knew the lead story in our paper was going to be a new development in the investigation of the crash, I started to brace you, but figured somebody probably had let you know.*
Tracey: No. That was news to me when I saw the paper. Not a very good deal, I don't think. There's definitely a problem there somewhere.

Q: *When did President Clinton call? The next day?*
Tracey: Yes, I believe that's right.

Q: *Can you share any of what he said?*

Tracey: Basically, that he was very sorry and that he knew about it from the beginning and that he was sending guys up [to the South Dakota crash site] to see what they could do. It was breaking his heart and they couldn't get any response. There were stories going around that they were going to shoot the plane down. He said that was ridiculous and was never an option. He said they'd rather a plane come down in one piece than in a thousand pieces. He was very nice, taking the time out to reassure me they were doing everything they could.

Q: *Who were the first people to arrive to give you help and support?*

Tracey: My girlfriends were all here straightaway. And [PGA Tour official] Jon Brendle from next door. Vivian [Silverton, daughter of Isleworth Country Club owner Joe Lewis] and a lot of my tennis friends were here immediately. Then the people from the church—pastors Jim Henry and J. B. Collingsworth. It seems like other people knew about it before I did because they were here straightaway. Billy Curry Jr. from Leader was here quickly and was a big help dealing with the media.

Q: *As much as you are comfortable doing so, can you take us through the start of that fateful day?*

Tracey: I was taking the children to school that morning. Van [Ardan, president of Leader Enterprises, which represented Payne] was coming to pick up Payne to take him to the airport. So, Payne had cooked the kids' breakfast while I was getting ready. I came down to say good-bye.

Q: *You kissed, I assume?*

Tracey: Yes, we hugged and kissed and told each other, "I love you." And I was supposed to join him that Sunday in Houston at the Tour Championship. We were going from there on to Valderrama [in Spain, for the World Golf Championship series event] together. The kids and I went out and got in the car. But I had forgot something, so I called back to Payne and he brought it out to the car. We kissed again. And as he was walking back up the stairs and I was backing out, we were blowing each other kisses. It was about eight o'clock.

Q: *What had you forgotten?*
Tracey: An ice pack. I had a bad neck that weekend. I had injured my neck and actually that's why I was taking the kids to school—because I had a chiropractor appointment. So Payne had brought that out. So I dropped the kids off at The First Academy. I went to the chiropractor and then went on about my business. I came home about noon. When I walked in from the garage, Gloria [Baker, the Stewart family secretary] was in the office talking on the phone. I noticed she had a strange look on her face. When she got off, she said, "That was a weird phone call." I said, "Why? What do you mean?" She said, "That was one of Payne's friends, saying F-16 fighter pilots are following Payne's plane." I looked at my watch and said, "That can't be true, because he would have been in Dallas an hour ago." Then the phone rang again and it was another friend saying the same thing. So I got on the phone and said, "Barry, where are you hearing this?" He said, "It's on TV." So I turned on the TV to CNN and began watching what everyone else was seeing. I called Cindy, one of the secretaries at Leader, and she said they had been called and told the pilots were incapacitated and that they were trying everything they could to get some response.

Q: *So that's when you tried Payne's cell phone?*
Tracey: Yes.

Q: *Once? Twice? Twenty times?*
Tracey: No. Just once. It rang and his voice came on.

Q: *It was his answering message?*
Tracey: Yes. He just says, "This is Payne Stewart's phone. Sorry,

he's not here right now. Leave him a message and I'll get it to him."

Q: *But it was Payne's voice, even though he was speaking in the third person?*
Tracey: Yes. Yes. So then I just kind of watched it on TV.

Q: *At that point, you had a pretty good idea . . .*
Tracey: Well, I knew it was his plane because Cindy had said they had called to say it was the right plane by the numbers on the tail. And I knew if he knew anything about all this and was on the ground he would call me. If he wasn't . . . well, I knew if they couldn't wake somebody up, the plane would run out of fuel because they had been going since they left Orlando, about nine o'clock. So, basically, I knew at that point what was coming. . . . That was it.

chapter 1

The Flight

ondale, October 25, 1999, broke brilliant and blue in central Florida, offering a perfect morning for flying as forty-three-year-old pilot Michael Kling and twenty-seven-year-old copilot Stephanie Bellegarrigue shuttled one of Sunjet Aviation's Learjet 35s across town to Orlando International Airport. The temperature was expected to climb to a chamber-of-commerce-proud seventy-eight degrees.

Kling and Bellegarrigue were making the minutes-long hop from Sunjet's headquarters at an airport in Sanford, a lake-dotted community on the northern edge of greater Orlando's three-county sprawl, to fetch passengers for a routine charter. All that might seem out of the ordinary was that one of the passengers on the flight-plan manifest was a world-famous celebrity, knickers-wearing professional golf champion Payne Stewart. But then both Kling and Bellegarrigue had long since grown accustomed to chauffeuring the rich and famous in and out of Orlando air space in well-appointed eight-seat private jets.

Entertainers. Sports stars. Captains of industry. Few others can afford the tariff for such convenience and luxury, even if they book from Sunjet's small fleet of older planes. Bellegarrigue had bragged just a few days earlier to her younger brother, Bobby, about meeting stock-car racing legend Richard Petty.

Kling, a former Air Force pilot with more than four thousand flight hours in jet aircraft, held an airline transport pilot's certificate with a rating for Learjets—although he had logged only about thirty-five hours in the command seat of a Lear. Married with three stepchildren, Kling was also an ordained minister working to launch his own international outreach effort, called Eagles Wings International. It would meld his love of flying and his love of mankind by transporting food and goods on missions to developing nations.

Bellegarrigue held the lesser commercial pilot's certificate and, according to Sunjet, had logged seventeen hundred hours. Born in El Salvador, the daughter of a physician, she had dropped out of Ohio State University to pursue her passion for flying at an aviation school, Embry-Riddle, in Daytona Beach.

The hop across town was to accommodate Stewart and his agents, Robert Fraley and Van Ardan, all of whom resided on the south side of Orlando. Negotiating Monday morning rush-hour traffic on crowded Interstate 4, which runs smack through downtown and all the way to the Sanford airport, would have required more than an hour and a considerable measure of self-restraint. So the charter was to commence at the Aircraft Service International Group's private terminal on the west side of Orlando International, where Stewart was accustomed to boarding one of the planes for which he owned a time-share segment with Flexjet, a subsidiary of the company that manufactures Learjets.

Stewart, in an arrangement similar to those used by fellow Orlando golf stars Scott Hoch, Lee Janzen, and Tiger Woods, leased one hundred hours of flying time annually from Flexjet to be whisked to and from golf's far-flung datelines in one of the company's gleaming, late-model Learjet 35A business jets. But the day's objective, a stopover in Dallas before Stewart reported for duty at the 1999 Tour Championship in Houston, was a prospective business deal arranged by Fraley and Ardan, the top two men at Leader Enterprises. So the excursion was on Leader's dime.

Fraley, forty-six, a former quarterback at the University of Alabama under coach Bear Bryant, founded Leader in the 1980s and built it into national prominence. Its clients included numerous NFL head coaches and athletes, such as Stewart, golfer Paul Azinger, and baseball pitcher Orel Hershiser. Family and friends would depict Fraley as a man softened in recent years.

Ardan, forty-five, was number two in the firm's pecking order, a civil engineer by education and a former stockbroker who was devoted to his wife and four children. His wife says he would leave "sweet, silly notes" of endearment for her to find, she said, "in funny places" like the laundry bin. While driving himself and Payne to the airport that morning, he had phoned her to say, "Debbie, I love you more than anything in the world."

A fourth passenger, Bruce Borland, a golf course architect out of Jack Nicklaus's stable, had been a late addition. The previous evening, he had been talked into taking the trip, possibly to partner with Stewart on the Dallas design project. Borland, forty, left his home near West Palm Beach very early that morning to make the two-hour drive to Orlando to catch the charter flight.

The day's main item of business, promoted by Fraley and Ardan, was a potential course design by Stewart for a residential country club development outside Dallas.

Fraley booked the Sunjet charter to take them to Dallas, drop off Stewart in Houston that evening, and return to Orlando. They might have used Payne's time-share arrangement and reimbursed him, but Sunjet's lower rates would save Leader several hundred dollars.

The tradeoffs were an older plane and a charter service that has acquired, in the Orlando aviation community, a reputation for cutting corners.

The company's founder and chief pilot, Jim Watkins, sixty-four, is something of a throwback aviator/adventurer with limited enthusiasm for contemporary paperwork and policies. In 1998, he brought in seventy-year-old Tom Turner, a veteran aviator respected in the industry, as director of operations to help improve Sunjet's standing with the Federal Aviation Administration (FAA).

The company had attracted the FAA's attention for several reasons, including the discovery of a secondary set of Hobbs meters—which measure hours of flying time—installed on planes under Sunjet management, bypassing the planes' primary Hobbs meters.

Such a practice could, in theory, shortchange the planes' owners of their share of charter-rental fees, since the secondary Hobbs meters could be used to hide hours actually flown. That also would permit extra flying hours to be squeezed in between required inspections and maintenance, which are pegged to Hobbs meter readings. The latter was the FAA's main concern. Turner said Sunjet had none of the required maintenance records for installation of the extra Hobbs meters. No one seemed to know how the secondary Hobbs meters got on the planes, said Turner, and the whole affair "turned into a sticky situation." The FAA, he added, ended up giving Sunjet an administrative slap on the wrist.

Another disturbing situation emerged in April 2000 when agents from the FBI, the FAA, and the Department of Transportation's Office of the Inspector General raided Sunjet with warrants to seize four executive jets and all records pertaining to aircraft maintenance, apparently in connection with Stewart's chartered flight. An FBI agent said the probe centered on "possible violations of federal law pertaining to maintenance and record-keeping and making false statements" during an investigation.

Although he described Sunjet as a "mom-and-pop operation that began growing fast and developed personnel problems," Turner said those issues were "all in the past now." He also emphasized that the plane sent to pick up Payne Stewart and his two agents that October morning had been maintained to government regulation.

KLING AND BELLEGARRIGUE WERE PARKED on the tarmac behind Aircraft Service's terminal, the plane's cabin door open, when Stewart and Ardan arrived in Ardan's car. They passed under a banner, hung four months earlier, that hinted at the state of Stewart's life. CONGRATULATIONS, PAYNE, it shouted, in tribute to his victory the previous June in the United States Open Championship. Stewart had notched his third major golf title (among eleven PGA Tour wins) for membership in golf's elite, and he was riding the crest of public adulation. A member of the winning U.S. Ryder Cup team just weeks earlier, he had become a popular and compelling national hero, imminently recognizable to even nongolfers, thanks to the distinctive and stylish knickers ensemble he wore in competition.

Passing through the terminal, he waved to Aircraft Service's manager Steve Smart, telling him they were on their way to Dallas. "See you next week," Stewart said brightly, then walked through the back doorway to the waiting aircraft. He smiled and shook hands in a friendly manner when introduced to the two pilots, exchanging pleasant small talk while his luggage and golf clubs were being loaded.

On this particular Learjet 35, with its assigned registration number of N47BA emblazoned in large black characters across its glistening white tail, the seating arrangement in the snug cabin featured the usual cluster of four seats in the middle, two facing forward and two facing aft, with a narrow aisle between them. A bench seat, capable of seating three, stretched across the back wall. A single, side-facing seat was forward, on the right side, just behind the cockpit and across from the entry door and compact galley. All of the seats were covered in plush gray upholstery with light gray trim.

Assuming this flight would be like a hundred others, Stewart settled into what he called the "Payne seat"—one of the forward-facing single seats.

Kling taxied the plane out toward the overly long Orlando International west runway, originally built to handle Strategic Air Command long-range bombers during the Cold War, and was quickly cleared by the tower. He pushed the dual throttles, and the little jet lurched forward, the twin Garrett turbofan engines providing the thirty-five hundred pounds of thrust that always startles first-time executive jet passengers, who must exert extra effort to hold their position if seated in one of the side- or aft-facing seats.

The plane rotated upward and streaked into the azure-blue Florida sky at 9:19 A.M., its monitoring passed within minutes from Orlando International air traffic controllers to those in Jacksonville. There are indications, explained in a later chapter, that within the first few minutes of the flight Payne fetched from his briefcase a little book given to him by its coauthor, former Tour pro Wally Armstrong. *In His Grip* is an inspirational tome that parallels religious principles in life and in golf.

Because the crew had filed an instrument flight plan, controllers would be following their movements from Orlando all the way to Love Field in Dallas. They were vectored on a northwesterly heading to a VOR—a stationary navigational device that sends out an electronic Morse code signal—in north Florida. From there, they would turn almost due west for the long leg to Dallas.

As the flight approached Gainesville, an air traffic controller's voice came over the little jet's radio.

"Lear Four Seven Bravo Alpha. This is Jacksonville Center."

"Good morning, Jax," Bellegarrigue answered. "Four Seven Bravo Alpha. Two-three-oh for two-six-oh," she said, explaining that they had climbed from 23,000 feet to their assigned intermediate altitude of 26,000 feet.

"Lear Four Seven Bravo Alpha. Jacksonville Center. Climb and maintain flight level three niner zero."

"Three nine oh. Bravo Alpha," she acknowledged. Kling began nosing the plane upward toward 39,000 feet.

That response would be the last anyone would receive from Bravo Alpha.

At 9:34 the Jacksonville controller tried to reestablish radio contact in regard to the flight-planned turn west. "November Four Seven Bravo Alpha. Contact Jacksonville Center on one three five point six five."

Nothing.

"November Four Seven Bravo Alpha. Contact Jacksonville Center on one three five point six five."

Still nothing.

The controller tried again. And a fourth try.

Nothing.

Instead of turning at the VOR, the plane kept climbing and holding that northwesterly course.

Over the next three hours, it became apparent that what had happened over north Florida was that the plane, for whatever reason, had lost cabin pressure, and the pilots, for whatever reason, were unable to correct that rapidly fatal circumstance. Stewart and the five others quickly succumbed to hypoxia, or oxygen starvation. Medical science and simulations in a hyperbaric chamber tell us that this is likely what happened that Monday morning over north Florida:

An alarm sounded when the air pressure level inside the cabin plunged. Stewart and the others were startled by their eyes watering and popping out of their sockets. Dust swirled about the little cabin, and the temperature plunged quickly to below freezing. Within a matter of seconds, water vapor inside the cabin condensed as fog, and the windows began frosting over.

The passengers began experiencing sudden hot and cold flashes and the feeling of ants crawling across their skin. Stewart, no doubt, curiously noticed the skin beneath his fingernails turning blue and his senses of touch and pain diminishing as dizziness, blurred vision, and slurred speech gave way to a moment of euphoria before he lost consciousness. In short order, his oxygen-deprived heart shut down in a fatal coronary.

Within a matter of minutes, the reigning U.S. Open champion, his two agents, the golf architect, and the two pilots essentially died in their sleep. Aviation officials refer to humans aloft as "souls." The irony is that probably before N47BA had even crossed into the southwest corner of Georgia, the six "souls" had departed the craft, leaving six frozen cadavers to endure a bizarre trek through America's heartland on a three-hour ride to oblivion. What would happen during the remainder of the flight, from the standpoint of the six "souls" who had taken off from Orlando, had become both moot and inevitable.

AT 10:08, EASTERN TIME, at the FAA's request, two F-16 Air Force fighter jets scrambled from Tyndall Air Force Base to overtake and visually inspect the unresponsive Learjet. Ten minutes later, the Tyndall jets deferred to an Eglin Air Force Base jet that was aloft on a routine training maneuver over the Florida panhandle. Captain Chris Hamilton, thirty-two, topped off his tanks from an airborne fuel tanker, then sped north at 600 miles per hour for fifty minutes, finally overtaking the craft as it approached Memphis, Tennessee.

"When I closed in, I expected to just look in the cockpit and make eye contact with the pilot and get a thumbs-up that everything was okay," Hamilton would recount months later. "I was figuring it was just a radio malfunction or something. I never expected to see anything as catastrophic as what I saw."

Flying alongside about fifty feet off the Learjet's left wing, Hamilton could see that the cockpit windows were frosted over completely, a certain sign of cabin depressurization. Authorities said the plane continued cruising along on the fixed-course setting and was gradually "porpoising"—dipping to 38,000 and peaking as high as 51,000 feet. There was no movement apparent inside the craft.

"It's a very helpless feeling to pull up alongside another aircraft," Hamilton said after returning to base, "and realize the people inside that aircraft potentially are unconscious or in some other way incapacitated. And there's nothing I can do, even though I'm just fifty feet away, to help them at all."

Hamilton gave way to two more F-16s dispatched from the Oklahoma Air National Guard in Tulsa, which would later be relieved by two pairs of

F-16s scrambled out of the Dakotas. They would escort the mute Learjet on the final segment of its doomed flight.

As the plane streaked past St. Louis, Payne's cell phone would ring, drowned out by the depressurization alarm blaring nonstop inside the foggy, icy cabin. The call was Tracey Stewart's desperate attempt to reach him; she had just returned home from a chiropractic treatment only to be jolted by the horrific televised reports speculating that Payne was on board. If he were not on the plane, then surely he would answer. She hoped with all her might that he would come on, say he was on the ground in Dallas, and curiously ask why she was calling. Instead, the answering mode kicked in with a recording of Payne's own voice instructing the caller to leave a message at the tone. Tracey did, but knew in her sinking heart it was futile.

At 12:13 P.M. eastern time, almost three hours after the Learjet had taken off, officials of the Northeast Air Defense sector notified all parties involved that calculations projected one hour of fuel remaining in the jet, based on information that it had taken on a full load of slightly more than six hundred gallons that morning. Another hour of flight would take the runaway Lear comfortably beyond Des Moines and other midwestern urban areas to the more sparsely populated Dakotas.

OFFICIAL U.S AIR FORCE TIMELINE LOG
OF N47BA EMERGENCY
(All times are eastern daylight.)

10:08—Tyndall AFB alert. Fighters scrambled for civilian in-flight emergency. FAA requested emergency escort.

10:10—Tyndall fighters airborne.

10:22—Tyndall fighters released. F-16A from Eglin diverted to escort.

10:52—Emergency track on flight plan from Orlando to Dallas at 39,000 feet. Aircraft jumped to 44,000. Air traffic controllers unable to talk to pilot. Type aircraft—Lear 35. Aircraft departed Orlando at 9:09.

11:00—Emergency track has five souls on board. Still no contact.

11:09—Memphis Center reports F-16 intercepted the aircraft. No movement in cockpit. Probable autopilot.

11:14—Memphis Center requests additional support. Southeast Air Defense sector reports emergency out of their area of responsibility. Recommend Western Air Defense sector take over.

11:25—Lear 35 tail number N47BA.

11:44—Eglin fighter diverts to St. Louis for fuel.

11:59—FAA advises four F-16s from Tulsa and a tanker (KC-135) moving to escort.

12:03—Northeast Air Defense scrambles two F-16s from Fargo, North Dakota (unarmed).

12:13—Northeast Air Defense sector reports aircraft should have one hour of fuel remaining. Flight path on 320 heading over mostly sparsely populated area.

12:16—Northeast Air Defense sector reports aircraft will run out of fuel in the vicinity of Pierre, South Dakota.

12:22—Fargo fighters airborne.

12:35—Fargo has two more F-16s on runway alert.

12:50—Second set of jets scrambled from Fargo. Western Air Defense sector has radar contact on emergency aircraft.

12:54—Fargo, North Dakota, fighters intercept emergency aircraft.

1:00—Fargo F-16s relay windows are fogged with ice. No flight control movement noted. Fargo F-16s thirty minutes fuel remaining.

1:05—Four Tulsa F-16s on KC-135 refueling on standby.

1:13—Second set of Fargo F-16s suited up [armed] on immediate alert.

1:14—Western Air Defense sector reports in-flight emergency beginning to spiral.

1:16—F-16s report Lear 35 spiraling through clouds at 4620N, 9855W.

1:20—Contact lost. Western Air Defense sector passes all information to Air Force Rescue Center.

1:24—Western Air Defense reports possible field on fire. Two farmers on ground investigating.

1:35—Western Air Defense sector reports crash five to ten miles south of Mina, South Dakota, in swampland.

1:36—Tulsa F-16s return to base.

1:40—Fargo fighters maintain cap over field while two others refuel.

1:47—Western Air Defense sector reports troopers on the scene, FAA no longer requires assistance. All assets return to base.

THE POSSIBILITY THAT THE JET MIGHT CRASH into a population center had raised the ugly specter of shooting down the Learjet 35 over open terrain. Pentagon spokesman Kenneth Bacon would later say that the military had never considered a shoot-down. However, two armed F-16s—"suited up," in military parlance—were placed on alert at Fargo, North Dakota, just moments before the daunting episode ended. Bacon said they were never ordered to take off.

Almost four hours to the minute after takeoff from Orlando International, one engine shut down. The little craft nosed over and began spiraling down through the clouds, gathering speed as it hurtled in a steep, eight-mile dive. With one engine still running and providing thrust, the plane reached about 600 miles per hour before impact at more than one hundred times the force of gravity.

"We know that," National Transportation Safety Board investigator Bob Benzon would say, "based on the fact that the flight recorder is guaranteed to one hundred Gs, and it broke." In fact, the virtually indestructible device was so damaged that the NTSB would send it to its manufacturer in Seattle for help in decoding flight sounds from the memory chips that were found dangling from the recorder.

When the jet plowed into that soft field a few miles outside the village of Mina, South Dakota, its nose penetrated more than ten feet below the surface, reaching the subterranean water level. The plane and its inhabitants instantly disintegrated as the rear of the plane telescoped against the front. Two of Payne's golf clubs, which had been stowed in a rear baggage compartment, would be found mangled against the nose cone. Except for a few scattered pieces, the wreckage was contained in its own thirty-by-forty-foot crater.

South Dakota Governor William Janklow, who visited the scene two hours after the crash, said, "There was one engine and a wing tank.

Otherwise, the next biggest pieces were only a couple of square feet. The airplane was totally obliterated. The human beings inside were destroyed just like the airplane."

A Careflight emergency medical helicopter was dispatched to the scene but returned to its Aberdeen hospital empty. One investigator would later confide that he and other members of the team "were literally collecting human remains in sandwich bags." Of the combined nine hundred pounds of body weight among the two pilots and four passengers, less than thirty pounds of identifiable human remains were recovered.

THE TEAM OF INVESTIGATORS began the tedious assignment of examining and reassembling portions of the plane fragments in hopes of determining cause. By the early spring of 2000, some five months after the crash, the NTSB had not released its findings, although it was known the probe centered on various components of the Learjet 35 pressurization system and the backup oxygen system that could have—*should have*—saved the day. Cabin pressure and heat are supplied by compressed bleed air flowing over the engines. Outflow valves at each end of the cabin regulate the pressure, allowing just enough air to escape to keep the cabin air pressure close to what it is at 8,000 feet while the craft climbs into the thinner air of much higher altitudes, where there is insufficient oxygen to support human life.

An FAA source, speaking on condition of anonymity, said the main focus of the investigation centered on those outflow valves and the emergency oxygen supply, which has to have its control knob turned to the "on" position to function in an emergency. The cabin outflow valves and the emergency oxygen control, which is located at the copilot's knee, are both items on the copilot's preflight walk-around inspection and on in-cabin safety checklists. The possibility that the emergency oxygen system malfunctioned or that the control knob was not positioned properly would be considered logical reasons why the pilots were unable to engage the system to save themselves and their passengers when the cabin pressure alarm went off.

When hypoxia sets in, the period of useful consciousness is a matter of seconds; for that reason, many pilots undergo training in hyperbaric chambers to recognize hypoxia symptoms quickly and react swiftly. The higher the altitude, the shorter the reaction time. Aviation medical experts say the time of useful consciousness at 22,000 feet is five to ten minutes. At 25,000 feet, it's three to five minutes; at 30,000 feet, one to two minutes. If Payne's jet was nearing its assigned 39,000 feet when cabin pressure was lost, the pilots may have had as little as twelve seconds in which to put on their quick-don masks and send the plane into a saving dive to lower altitudes.

Yet eight of ten pilots who haven't rehearsed the event take fifteen seconds or longer to respond with corrective action when they experience a loss of cabin pressure, according to U.S. Air Force research using simulators. What's more, during an actual emergency, a loss of cabin pressure is not as obvious as it is in the hyperbaric chamber. The oxygen depletion and its ensuing symptoms, initially undetected by a plane's crew or passengers, are usually more insidious.

If an outflow valve were to allow too much air to escape, the cabin pressure would mimic the steadily diminishing outside pressure as the plane climbed to its assigned altitude. That scenario would appear to be consistent with all that could be observed as Stewart's flight hurtled northwest on autopilot, bound for oblivion. A rupture in the cabin fuselage, a cracked window or an unsealed door would have created a sudden, or "explosive," loss of pressurization. But none of the military chase pilots who flew alongside could see any signs of visible damage.

That suggests the problem was more like the vast majority of pressure-loss cases in commercial aircraft, where the loss is gradual, or insidious, rather than instantaneous. However, a prevalent theory within the investigative team was that the outflow valve located on the forward wall of the cockpit blew out and into the front bulkhead.

That would result in explosive loss of cabin pressure and the damage would not have been visible to the F-16 chase pilots. Turner, the Sunjet operations director, noted that the emergency oxygen lines are in close proximity to that outflow valve and subject to damage if the valve blows out.

This particular Lear had experienced a problem during its previous flight. There were reports that Sunjet replaced a valve two days before Payne's ill-fated flight and had failed to flight-test the repair properly.

Sunjet president James Watkins, son of the founder, said it was a

$12,000 engine modulation valve—another component of the pressurization system—that was replaced, not the outflow valve, and that the plane indeed had been taken aloft to test the repair. However, the Sunjet pilot who said he flew the test said he ascended only to 15,000 feet, less than half the altitude typically assigned to Learjets.

The flight recorder on board was of little help to investigators because it was the type that ran on a thirty-minute loop, constantly rerecording over itself. So after the memory chips were decoded, only the final thirty minutes of the flight could be heard. The chips confirmed that the cabin-pressure alarm had been activated, but gave no telltale sounds from the initial moments after cabin pressure was lost.

Of the nine documented instances over the past fifteen years when Learjet 35s have lost cabin pressure, Federal Aviation Administration records show that most were caused by malfunctions in the valves or regulators that control pressurization. The compromising of an outflow valve could be caused by something as simple, experts say, as a faulty landing-gear squat switch or an electrical short that would keep the solenoid of the valve in the full open, or ground-level-pressure, position. Falling cabin pressure becomes more critical in business aircraft than in commercial airliners because of the relatively small cabin-air volume in business planes. The Learjet 35's cabin is just 268 cubic feet, or roughly the size of a typical walk-in closet. The cabin measures just four feet, eleven inches at the widest point and has just four feet, four inches of headroom.

Pilots tend to scoff at the likelihood of depressurization, saying it only happens in hyperbaric simulators and aging planes. The plane Stewart's agent booked for this flight was twenty-three years old, having flown more than ten thousand hours and executed more than seventy-five hundred takeoffs and landings. In late 1977, Learjet began to include an emergency-pressurization backup system that automatically activates if the cabin pressure falls to what it would be at approximately 9,500 feet. But that was more than a year after this plane had rolled off the production line, in April 1976.

The Flexjet service that Stewart and other Orlando Tour pros more routinely use purges its fleet of any plane that reaches five years of age. Flexjet hires only highly experienced pilots, who are then put through a constant and rigid program of training and testing. "This isn't to suggest Sunjet's pilots are not capable," said Dave Franson, a spokesman for Flexjet's parent company, "but [the pilots who flew the Learjet 35] didn't have the same qualifications and training that we require."

ON NOVEMBER 10, more than two weeks after the crash, the NTSB investigation team released the recovered personal effects and human remains. That day would have been the Stewarts' eighteenth wedding anniversary. The family-assistance unit of the NTSB made the arrangements to ship the personal-effect items by air and to make them available to the victims' families that afternoon in Orlando.

Tracey Stewart and the widows of the two agents decided to go together to lend one another support for this emotionally charged moment. Tracey, Debbie Ardan, and Dixie Fraley, filled with anxiety, were somberly greeted by an official, who asked if they wanted him to accompany them into the room. They declined and, haltingly, entered the room containing the last vestiges of their husbands. Inside they found three small, sealed containers of the personal effects, each carrying a neatly stenciled name.

Tracey reached out and took the other women's hands. "Let's pray," she said, and began praying aloud.

Later she would tell a friend, "There was such a spirit of God in that room that we were overwhelmed by what was going on. And so grateful to have even partial remains and a few personal items."

The recovered items included Payne's wedding band, which had been bent into an oval, his Southern Methodist University college ring, and the simple, fabric WWJD wristband that Aaron Stewart had given his father. Only the clasp of the wristband—carrying the abbreviation of the guideline for daily Christian living What Would Jesus Do?—had been damaged. Tracey had the clasp replaced and began wearing the bracelet.

Also recovered was Payne's briefcase, damaged and bloody. And the little inspirational book from Wally Armstrong was so soiled, Tracey would tell Armstrong, that it looked as if it had been in a cornfield for months.

The sparse human remains were in the control of Edmunds County (South Dakota) coroner John Hein, who contacted the six families and was instructed to cremate the remains, except for Payne's. Tracey instructed Hein to put her husband's remains—no matter how limited—in a full-sized casket and ship it to Orlando.

Hein complied, placing the body parts—Payne's left hand, part of a hip, and several teeth identified with the help of X-rays sent from his old hometown dentist in Springfield—in a vinyl body pouch. He anchored the pouch inside a sealing casket.

The casket was shipped that day from Sioux Falls on a Northwest Airlines connection through Minneapolis and on to Orlando, where it was received that evening by Baldwin-Fairchild Funeral Home under a veil of strict confidentiality. Tracey visited the funeral home, where one of the directors urged her not to open the casket. The gruesome sight, he reasoned, would not make for a pleasant lasting memory. She agreed, gave the man a few of Payne's personal items she had brought from home to place inside the casket, and finalized plans for a very private burial.

That Sunday afternoon, November 14, as the Florida sports world began focusing on the heated annual University of Florida–Florida State football clash in the week ahead, workers at the Dr. Phillips Cemetery, just a few blocks from Payne and Tracey's first Orlando home, bought sixteen years earlier, lowered the casket without ceremony or ritual. Only Tracey and the two children looked on.

The Dr. Phillips Cemetery is an idyllic little patch of central Florida, green and manicured, that slopes down to a central pond with a fountain spraying constantly in the breeze. Dotted around the pond are picturesque gnarled oaks. It has more the look of an airy park than a cemetery, in part because there is no signage to identify it as such and above-ground headstones are not permitted. Each grave is required to have a simple, rectangular marker, recessed to ground level. Those driving by on Apopka-Vineland Road, the busy four-lane boulevard that runs across the front of the grounds, hardly realize it is a cemetery. Giving it away is an occasional spray of flowers at a gravesite—like the one on the grassy slope where Payne is interred, in the afternoon shade of one of those oaks and not far from the edge of the pond.

Payne's marker, placed four months later, is etched with his familiar silhouette in a golf swing follow-through, one of his favorite verses of scripture from the Psalms, and an endearing phrase Tracey had used in her eulogy at the memorial service four days after the tragedy. In Springfield, Missouri, Bee Payne-Stewart had ordered a small four-sided monument that she said would be placed in Hazelwood Cemetery in her son's honor. "We need that for history," she reasoned.

Bee and Payne's two sisters had become upset about being told of the burial days after the fact. In an attempt to make amends for that oversight, Tracey began sharing little updates with the family. These included her visit to the gravesite on January 30—Super Bowl Sunday—which would have been Payne's forty-third birthday. She and the two children placed an arrangement of lilies at the head of Payne's still-unmarked grave, joined hands for a moment of prayer, and departed.

Tracey eased her car back up the unpaved driveway some fifty yards to that four-lane road, which local government officials were trying to rename. By early spring, they were anticipating Florida Department of Transportation approvals to officially rededicate it as Payne Stewart Boulevard.

chapter 2

The Dark Bulletin

L unchtime on this particular Monday found Randall James and Jim Henry over their noon meal in Faith Hall in the sprawling campus complex that is First Baptist Church of Orlando. They shared the meal to discuss church business.

James, fifty-three, is an Orlando institution, a sad-eyed and soft-spoken survivor of colon cancer, lung cancer, and twenty years as the top aide to three Orlando mayors. After retiring from politics, he took on the post of president of The First Orlando Foundation, the church's fund-raising arm that supports various outreach programs, including the one-thousand-student K-through-12 First Academy, where young Chelsea and Aaron Stewart have attended the past five years. It is a labor of love for James.

Henry, sixty-two, is the longtime pastor of First Baptist and a former two-term president of the Southern Baptist Convention. A charismatic and gifted pulpiteer, he fashions gripping contemporary sermons by deftly blending scripture with folksy humor acquired from his Tennessee rearing. A visible and inspirational figure throughout the region, Henry was honored as the 1997 Floridian of the Year.

Shortly before one o'clock, the two men departed for their respective offices, Henry's in the expansive main sanctuary building just across the lawn and James's in downtown Orlando some five miles up Interstate 4. But a moment before James reached his black Buick Park Avenue sedan, his pager went off. He recognized the red numbers on the digital display as those of his office phone. He punched the numbers into his cell phone and a staffer blurted the numbing news: There were myriad media reports that a private jet was out of control, and speculation that it was a flight chartered by the pro golfer Payne Stewart.

Just ten days earlier James had presided over the foundation's upscale annual banquet, whose purpose on that occasion was to bestow Payne with the organization's Legacy Award. The golfer had been selected mainly for his brief but effective religious witness to the world media on the eighteenth green at Pinehurst, moments after winning the U.S. Open in June 1999. In the course of several discussions and meetings with Payne concerning the award and the approaching banquet, James had become enamored of this gregarious sports star, whom he had previously known only from a distance. Then, just three weeks before the banquet, James had been overwhelmed when Payne informed him that he and Tracey had decided to give $500,000 to the foundation, to be earmarked for the budding athletic complex at The First Academy.

James clicked off his cell phone, wheeled around, and *ran* across the lawn, up a flight of stairs, and down the long corridor leading to Henry's office. Standing in front of Sandi Mathis, Henry's secretary, he delivered the emergency request to see Henry in single words separated by gulps of air. She poked her head into Henry's office and said, "It's Randall James, and it's an emergency."

Baffled, Henry said, "How could it be an emergency? I just left him not two minutes ago."

In an instant, James, his chest still rising and falling, delivered the dark bulletin.

"I don't know what the truth of this is, but that's the information I just received," he said.

Before they knelt in prayer for Stewart's safety, James looked the pastor right in the face and could see his eyes welling up.

"He appeared broken just at the prospect all this could be true," James later recalled. "I had kind of a feeling of shock. I was scared and felt a big knot in my stomach. And I could tell Jim felt the same way."

James returned to his car and drove quickly to his office, pushing the speed limits as he does when suffering occasional and excruciatingly painful kidney-stone attacks in the middle of the night. At his office, James joined his two staffers, who sat mesmerized by the ongoing TV coverage.

When confirmation came that it was, indeed, Payne's plane and that it had crashed, James quickly called back to the church for Henry, who said he and First Academy headmaster Ed Gamble were leaving for the Stewart house. James agreed to meet them there.

As James was scurrying out of the foundation's offices, he passed the postman, who dropped off the day's batch of mail. Chillingly, one of the envelopes held a check from Payne for $150,000—the first installment of that $500,000 donation.

Looking back on the day six weeks later, Henry attempted to put it all into perspective. "I would say in all my years of pastoring, Payne's death, combined with the memorial service that followed, has been the most dramatic impact of affecting other people across the board, of any single event I can remember. The only thing I can think of that would come close to it would be when President Kennedy was assassinated. The drama—the trauma, the thing of so many people remembering where they were and what they were doing when it happened—was unique. That's only the second time in my forty years of pastoring that I can remember so many people comparing and relating that they'd never forget where they were when Payne's plane went down."

BEE PAYNE-STEWART, who joined her maiden and married names after Payne's father died, had gone to her regular water aerobics class in Springfield, Missouri, that October Monday morning, then joined her friend Lavonne Wilson for lunch at McSalty's, their favorite pizza place. Arriving home after lunch, she discovered one of her daughters, Lora Stewart Thomas, waiting at the door with a look of distress.

"Mom, why are all the radio stations trying to reach you?"

They went inside, clicked on the TV, and discovered why. CNN was reporting on the runaway plane nearing the Dakotas and speculating that Payne was aboard. "That can't be true," Bee insisted to Lora, her tone more hopeful than confident. She reasoned that Payne had called her that very morning on his cell phone on the way to the airport in Orlando. He was flying to Dallas, not the Dakotas.

"He said he was going to Dallas a day early on his way to the tournament in Houston," she recalled a month later. "He said they want to build a golf course and sell some lots around it. I kept watching the TV and kept thinking it isn't right, it isn't right. My friends all started coming in. I was just crazy. No one was calling to tell me anything officially. I still haven't heard anything officially from anybody. I only knew what was in the news."

CHUCK COOK, WHO HAD BECOME much more than merely the swing coach in Payne Stewart's life, was scheduled for a working session with him the next day in Houston. To break free, Cook had lumped several of his amateur students into sessions that Monday at the Barton Creek Country Club's Lakeside Course, outside Austin. Had he followed his usual routine, Cook would have taught until noon, then had lunch in the clubhouse. But on this particular day, he had inadvertently failed to take along enough blank videotapes for his lessons. So at lunchtime, he drove to a nearby convenience store where he could buy some tapes and top off the gas in his boat, anchored in the marina alongside the store.

Ordinarily, Cook doesn't check his phone messages during lunch. But while still sitting in his car after driving back to the club, he decided to click on his cell phone and see if anyone had called. The display lit up and noted that he had twenty-one messages. "What in the world!" he blurted aloud, punching up the first one.

It was from Bob Estes, one of his other Tour pros, calling from Houston. "I don't know if you've heard or not, but there's a plane out of control that's flying across the United States and they think it's Payne."

Jolted by the message, Cook clicked on the next three, all similar to the first.

He started his car and swung by the Lakeside pro shop to ask one of the staff assistants to call his students and cancel his afternoon lessons. He gunned his car toward his home nearby, listening to more messages on his cell phone as he went. They were all the same: frantic bulletins from relatives, from Payne's caddie, Mike Hicks, from another of Cook's Tour pro students, Omar Uresti, from a reporter with the Austin newspaper. Because the passenger list on the plane wasn't known initially, many had feared that Cook, who occasionally flew with Stewart, also might be on board.

Cook raced into his house and flipped on CNN. The first report he saw was speculation that five people were aboard the plane. The knot in his stomach doubled at the thought that Payne's entire family was on the runaway jet. He flashed back to the many nights he had spent in Payne's lake-front mansion, his children sweetly offering dinner-table blessings that always included thanks for Cook's safe journey to Orlando.

Then he realized that two of the five people on board were pilots, leaving Payne and two unnamed passengers.

"I knew Tracey's parents [Shirley and Norm Ferguson] were in Orlando at the time to keep the kids, which allowed Tracey to travel with Payne on some of these trips," Cook later recalled. "So I thought for sure Tracey was on the plane. Then I thought that maybe Shirley was watching the kids and Norm had gone with Payne. I kept going through scenarios. I knew they had just completed the Disney tournament, and I had talked to him and he had mentioned he was going to Dallas to look at a golf course. But at that moment I didn't remember that. I was too upset to think. And I thought maybe he'd taken [Tour pro] Justin [Leonard], because they had gotten very close before and after the Ryder Cup, and he was just giving Justin a ride home to Dallas and was going down to Houston after dropping off Justin."

Cook resisted calling Tracey and instead called Payne's Orlando representation firm, Leader Enterprises, only to hear a recorded message that the offices had closed. Within moments, CNN reported that the plane had crashed in the Dakotas. Cook dialed the Stewart home. He reached Gloria Baker, the family secretary, who gave him the passenger list. All gone.

Cook and his wife immediately began packing for Orlando. Cook's daughter, a student just across town at the University of Texas, also wanted to make the trip. "She and Payne really hit it off," said Cook "She'd tease Payne by gigging him with some SMU joke and he'd come back with a U.T. joke."

LARRY RINKER, A JOURNEYMAN PRO who'd enjoyed an off-and-on friendship with Payne since they'd first earned their Tour cards in the 1981 spring qualifying school, strolled into a Hallmark store not far from his home in Winter Park, a tony suburb of Orlando, at lunchtime that Monday. His wife, Jan, had a birthday in two days, and Larry wanted to buy her a card before he headed off the next morning to play in that week's Tour stop, the Southern Farm Bureau Classic outside Jackson,

Mississippi. He was just reaching for his first card when his cell phone rang. It was Jan: "Have you heard about this plane that's flying off course? There are a couple of Air Force F-16s flying alongside it. . . . It's a Learjet, a private plane, headed for Dallas."

She needed to say no more. Rinker filled in the blank: "It's Payne."

Rinker had immediately drawn on a conversation with fellow pro Lee Janzen the previous day in the parking lot at the Disney World Classic. Just making small talk, Rinker had asked Janzen if he was flying with Payne, as he often does, to Houston for the Tour Championship that week. Actually, Janzen had failed to make the field, but he'd replied only that Payne was going Monday to take care of some sort of business in Dallas. When Jan told Rinker that a Lear bound for Dallas was in serious jeopardy, a vision of Payne seated in the plane raced into his mind's eye.

"I just hoped it wasn't him. We didn't know anything for sure at that time. I don't know why I said it, but I just said, 'It's Payne.' So Jan called [Tour pro Scott] Hoch and called me right back and said the Hochs think it is Payne's plane. I then called the commissioner [PGA Tour commissioner Tim Finchem] and got a secretary and said it was an emergency. I told her what I knew and she said the FAA already had called and that they think it's Payne's plane. So now I'm just in shock. I remember looking down at the cards and I couldn't even go there. I mean, I couldn't even begin to think about getting a card for my wife. So I drove home, which was only a few minutes away.

"All this time the plane was still in the air and, on TV, they were talking about maybe having to shoot it down. They were concerned that it might hit a populated area. So this whole time, now, I'm hoping it's not Payne's plane. As I watched it for a while, nobody on CNN was saying it is Payne's plane. Then they say they think it is. I never thought things like, 'Are there other golfers on the plane?' I still was hoping it wasn't his plane. But then they confirmed it and the plane crashed. I still had to pack to go to Mississippi the next morning. I began putting a few things together and then wandered back in where the TV was on."

On the screen was a still photograph of his friend, with the caption "Payne Stewart, 1957–1999."

"I just went into the garage and cried my eyes out."

LEE JANZEN, PAYNE'S CLOSE FRIEND, Orlando neighbor, and U.S. Open nemesis—he edged Payne down the stretch of both the '93 and '98 Opens—had just reached the Bay Hill Club's third hole in a charity pro-am when his cell phone jangled. It was a friend who had seen the initial reports and was concerned that Janzen might be on this runaway jet that had been bound for Dallas.

"At the time, the reports didn't say who was on the plane," Janzen recalled. "But I knew immediately it was Payne because he had just told me two days earlier that he had to go to Dallas that day. It was awful. My knees got weak. I almost threw up."

Because he was still unsure just who was on the troubled flight, Janzen dutifully tried to hit his tee shot, but the ball squirted low into the right rough. He couldn't shake the strong feeling that the worst was probably true. As the group departed the tee, one of his amateur partners answered a cell phone call, and from the one side of the conversation he could hear and the grave look on the man's face, Janzen sensed that the news reports were increasingly grim.

"So I called my wife immediately. She was at Scott Hoch's house and they were all hysterical. So I left right then. I never got to my second shot."

MIDMORNING IN THE PORTLAND, OREGON, suburb of Lake Oswego found flamboyant Tour veteran Peter Jacobsen at home just starting his usual four-mile treadmill workout. He was watching a rerun of *Matlock* on the wall-mounted television set. The phone rang, and after a moment, Jacobsen's wife, Jan, advised him that the caller was Ed Ellis, president of Peter Jacobsen Productions. Just ten minutes into his forty-five-minute run, Peter asked her to take a message, but Jan, with a strange look on her face, countered that this was a call he really needed to take. So Jacobsen jumped off the treadmill, grabbed the extension, and hopped back on, hardly missing a stride.

"Hi, Ed. What's up?"

"You need to turn on CNN."

"Why? What's up?"

"I think Payne's in trouble."

Jacobsen's first thought was that there had been repercussions over Payne's Chinese impression on ESPN a few days earlier at the Disney

World Classic. British golf commentator Peter Alliss had criticized the U.S. Ryder Cup team's behavior by saying that the Americans were no closer to being like the British than were the Chinese. Payne had playfully fired back in an ESPN on-course interview with a stereotypical Chinese impression, and the politically correct police had briefly erupted.

"If it's that Chinese thing, I know Payne never meant any harm," Jacobsen told Ellis. "Just like Fuzzy [Zoeller] never meant any harm in that Tiger Woods thing."

"No, I think Payne's in *real* trouble," said Ellis, who was finding it difficult to say anything more than just that Payne was in trouble. Peter flipped the TV over to CNN.

The workout stopped. He sat in front of the TV for the next hour and a half. This was one of his fun-mates on Tour, a fellow jokester whose company he adored. This was his costar in their jocular Tour rock band Jake Trout and the Flounders. And his life was in danger.

"I started crying. I cried for four days," Jacobsen said a month later. "In fact, I'm starting to cry right now just recalling this. I remember getting off the treadmill and sitting in front of that TV, literally in shock. I didn't move for two hours, and that's hard for me to do."

When the TV news reported the plane had crashed, Jacobsen recalls that he actually lost his breath. "I had an intake and I couldn't breathe. I couldn't speak and I couldn't think. I remember my wife and I were bawling our eyes out."

PGA TOUR OFFICIAL MARK RUSSELL was changing planes in Atlanta, en route to Houston, when his cell phone buzzed. His wife, Laura, was calling from their home in Orlando with the disturbing early reports on television. Just before stepping onto his connecting flight to Houston, Russell called the Tour office near Jacksonville and was told that authorities feared that Payne Stewart was aboard the runaway aircraft.

A feeling of disbelief consumed him as he settled into his seat. One thought kept ringing in his mind: "How could this possibly happen?" As he deplaned in Houston, he pulled the captain aside and asked if he had any news. The captain was unaware of the Stewart flight problems, but after listening to what Russell had been told about the unresponsive pilots, he said that he used to fly Learjets, which are typically assigned to higher altitudes—40,000 feet and higher, above commercial air traffic.

"If there is an oxygen problem at that altitude," the captain told Russell, "you have only five to ten seconds to react."

PHIL MICKELSON, WHOM PAYNE HAD BEAT in dramatic fashion on the eighteenth green at Pinehurst five months earlier, was in his bedroom in Scottsdale, packing late that Monday morning for the Tour Championship. His mother-in-law called and told Phil and Amy to turn on CNN. There was an urgency in her voice as she relayed news of a plane in trouble and the chance that a professional golfer was aboard.

"For the next four hours, we just sat in our room and watched the news, flipping from station to station," Mickelson recalls. "I can't describe the feeling. It was awful."

FORMER PGA CHAMPION HAL SUTTON, whom Stewart already had promised would be his assistant captain if he were ever selected to captain the U.S. Ryder Cup team, was having lunch with his father, Howard, at the Roadhouse Grill, not far from his home in Shreveport, Louisiana. An acquaintance walked up to the table and asked if he knew that Payne's plane had just crashed.

"It was the most sinking feeling I've ever had in my life," said Sutton, whose thoughts turned to Payne's wife and their two beautiful children. "You put yourself in that situation and think about how often you fly, putting your own life and the lives of your family in the hands of others."

Sutton managed another bite of his lunch, then pushed the plate away. He looked at his father and shook his head silently, then excused himself. Driving home, Sutton silently reflected that he and Payne had lockered next to each other for eighteen years, an alphabetical happenstance. No more would they share a bench and small talk in front of their lockers. Tears blurred Sutton's vision, and he pulled over to the curb long enough to compose himself. At the Tour Championship in Houston the next day, Sutton would sit and gaze wistfully and painfully at the locker next to his, the one with his departed friend's name on it.

FRANK VIOLA, A FORMER BASEBALL PITCHER who lives in Orlando, had been overwhelmed by Payne's thoughtfulness six months earlier, when, as a birthday surprise, the golfer had fulfilled one of Viola's lifetime dreams. Payne had invited his good friend to fly with him to Augusta the week before the '99 Masters to play a practice round at the revered Augusta National Golf Club. For an avid amateur golfer like Viola, that was indeed a happy birthday.

Now Viola was on another golfing junket with several pals in North Carolina. They had played one course that fateful Monday morning, then driven to another for an afternoon round. It was about two o'clock, almost an hour after Payne's plane had gone down, when Viola walked into the pro shop.

The friendly, unassuming former big-league lefty makes a habit of introducing himself in the company of strangers, and now he stuck his hand across the counter at a twenty-something assistant pro. As he did, Viola noticed that the young man had tears in his eyes. Giving the pro his name, Viola said he couldn't help noticing that the young man was upset about something.

"Didn't you hear the news?" the pro asked.

"No. What happened?"

"Mr. Payne Stewart's plane has gone down."

Weeks later, Viola recalls his legs buckling, a vast emptiness consuming his innards.

"It just about knocked me to my knees. After I got myself together, I got on the phone to my wife and she caught me up on the situation," Viola said. "It's easier to talk about that moment now. It was impossible for days after it happened."

CHUCK DALY, WHO HAD RETIRED as the Orlando Magic coach four months earlier, flew to Chicago that Monday to address the fourteen head coaches of the Continental Basketball Association at the behest of CBA official Brendan Suhr, his longtime assistant at Detroit, New Jersey, and Orlando. Daly arrived in the lobby of the O'Hare Wyndham late that morning, embraced his old friend, and excused himself to freshen up in his room before lunch.

He flipped on the TV and was jolted by an early report of a private jet out of control, including speculation that a pro golfer might be on board. Daly remembers the tingle that ran through his scalp, accompanying the unshakable thought that one of his famous, former neighbors at Orlando's Isleworth Country Club was probably on the doomed jet. Back downstairs, he shared the grim news with Suhr. "I'm afraid it's one of our friends," Daly added, noting that Tiger Woods, Mark O'Meara, Lee Janzen, and Payne Stewart routinely booked Learjets.

After a quick lunch, Daly hustled back to his room to watch updates. In a moment, his worst fear materialized.

"When they confirmed it was Payne, it really hit me hard. It was very much like the same feeling I had when President Kennedy was killed. My heart sank. Suddenly, I was half sick," recalls Daly, who flashed back to that warm Payne Stewart smile he had so often enjoyed.

One of those smiles had come when Daly had first moved into Isleworth after taking over as Magic coach, in 1997.

"Payne was the first person to come and literally knock on the door and welcome me to the club," said Daly. "He came in and we had a wonderful visit, remembering the golf we shared at Barcelona during the Olympics. He was over there almost the entire time, playing with me and Michael [Jordan] and [Charles] Barkley. When I moved to Orlando, he was always so generous with me, coming over to the table at lunch, or giving me tips on the range or asking me to join him for several rounds of golf. A guy like me who is not a very good golfer can be disruptive to those guys' games, but he was always so gracious about it."

Suhr recalls Daly coming back downstairs at the Wyndham. "Chuck is a guy who is the greatest at keeping a tight rein on his emotions. He maintains his composure so well," said Suhr. "But he was in shock. It really affected him."

Last summer, right after Daly retired, his wife, Terry, sought some trinkets from several of the Isleworth Tour pros for Chuck's birthday. One was a pin flag from Pinehurst signed by the Open champ, Payne Stewart. "You can only imagine how special that is to me now," said Daly.

JOHN SHELTON WAS EN ROUTE from a reunion of his old University of Louisville football team to Jackson, Mississippi, that

Monday morning to spend a few days with his daughter, Susan; her husband, Dan Bennett; and the light of John's life, five-year-old grandson John Daniel Bennett. A folksy and likable sort with an active sense of humor and a selfless nature, Shelton had become an Orlando Realtor, residing and specializing in the Bay Hill area, following his career as a high school and college assistant football coach. Early in his playing career, Shelton had been the starting quarterback at the University of Louisville. He became a defensive back the day the coaches brought in a young signee with a crooked smile and asked Shelton to take the kid under his wing: a kid named John Unitas.

In 1983, Shelton showed Payne and Tracey Stewart around the Bay Hill area and sold them their first Orlando home. Payne and John became fast friends. The old coach occasionally played golf with the gregarious young Tour pro, or took him along on bird-hunting trips to south Georgia and fishing junkets to the private fish camp an hour out of Orlando where Shelton and former Louisiana State University football coach Charlie McClendon are members.

Now Shelton was scurrying through the Birmingham airport to make a tight connection to Jackson. He noticed a cluster of people intently watching a news report on TV and paused long enough to ask a man at the back of the pack what the story was. The man said there was a private plane in trouble, flying from Orlando to Dallas. Shelton, well-connected in Orlando, shuddered at the likelihood that he would know people on the plane. He hurried on to his gate and boarded for the short hop to Jackson; there he was met by his daughter.

"Daddy, have you been watching TV?" Susan asked. "There's a jet from Orlando to Dallas that's out of communication." Shelton mentioned hearing something about that in the Birmingham airport.

Moments later, they were at Susan's house and John was unpacking in the guest room when he heard the phone ring. Susan walked in and announced, "Daddy, it's Payne Stewart."

At first, he thought she had meant that Payne was on the phone and wondered aloud how in the world Payne would have known to call him at Susan's. He noticed tears welling up in her eyes as she softly corrected: "No, Daddy. It's Payne on that plane."

ALERTED TO THE EARLY NEWS REPORTS by one of his office staff, Ed Gamble, the hulking and good-natured headmaster at The First Academy, strode briskly into the school's library, where he could access CNN. His mind spun as he watched the ongoing coverage of Payne's unwavering and unresponsive jet. He flashed back to the good-natured ribbing he and Payne had often exchanged while in the stands watching their sons playing on the same basketball team the previous winter.

Payne's son, Aaron, was in the adjacent building in the same fifth-grade class as Gamble's son, Joseph. Payne's daughter, Chelsea, a ninth-grader, was in the next building, the middle school wing.

Gamble is a devoted, thirty-year educator, the son of an Army chaplain. But little had prepared him for this bizarre and troubling moment. "By that time, they had scrambled the military jets tailing the plane and were seeing that the windows were frosted and they couldn't see any life or motion inside," Gamble later recounted. "I'm thinking, 'Let's get Payne's kids out of class. Let's don't let them hear this by accident.' At this point, I didn't know that Van Ardan was also on the plane. The Ardans have three children in our school."

Gamble phoned Larry Taylor, the middle school principal, and instructed him to get the Stewart kids out of class, using whatever excuse he wanted, and to get them to the office in preparation for going home. His instinct was to call Tracey Stewart, though he didn't know if she was aware of what was happening. Thankfully, she said she was also watching CNN and had already sent a friend to the school to pick up Aaron and Chelsea.

Then he was advised that Van Ardan also was on the flight. He went through the same process, fetching the Ardan children from class and phoning Debbie Ardan. She was unaware of the situation. "So it was my unpleasant duty to inform her the plane was in distress," said Gamble, who then hooked up with Pastor Jim Henry and accompanied him to the Stewart home.

JIM HENRY AND ED GAMBLE found an Orange County sheriff's deputy at the Stewarts' driveway entrance, along with several print and television reporters, photographers, and cameramen. Henry and Gamble were waved through. They glided down the winding driveway past the tennis court and eased to a stop in the sprawling, three-story home's circular driveway, where Tracey Stewart was standing with a friend.

Henry walked toward Tracey, who grabbed him in a tight embrace. They both began crying. It was now 1:30 and the report had just come that the plane had crashed. They walked though the front door and into the house, where three wives of Tour players, Alicia O'Meara, Beverly Janzen, and Sally Hoch, were in conversation with several members of the Stewart family. Henry advised Tracey that the staff at The First Academy had not informed Aaron and Chelsea of the specifics of the emergency and asked if she wanted him with her when she broke the shocking news.

Tracey said she preferred to tell the children alone and then ask Henry to come in and counsel them. Within a few moments, the children arrived.

"Mommy, Dad's got my cell phone," said Aaron. "He'd call if something's wrong."

Tracey smiled sweetly at him, put her arms around her children's shoulders, and led them up the stairs to her bedroom. Fifteen minutes later, she emerged and asked Henry to come in. She returned to the bedroom, and when Henry entered he found the children sitting red-eyed but stoic on each side of their mother at the edge of the bed. Henry read a scripture, then led them in prayer.

By this time, Randall James and golfers Paul Azinger and Lee Janzen had joined the growing crowd of supporters. The pastor approached James and softly asked that he help Tracey draft a public response, a press release—a task James had performed many times during his long stint in the mayor's office. James went downstairs with Gloria Baker, the family secretary, and they crafted a statement in the ground-floor office. Baker typed it into a word processor and printed it out:

> We appreciate the heartfelt love and kindness shown by our friends and loved ones in our loss of Payne. We know he is with the Lord, and in that we take comfort. Please keep the Stewart family in your prayers along with the families of Robert Fraley, Van Ardan and the two pilots.

James took the one-paragraph draft back upstairs, to where Tracey and the two children were still seated on the edge of the bed.

"The kids obviously had been crying, but they were in a somber mood, just staring at the wall. I embraced Tracey and we cried and we hugged. I handed her the release. She read it and said it was fine. She didn't change anything," James recalled. "Right after that, she asked me to stay in the room with the two children for a few minutes while she went downstairs to talk with some of the other people who had started to gather."

Alone with the children, James attempted to comfort them, saying Payne was in Paradise now. Turning to Chelsea, he said, "You know, it won't be too long before your dad will be looking down and seeing you play on that brand-new softball field. And he's going to be so proud of you."

James was pleased that they seemed to take a measure of comfort from his words. "Their faith was steadfast," he would recount weeks later. "I just hugged them and told them how much their daddy loved them and how much God loved them and that this was not a mistake. I told them He would use this for something that we may see later on, that right then, we didn't understand why.

"We would soon see why," James added, alluding to all those who have been inspired to rededicate their faith in the wake of Stewart's death, "but at the time, we didn't."

MISSING FROM THE INITIAL SUPPORT GROUP on the day of the tragedy, through unfortunate happenstance, were Tracey's parents, Norm and Shirley Ferguson, who happened to be visiting from their home in Australia. The Fergusons had chosen this particular day to tour nearby Disney World and were blissfully unaware of the traumatic scenario that was rocking the rest of the family. Attempts were made to contact them, but they weren't carrying a cell phone and could not be reached. Inside the Magic Kingdom, there are few visible TV sets that might have alerted them to the tragic saga.

Almost eight hours after Payne's plane crashed in South Dakota, the Fergusons casually turned onto Charles Limpus Road and were startled by all the hubbub swirling around the gated entrance to their daughter's home. The explanation that would come was devastating.

The Fergusons had planned to return to Australia the next week but promptly decided to extend their visit a couple of months to be with Tracey and the children in their time of need. At first, however, there was bureaucratic resistance to extending their visas on such short notice. Then they made contact with a man in Washington, who used his connections to successfully eliminate the red tape. A guy named Clinton.

ACROSS TOWN, LARRY RINKER was having trouble making himself pack. He didn't feel like going off to the Mississippi tournament and told his wife so. She encouraged him, reasoning that Payne would want him to play. Larry nodded, thinking that Payne would laugh that silly laugh of his and say, "You have to go play unless you want to go back to Tour school."

The Rinkers were trying to decide whether they should visit the Stewart home. When they started seeing on TV some of the other pros entering and leaving the house, they decided they would go there later, in the early evening.

"It was tough," Rinker recounted. "When we got there at about seven-thirty, there weren't quite so many people in the house. I'd say less than twenty-five. So it wasn't mayhem. There were still some newspeople outside the gate. Everything was well under control. There was a policeman at the gate. I just said, 'Larry Rinker,' and he waved me right through."

Tracey was with someone when the Rinkers walked into the house. Alicia O'Meara greeted them: "It's great that you guys came." When Tracey became free, she and Larry hugged and cried for a full minute.

Jan Rinker tried to console her: "You have to be really proud of Payne and what he has done and how he had changed."

Rinker was proud of his wife for saying what he couldn't at that awkward moment. He thought about how it was bad enough for a woman to lose her husband, but she'd also lost the two people—Ardan and Fraley—who ran their lives. Those were the two people Tracey would have turned to for support and guidance, except that they had been snatched away by the same tragedy.

Looking back, Rinker said he felt even prouder of Tracey, whose handling of the situation has been a source of inspiration, as much as Payne's life, to so many.

"And the children, too," he said. "That's one thing that really got to me. When we first got to the house that night, the children were upstairs in their rooms, with some of their friends who had come over. I didn't know Payne's kids that well but I just wanted to see them—especially Aaron."

After asking directions to Aaron's room, Rinker climbed the stairs. The door was open, and Rinker eased inside. The boy turned from his two buddies to greet Rinker.

"Aaron, do you know who I am?"

Aaron shrugged.

"I'm Larry Rinker. My son is Devon," he said, smiling.

"Yes, sir. I know who you are," said the boy, sliding into Rinker's embrace.

"I'm really sorry about your dad," said Rinker.

Rinker picks up the story here: "He looked me right in the eye, with no tears, and said, 'He's in a better place now.' . . . That just blew me away. The strength of that ten-year-old kid was just incredible. I had been hesitant about whether to go up there, but I was so glad I did."

Sweet Eulogy

S hugie Collingsworth often says her husband's gift is that in times of crisis he typically focuses on the task at hand. J.B. lived up to his rep in the Stewart home in the moments following Payne's death. The First Baptist Church associate pastor kept looking for the person who would take charge of all the arrangements that needed to be made.

In short order, he realized that person would have been agent Robert Fraley, head of the Leader Enterprises firm, which guided Payne and Tracey Stewart in virtually all matters outside of golf club selection. But Fraley had just died alongside Payne. A young Leader staffer, Bill Curry Jr., the son of the former coach and NFL All-Pro center, was beginning to tend to some details, but Collingsworth could tell he was young and needed direction.

"So he diverted to me," recalls Collingsworth, who called an early-evening huddle with Curry, Tracey, and next-door-neighbor Jon Brendle—a PGA Tour official who has practically become a Stewart family member in recent years. The pastor suggested a memorial service and sought Tracey's preferences so a plan of action could be launched.

She embraced the notion and insisted that it be open to the public to accommodate anyone Payne had touched. She wanted to include the hit pop song "You Are the Wind Beneath My Wings," explaining, "That song exemplifies how I feel about Payne." She wanted the memorial centerpiece to include the new photo portrait of Payne in a tuxedo with his striking crystal-eagle Legacy Award. She wanted Paul Azinger among those who delivered eulogies.

At least two of the men would later remark that it was both eerie and inspirational that the new widow could function so purposefully just hours after her husband's shockingly tragic mishap. But her participation in the initial planning would be but a tune-up for her remarkable role during the memorial service itself.

Brendle conferred with Tour headquarters the next morning. Arrangements were made for a one-day suspension of that week's Tour Championship in Houston and Southern Farm Bureau Classic outside Jackson, Mississippi, to allow Tour pros to attend the Friday service at First Baptist. Television coverage was added. The church's 1998 investment in an in-house mini-studio and built-in equipment in the sanctuary made it possible to offer a single feed to the various stations and cable networks expressing interest in carrying the service.

Tracey signed off on live television, assured that the single feed would not compromise the dignity of the service. The number and placement of cameras would be the same as they would be at any routine Sunday service.

"We knew that this was going to be big, but it just kept exploding, kept getting bigger," pastor Jim Henry recalls. "We were getting calls and requests from Reuters and Associated Press and The Golf Channel and other networks in addition to the local stations. We had no idea that CNN was going to carry the whole thing and keep it going all over the world. I don't know who made that decision or how they made it, but that was simply astounding."

There was growing concern that even the church's expansive, six-thousand-seat sanctuary might not accommodate all who wanted to attend. There was a discussion about a closed-circuit feed for the overflow in the gym-sized Faith Hall, just across the courtyard, but that was scrapped.

"The whole thing didn't really come together until that Wednesday, when I got about thirty people together at the church to make plans," said Collingsworth. "It's just a miracle that so much fell together in such a short time."

Henry and Collingsworth became convinced that divine intervention was at work.

The week before, Collingsworth had arranged for Payne and spiritual singer Michael W. Smith to play golf. Smith welcomed the invitation to sing at the Friday memorial, but he also was scheduled to perform in Calgary, Alberta, that Thursday evening and was booked in concert the next night in Michigan. Disappointed, Collingsworth said he especially "wanted Michael to do the song 'Friends,' which sort of summed up who Payne was." Smith phoned back three hours later to say a flight had been arranged for him to fly all night Thursday to arrive in time for the service, then be whisked off to Michigan that afternoon. For reasons that remain vague to those involved, the memorial already had been scheduled to start at 11:00 A.M., somewhat unusual for a weekday service. An hour in either direction and Smith would not have been able to pull off his cameo appearance.

Henry, who was asked to deliver the closing comments, said that just two weeks earlier he had been inspired to write three principal sermons in the same week, something he had never before managed in his forty years as a pastor. "I thought, 'Lord, you have given me this to get ahead—time that I will need soon,'" Henry recounted. The day before the service, Henry would use that time to craft a message around the phrase "Payne's in the gallery," which had been echoing in his mind at home the previous evening.

Then there was the photo that Collingsworth's daughter found on the Internet, depicting Payne at some tournament looking skyward, his arms reaching high. Perfect, Collingsworth thought, to put on the large video display during Vince Gill's song "Hey, God!" It was near 11:00 P.M. on the eve of the service, but he phoned The Golf Channel, whose headquarters are in Orlando just minutes from the church. If he faxed the photo to them, could they possibly find it by nine the next morning?

Not only did the cable network come up with that precise photo, but several of its staffers worked through the night to produce a heart-tugging video of still shots and interview clips that was shown near the end of the memorial. "It was all so perfect," Collingsworth said. "And during the service was the first time I had seen it."

Most remarkable of all were the bracelets.

Two days earlier, Collingsworth had hit upon the thought of giving out a WWJD ("What Would Jesus Do?") bracelet—like the gift from Aaron that Payne wore constantly during his final five months on earth—to each person at the service. He was driving past Universal Studios on Interstate 4 when the brainstorm hit. Just as quickly, he pushed it aside as impossible to pull off. Six thousand bracelets in less than two days? He had neither the time nor the money.

That night, he received an E-mail message from an old friend, Linda Septien Blackard of Dallas, asking him to call. She had sung at the Collingsworths' wedding some twenty years earlier. J.B. placed the call and discovered it was Linda and her husband, Jeff, who had lured Stewart to Dallas that fateful Monday for the golf-course development meeting, thus burdening themselves with a sense of guilt. Collingsworth reassured Jeff Blackard, who said, "I was so impressed with what Payne did at the Open, to give credit to the Lord. Wouldn't it be great to give out one of those WWJD bracelets to everyone there?"

J.B. Collingsworth nearly dropped the phone.

He said he loved the idea but didn't have the money. Blackard offered to pick up the tab if Collingsworth could rustle up the bracelets. Collingsworth placed one call the next morning to Rodger Long, of Long's Christian Bookstore in Orlando, with the absurd request. Long had only a handful of bracelets but offered to check with another bookstore owner, Larry Meeks, in Leesburg, forty miles northwest of Orlando. An importer had just dropped off a shipment of three thousand of the bracelets to Meeks the previous day. Meeks's wife then made a call and found that the same importer had delivered another three thousand to a bookstore in the Orlando suburb of Winter Park. She drove there late that Thursday afternoon, picked them up, and delivered to the church six thousand WWJD bracelets—*exactly* the amount desired. No more. No less.

The passing out of the bracelets during Collingsworth's closing benediction became a special moment during the two-hour "coronation," as it was called, that took the estimated forty-five hundred people in the church and the millions more watching worldwide on a riveting, emotional rollercoaster. Many in attendance, including some of the seventy-five Tour pros present, vowed months later that their "Payne bracelet" had not left their wrists since that special moment.

ONE OF THE MOST POWERFUL MOMENTS came when Paul Azinger haltingly approached the lectern and, before uttering a word of his eulogy, pulled on a navy blue tam-o'-shanter cap and bent over to tuck his trouser legs into long argyle socks for a faux-Stewart ensemble. The congregation emitted chuckles, which escalated to laughter, which escalated to a stirring ovation as Azinger completed the transformation.

The response was a boon to Azinger, who was fighting a monster lump in his throat.

"Tracey had asked for some levity," Azinger related later. "She said, 'I don't want this to be too sad.' I didn't know how that was going to go over. But it worked well and it helped me to step up there, get situated. Everybody knew how hard that was going to be for me. To be able to step back and do that really helped. The reaction was better than I could have hoped.

"My fear, getting up there to speak, wasn't not knowing what to say but being able to say anything at all. I was afraid all I would be able to do was sob and not be able to get through it at all."

Collingsworth had selected Azinger to bat cleanup in the eulogy line-up of friends and associates, which consisted of the wry Cook, Payne's teacher ("Not a difficult job as you might imagine. Nice shot . . . nice shot . . . that's better"), and SMU golf teammates Todd Awe and Barry Snyder. One by one, they strode to the lectern and fought for composure while reflecting on their special friend—alternately saluting his character and sharing his mirthful foibles. Before them, among sprays of red and yellow blooms, was spread a virtual museum collection of artifacts connected to Payne's eventful life. Photos of him in competition and with family, two U.S. Open trophies, the Ryder Cup that he helped recapture for America just a month earlier, his '89 PGA trophy, the glittering Legacy Award, his harmonica, the hideous fake teeth he sprung on so many in slapstick mischievousness, and, finally, a bottle of Rogaine playfully placed there by two children who had learned to tease from a master.

Moments before the service, Henry and Collingsworth had gathered the speakers in a small office tucked behind the altar. Azinger later confided to Henry that at that moment he was scared to death that the knickers gag would be taken the wrong way. "If they hadn't laughed," he told Henry during the lunch reception that followed, "I would have melted right there!"

After relating several of Payne's jocular misadventures, Azinger, whose serene handling of his 1993 cancer diagnosis had launched Payne's spiritual examination, closed his stint at the lectern with a salute to the golfer and the two lost business agents, repeating the theme "Only God can change hearts." The phrase would linger with many of the millions watching.

Another tingling moment was captured in the sweetly ironic comments from Payne on The Golf Channel video, part of an interview aired live one year earlier. Host Peter Kessler asked what Payne had learned from his buddy when Azinger was gravely sick with bone cancer and undergoing chemotherapy during most of the 1994 Tour season.

"It put a different perspective on my life," Payne responded. "I know it definitely put a different perspective on his life. You know, golf isn't everything in my life. . . . And that's one thing that Paul taught me—that golf isn't everything. God's gonna call us home sometime. And Paul thought he was going to be called home early. . . . But, hey, I'm going to a special place when I die, but I want to make sure my life is special while I'm here."

Forty-five hundred heads spun, and silent expressions shouted, *"Did you hear that?!!"*

Azinger would later say he didn't realize the truth of what Tracey had said about his impact on Payne until watching that interview for the first time, there in the church. Payne had been the first friend to call when the cancer was diagnosed and had made several trips to Azinger's home outside Bradenton to offer support. Unexpectedly, Payne would receive more than he gave.

"I don't know how to explain it," said Azinger. "There are no words to describe what he saw. I was more *example,* I guess. Until then, I don't think he understood the faith aspect of my life. I thought he looked at me kind of strange. We had never talked that much about it. A few times over dinner I gave him my thoughts. And when I was sick, I think maybe he saw something in me. It's hard to describe. *Comfort* is a good word. It's like a peace. Chances are he sensed that."

Cook sensed other forces in the early to mid-1990s that helped begin pointing Payne to a higher plateau. He and Tracey hired a nanny, a very rigid and proper Englishwoman named Theresa Selby, who raised the standards of decorum in the Stewart household.

"When Chelsea was very young, she was a spoiled little brat and Theresa wasn't going to have any of that," Cook confided. "Theresa was a hard-line nanny. So she started making those kids toe the line—making them do their home work, insisting they say 'Yes, sir' and 'Yes, ma'am.' Very quickly, the attitude in that house changed dramatically. Then the kids started going to The First Academy, and a lot of the things they brought home were related to the religious ideals they had learned at school."

Cook also was aware that others in Payne's life, besides Azinger, had begun to boost his faith. Fraley. The legendary Byron Nelson. Orel Hershiser. Van Ardan. The old parable was proving true: You are who you associate with.

Payne even began talking to Cook about his growing faith, but it never hit the kindly little swing coach just how serious Payne had become until he won the 1999 AT&T at Pebble and praised God in his acceptance. "I knew he had changed and had become more active in his Christianity, but I hadn't realized he had become as devoted to it. He was never one to carry it on his sleeve—and this was but a brief mention—but he did come out and express himself in public. And that surprised me."

PAYNE'S PUBLIC AFFIRMATIONS provided yet another peg for the memorial service. Collingsworth had been nurturing Payne's spiritual growth and saw it spectacularly burst forth in full bloom a few nights after Payne had won the Open at Pinehurst.

Friends gathered to pay tribute to the second-time Open champ. The focal point of the party was a big-screen replay of final-day TV coverage. Seeing the tape for the first time, Payne watched images of himself sinking the winning putt and moments later giving credit to God. At the party, Collingsworth noticed Payne walking away, trying to hide the tears welling up in his eyes. In a moment, he faced his pastor, the tears beginning to flow.

"I loved it, because I love to cry," Collingsworth said, picking up the story during his memorial address. "I put my arm around him and said, 'Payne, I just want you to know I appreciate what God's doing with your heart.' He looked at me as hard as he could, tears now streaming down his face. He said, 'J.B., I'm not going to be a Bible-thumper. I'm not going to stand up on some stump. But I want everybody to know—it's Jesus.'"

The tearful proclamation defined Payne's immense evangelical clout, doubly effective in its low-key, witness-by-example style. Like so many others, Payne had been turned off by the overly aggressive Christians among his athletic peers, those who would corner you in the locker room and beat you over the head with their beliefs. Here, instead, was a compelling, increasingly embraceable global superstar who wasn't about *telling* you how faith could lift your life; he wanted only to *show* you.

"I think he felt it wasn't his position to try to persuade people about his religious beliefs," fellow pro Phil Mickelson said after the memorial service. "He was comfortable in his own faith and didn't feel he needed to sell it to other people to validate it. I think he may have had a more inspirational effect on people the way he chose to handle that."

There was another moving moment at the memorial's conclusion as the seventy-five gathered Tour pros formed a cordon up the center aisle for Tracey, the children, and other family members to depart. Tracey paused for hugs and consoling exchanges with the likes of Greg Norman, Peter Jacobsen, Scott Hoch, Mark Wiebe, Lee Janzen, Mark O'Meara, Jack Nicklaus, and other headliners. A church staffer gently suggested she save those for the reception, lest the two-hour service be extended yet another hour.

"Looking back on it," Wiebe would say much later, "that was probably one of the coolest things I'll ever do. It was literally hard to stand."

Mickelson, whom Payne had nipped for the Pinehurst spoils, would later observe that watching Tracey and the two children making their way between the two rows of Tour golfers "was one of the most difficult things that I've ever witnessed. It was difficult to watch.

"I'll tell you what went through my mind that really hurt," he continued. "That weekend, Payne had missed the cut at Disney and had gone to Aaron's football game and watched him catch a touchdown pass. I remember thinking that these two kids were going to grow up knowing that Payne went to all of their games and other functions. And that every game or function they were involved in, they were going to miss him. I just thought that was one of the saddest things I've ever felt."

Aaron's Pop Warner team, the Panthers, sat together during the service in their blue jerseys. Days before bursting with pride over Aaron's touchdown, Payne also had served as a line judge for a First Academy junior varsity volleyball game in which Chelsea had served out fourteen straight winning points in a fifteen-point game.

BUT THE MOST MOVING AND STUNNING MOMENT of the service belonged to Stewart's widow. Audible gasps of disbelief were heard when, accompanied by her brother for support, Tracey approached the altar and walked to the lectern to personally deliver her own eulogy barely four days after her husband had been snatched out of thin air.

She had been emboldened by the other two widows in her tight friendship circle, Dixie Fraley and Debbie Ardan, who, a day earlier, had similarly spoken at the memorials for their own lost husbands. The three women had discussed the unusual tactic among themselves earlier in the week and collectively decided that they were best armed to render the proper perspectives on what their husbands had meant to them.

Even a strong force like New York Jets coach Bill Parcells, also a Leader client, was blown away by the sight of Dixie Fraley approaching the lectern the previous day during the Fraley memorial across town, in the auditorium of Orangewood School. The macho football icon had already been reduced to a sniveling mess by the first speakers, but he was truly jolted when Dixie walked forward. "Oh [expletive]! I can't *believe* this!"

Neither could Chuck Cook when Collingsworth told him at midweek that Tracey would be one of the speakers at Payne's memorial.

"I couldn't believe it. I wondered how clearly she was thinking," he said six weeks later. "But she was an unbelievable rock and still is. Those three wives were so brave. I still hear people ask, 'Is that common?' 'You ever hear of that before?' It was truly unbelievable, and all three did a marvelous job."

Tracey began by recounting when she and Payne first met, at the 1980 Malaysian Open. She was at the tournament with her brother Mike, then an aspiring Tour pro and now at her side in front of a spellbound crowd. Tracey and Payne spotted each other across the room at a pretournament reception.

"It was love at first sight, and he would later say it was the same for him. He was the most beautiful man I'd ever seen," she recounted. "And I didn't even know who he was. For two days, we played these little games until another golfer introduced us. He finally asked me out to dinner and I acted nonchalant. But inside I was screaming with joy."

Continuing with little sign of wavering, she detailed what a devoted husband and doting father he had been, always making time to be with their children. She noted his passion for fun and his immense pride that both Aaron and Chelsea had inherited his athletic abilities. Payne had showed that button-popping pride just six days earlier when he had watched Aaron catch the touchdown pass.

In the end, Tracey spoke not to the congregation but to Payne, as she read from her prepared text: "You will always be my soulmate and my friend. You are the light of my life, the tower of my strength. And even after eighteen years of marriage, you are still the most beautiful man I've known—not because of how you looked on the outside anymore, but because of what was on the inside."

She looked up to smile demurely to the congregation and conclude: "Let the party in Heaven begin."

JUST BEFORE LUNCH the previous afternoon in Mississippi, Payne's 1981 qualifying-schoolmates Wiebe and Rinker boarded a commercial flight connection for Orlando. They felt a bond with the subject far too strong merely to attend the Thursday memorial service being planned at Annandale Golf Club for the pros competing there at the Southern Farm Bureau Classic.

Both were shaken by the sudden loss of such a close and cherished comrade.

Staring blankly out the airplane's window at Mississippi pines falling away below him, Rinker began taking stock of his life. Here he'd been worrying about a trivial thing like making the top-125 exempt list for his playing card on the main Tour the next season. "Hey, I'm gonna play golf next year," he thought to himself. "Who cares where I play? Does it really matter?" Reared in a church where his father was a deacon, Rinker nevertheless felt a deeper peace at that moment, he recalls, that he wishes he could have for the rest of his life.

He had been in mourning since the first moment he'd heard the devastating news that Monday. But all of a sudden, he could see the whole story. Here was a guy who was cocky, but he was a great guy and a lot of fun to be around. All of a sudden he has this transformation in life that Rinker and others close to Payne all saw. And now he's gone. But enough people saw the change in him to realize that the only thing that had changed was his faith.

In the adjacent seat, Wiebe was on the same wavelength. "You have to take time to smell the roses," he told himself. "I have to take the extra time for my family, make the extra call to those who matter most."

"It made me realize how short our lives are," Rinker would say weeks later. "And it made me make choices that I wouldn't have made in my life—like making an effort to go do something that is fun, or sharing with friends. It really hit me where I am spiritually. I've never been the kind of Christian to ask why—'Why did you do that, God?' But this time I thought about Tracey and thought about those kids not having a father. It was so unreal."

Wiebe would spend the night at Rinker's house in Winter Park after they had picked up another mutual friend, Lane Morrey, who'd played on Payne's SMU golf team. The three of them stopped for dinner that evening at Dexter's, where Rinker has performed on jazz guitar, and they shared a special bottle of wine with dinner.

"Silver Oak cabernet sauvignon was Payne's favorite," Rinker explained. "He served that to me anytime I'd go over to his house. And that's what he ordered one night last year when we had dinner at Pebble Beach. He said that was the best. We felt certain that he would want us to get together and have some Silver Oak in his honor. So we did, the night before the memorial."

The three men shared funny stories about their upbeat friend. They swallowed hard at somber thoughts. They sipped Silver Oak. Until the bottle was as empty as their hearts.

ARRIVING FROM ACROSS TOWN BY CAR, from their far-flung homes by private jet, and from Houston by the Tour's chartered plane, the seventy-five pros and their wives were herded past eighteen television satellite trucks and a barricade of reporters and photographers just outside the entrance of the First Baptist Church's Welcome Center B. They wore dark suits and darker glasses, the latter to hide reddened eyes and to shield them against the brilliant, cloudless central-Florida morning.

They were ushered down a short staircase and into a lower corridor leading to the church's choir room. There would unfold a telling phenomenon that Payne Stewart would have loved dearly.

Because most of the pros and wives had not seen one another since the tragedy, they fell together in emotional embraces, tears flowing. But within minutes, little groups began to share favorite Payne Stewart stories. The tears gave way to smiles. The smiles gave way to laughter. In an adjacent office with the other memorial speakers, Collingsworth cracked open a door to check the cause of the clatter. He watched for a moment and smiled knowingly, then pulled the door shut.

In each little cluster, someone would rush the storyteller, having thought of another good one themselves. It was so perfectly Payne.

"Well, that was certainly the case," Phil Mickelson said, recalling the scene. "Payne was always one to evoke humor, with his fake teeth being the most infamous and repetitive example."

Mickelson shared recollections of Payne once wearing the jagged, fake teeth in a shootout before the Buick Invitational in San Diego, and "walking up to shake hands with fans and saying, 'Thank you so much for coming out.' With these big, horrible teeth protruding out and these people not really knowing what to say. Here was their first chance to meet Payne Stewart up close and they were shocked that he had such atrocious teeth. It was the first time I had seen the joke teeth and it gave me a start too. I remember thinking, 'Gee, I didn't realize Payne's teeth were like this.'"

Wiebe paused amid the din and looked around, impressed with what he saw. "I thought, 'How many people has this guy touched?' I kept seeing more and more people. Full of hugs and handshakes and sweet memories of Payne."

"There was a real brotherhood in there," remembered Rinker. He swapped amusing anecdotes with Loren Roberts and Tom Lehman, then spotted former University of Florida teammate Terry Anton, who had played the Asian Tour with Stewart and had been invited to return to Australia to serve as best man when Payne and Tracey married. Rinker smiled and playfully tweaked his old friend: "Oh, so you make the memorial service, but not the wedding."

Dozens of pros look back on that choir-room gathering with pride, as a time the PGA Tour proved itself as a caring family. The only disappointment was expressed in a question asked by several: "Where's Arnold?" The Bear and the Shark had each flown in from south Florida. The Tiger had returned with the group from Houston. Arnold Palmer was conspicuous by his absence.

Four days earlier, right after the crash, Palmer had waved off the local TV news crews that showed up at his Bay Hill Club, just five miles from the church. He was shown on the six o'clock news walking away, across the clubhouse lawn. His publicist, Doc Giffin, issued a prepared statement from Palmer, expressing sorrow over the tragedy, and suggested that Arnie was simply too emotionally distraught to give interviews that day. Two days before the memorial, Palmer flew to Latrobe, Pennsylvannia, to be with his ailing wife, Winnie.

In the choir room, when associate pastor Billy Mitchell climbed onto a riser in one corner, he blinked oddly at the sights and sounds of happy memories. He had to ask for quiet to begin explaining the planned procedure—the section of pews reserved for the pros and their spouses at the front of the sanctuary, the human corridor they were to form for Payne's family at the close of the service, the reception in Faith Hall that would follow.

They filed into the main sanctuary and were seated in time for Collingsworth's welcoming remarks, including this advisory: "You're going to cry and you're going to laugh."

"I cried and I laughed. I think everybody did," Rinker nodded. "The service was incredible."

That night, he called his parents, who had watched the service on CNN. They told Larry that in their lifetimes, they couldn't recall the death of anybody having the impact on so many people's spiritual lives that Payne's death had. Not even presidents.

part two

THE CLOWN PRINCE

Q&A

with   Larry   Rinker

Among the scores of fellow Tour pros who became close to Payne
Stewart, journeyman Larry Rinker is uniquely qualified to paint
the total portrait. Stewart and Rinker met and shared the fractious
uncertainties of Tour qualifying school at Disney World in the spring of
1981. Both earned their cards to play the PGA Tour, and as fellow rookies,
their new friendship grew. They frequently played practice rounds at the
glitzy golf datelines across the country and in Orlando, where Rinker had
moved from Stuart, Florida, and Payne from Springfield, Missouri. That
tight bond would last for several years, until Payne's ascension as one of the
Tour's stars pulled him apart from Rinker and others in the lower strata of
the money list.

The PGA Tour's policies contribute to creating kind of a caste system.
Past champions and leading money winners are paired together in the
opening rounds of most tournaments. Payne found himself playing in the
featured pro-am on Wednesdays; Rinker was often shuffled off to a backup course for the secondary pro-am. Headliners are whisked around between tournaments in lush, private jets; the Rinkers of the golf world more
often trudge through airport lobbies with the rest of us.

Officially winless over his nineteen Tour seasons, Rinker has earned
$1.9 million in official money. Two runner-up spots, in New Orleans
(1984) and Pebble Beach (1985), represent his highest finishes. A
Southeastern Conference champion while playing for the University of
Florida, Rinker teamed up with his sister Laurie Rinker of the LPGA for
his only Tour-related victory in the 1985 J.C. Penney Mixed Team Classic.

Payne's evolving personality also widened the gulf between himself
and Rinker for a span in the late 1980s and early 1990s. Rinker and the

other lesser lights began to notice that Payne had less time for them and preferred hanging out with champions like Paul Azinger and Mark O'Meara. Finding himself outside the inner circle, Rinker was accorded a different vantage point from which to view the Payne Stewart who began to stack up a few victories and lots of cash.

In more recent years, as Payne matured and redirected his priorities, he reached out to pull his old friend Rinker back into his circle. There, Rinker discovered the "new" Payne Stewart, the kinder, gentler, more caring fellow who Rinker was happy to reembrace. As the format for this book was being developed, we assumed that one of the more high-profile pros close to Payne—Paul Azinger or Peter Jacobsen, perhaps—would be preferred for the Q&A to launch this portion of the book, examining Payne's personality. And, indeed, Azinger and Jacobsen provided valuable insights and anecdotes. But less than halfway through a ninety-minute interview with Rinker, it became clear that his keen observations and his changing vantage points—from within Payne's inner circle *and* as an outsider for several years—made him a natural to begin the profile of the knickered guy who turned from ugly duckling to lovable goose . . .

Question: *What were your early impressions of Payne from that Qualifying school in the spring of 1981, when you two first met?*
Larry Rinker: Mark Wiebe roomed with him at that Tour school and the three of us played practice rounds together. Payne and I got our cards at that school and Mark missed, but got his later. I remember realizing Payne was good when we played those practice rounds. The great rhythm was already there in his swing. Then I remember realizing he also had lots of confidence. I bogeyed seventeen and eighteen in the last round and barely made my card by one stroke. I was playing conservatively coming in, knowing I had my card made if I just didn't have a major wreck. I was pretty nervous getting through a pretty tough ringer. We were standing at the scoreboard and Payne said *(in guttural tones)*, "I hit it gooooood today! I hit sixteen greens!" I remember thinking *(laughing)*, "Wow, that's pretty confident. More confident than I was out there today."

Q: *So the two of you set off on the adventure of playing the PGA Tour, expanding a new friendship in the process?*

Rinker: Yes. One of the first tournaments where we played was in Abilene, Texas, the old LaJet Classic. I asked Payne if he wanted to share a room there and he said, "I'll room with you as long as you don't philosophize about the golf swing." He was one that never liked to talk with other players about the swing. If you started talking swing theory, he wanted to leave the room. In my mind, I always wanted to get everything perfect so I could play well. I think his thing was that it's never going to be perfect, so just accept it and make the best of what you have.

Q: *So you were impressed with his swing and his level of self-confidence right off. What did you think of Payne the person back then?*

Rinker: Basically, you just didn't think he would go out of his way for you. And he would needle you to the point that it would hurt you. When I had to go back to the Q-school in '83 and '84, he'd say, "Hey, you're going back to your favorite tournament." And laugh. When you say things like that, it comes off hurtful. And I have heard similar things that he said to other guys. As for the guys like me and Wiebe that he was close to, it almost seemed like his way of being a friend and trying to get us to play better was to be a little arrogant in his criticism—to where you say, "Well, I'll show him!" In his way, he was trying to inspire us. But sometimes the knife cut a little too deep.

Payne was always the life of any party. If you were hanging out with just the guys, Payne was great. But there were a lot of times that getting together with him and doing a project, it was always, "Well, if it fits into my schedule." Payne had a tough time being real close to the players because he was so competitive. We had dinner at Pebble Beach one night last year, a group of us, and I overheard him say that he's just so competitive that his best friends were not golfers. There was a time when he would have made the top-ten list of least-liked guys on the Tour.

Q: *You mean in a vote of just players?*

Rinker: Yes. And I know many in the press were also put off with him. It's funny, because it got to the point where Mark and I said, "Well, he's being a jerk, but we're still going to be his friends." And we're still here.

Q: *Did you see some cracks in that early armor of confidence and cockiness?*

Rinker: Here's an interesting story. At the start of 1982, our first full year on the Tour, he hardly qualified for a tournament until the Magnolia Classic in April, at Hattiesburg, Mississippi. He had missed most of the Monday qualifiers that we had back then, made the field at Hattiesburg, then wins the tournament. But it wasn't an official Tour win that would exempt you into the other tournaments. So he wrote letters asking for sponsor exemptions into the other tournaments that year. And I'm not talking about the big prestigious events like the Memorial. I'm talking about the Kemper Open and all the rest. And nobody gave him an exemption. But he wins Quad Cities that summer, an official win, and that gets him exempt for the rest of that year and the next. I found it interesting that the week he died, the Mississippi tournament, which has since moved to Jackson, was making a big deal that "Payne Stewart won our tournament in 1982." And I'm thinking, "Yeah, and *(laughing)* nobody gave him an exemption after that, either. He was still a Monday qualifier."

Q: *He won Quad Cities wearing knickers, encouraging him to continue with the outfits that became his calling card. What were your first impressions of him playing "in costume"?*

Rinker: I had mixed emotions. In a way, I thought it was pretty cool. They were called plus fours down in Australia. But then on the other hand, I was thinking it was a little too much. But when he won Quad Cities wearing them every day, and with his father there, then it was over. The knickers were there to stay.

So the funny thing is, I played in the '86 Masters and I think that was the first year Payne put on the tux shirt with the cuff links and the bow tie with his knickers to play in the par-3 tournament. A friend of mine was up there and took a picture of him. It's the only thing I ever asked Payne to sign to me. He playfully signed, very formally: "My good friend, Larry. Hope everything is always perfect. Your friend, Payne" And that says it all. I didn't have the picture out in the house, but after he was killed, I dug it out and now have it hanging prominently in my office at home.

Q: *Looking back, do you agree with most that the outfit was a master-stroke in the way it galvanized an identity for him?*
Rinker: Without question. I mean, looking back, I would call him Sammy Davis Jr. in spikes. Payne was such a showman. Sammy Davis Jr. could do anything. He could sing and act and dance and tell jokes. Payne just had this aura of sparkle about him. Payne Stewart is an original. There won't be another like him.

Q: *And that knack as a showman led you to include Payne when former commissioner Deane Beman asked you to form a jocular Tour rock band?*
Rinker: Yes. I knew Payne played harmonica, so I asked him to be part of it. And I knew Peter Jacobsen, with his stage presence, would be good. Peter could be an actor any day and steal the show. So Peter and Payne became the main stars for what came to be known as Jake Trout and the Flounders. Deane pulled me aside during the West Coast swing early that year and asked if I would put together a band made up of players for the annual clambake we have for the players and their families at The Players Championship in the spring. I invited guys I thought would be interested in doing it and could contribute.

Mark Lye played guitar, so he was in. And John Inman was one of the guys at the start. He used to sing in a barbershop quartet up in North Carolina and could play the piano. And I was the fifth guy, on guitar, for the Jacksonville show. We were also asked to play for the pro-am party at the Memphis tournament later that year. But Inman didn't pan out after that and I dropped out later, leaving the official group as Payne, Mark, and Peter. They're the ones who later made a cassette tape and a CD with funny parody lyrics written to popular songs.

Q: *The final nine on Sundays usually makes the transition from medal play to virtual match play between two or three players. Could that have been part of Payne's problem closing victories in the first half of his career?*
Rinker: Yes. There was a time when Payne wasn't that great a match-play player. On Sunday, it gets down to, "Okay, you need to make this putt to win." I used to beat him a lot in practice rounds. And then he would just annihilate me in the tournament.

This is funny. We played a practice round one day early in the AT&T week and I beat him soundly. We played twenty-seven holes—eighteen at Cypress Point and the back nine at Spyglass. We were playing a ten-dollar Nassau and I birdied the ninth and eighteenth at Cypress and the eighteenth at Spyglass to beat him for a hundred and fifty dollars. Everybody knew Tracey held the family checkbook with an iron grip. If a caddie's percentage worked out to so many dollars and, say, forty-five cents, she made out the check right to the forty-five cents. There was no "rounding up." When the match is over *(laughing)*, I needled Payne by asking, "Do I need to get a check for this from Tracey?" He twisted up his face and snorted, "I'll pay you!" The point was that Payne probably wasn't allowed to have a hundred and fifty dollars in cash on him. But she has been a great wife to him. Stayed with him through thick and thin.

But back to how he came to handle the Sunday rounds. I think it was part experience and that he had been there enough that he figured out what he needed to do. Also, he had started working with Dick Coop, the sports psychologist, and he was working with Harvie Ward, who kept telling him to trust his swing down the stretch. The Tour used to have a match-play tournament at Tuscon. Payne's record wasn't that good in the match play at Tuscon or in the Ryder Cup in the individual matches. Look at what his singles record was the first few times. [Stewart was 1–2 in singles in the first three of his five Ryder Cup appearances.]

Q: *At least until he won his first Open title at Hazeltine in brave fashion, there was the feeling that his wins had come mostly not because Payne captured the tournament, but rather the other way around. The '89 PGA certainly seemed to fall in that category, Payne winning by one shot mainly because Mike Reid collapsed disastrously down the final few holes at Kemper Lakes.*

Rinker: You're right. When he won that PGA, he definitely played well, but if Mike Reid pars two of the last few holes, Mike is the winner.

Q: *Skeptics suggested that Payne played well the last day of that tournament in part because he was freewheeling, thinking he was playing only for second, behind Mike.*

Rinker: That's right.

Q: *So when Payne finished several groups ahead of Mike and was shown on TV in the scorer's tent laughing and yukking it up while watching on a monitor as Reid struggled, his image plummeted with the golf media.*

Rinker: With everybody. With the other players and everybody.

Q: *Knowing Payne, he could have been laughing about something totally unrelated to Mike's collapse, but the appearance was very damning.*

Rinker: That's right. Like I said, it was right about then, at that PGA, and right after then that I would probably say he was one of the ten least-liked guys on the Tour. But when the transformation came, there was definitely more compassion. Especially toward me. I don't feel he ever talked down to me as a golfer or treated me any differently over the years. There's no question he was a far better player than I was throughout our careers. One year I finished thirtieth on the money list and got near him. But other than that, he finished far higher on the money list than me every year. You almost would think he would be like a big brother, saying, "C'mon, what's wrong?" or call me up for encouragement. But I didn't get any of that. I'd get it when I'd see him occasionally.

Q: *When did you first notice that Payne was shedding that cloak of arrogance and becoming a more compassionate person?*

Rinker: It's hard to pinpoint. But I do remember in 1997 at the last tournament of the year at Las Vegas. I was number 125 [on the Tour money list]. My card for the next year was on the line. We had had dinner Tuesday night of that week. I ended up making the cut and keeping my card. Payne was one of two or three players who called my room to congratulate me late that afternoon. He said, "Way to go!" The next thing I know he started asking me about my round and I'm thinking *(laughing)*, "Wait a minute. Is this Payne?" I remember telling him about my round. And there was one hole, the eleventh hole, where I drove it in a fairway bunker and I went for the pin out of the bunker and made bogey. He said, "Look, you've got to protect par. I don't care if you hit it forty or fifty feet to the right of the hole. Hit it somewhere where you can make par. I remember thinking that I would have never thought of that. And that will be with me for the rest of my life.

After we talked, we ended up meeting over at the Hard Rock Cafe, because he was doing the VH-1 pro-am the next day. Our mutual friend Stephen Stills, the musician, was there and we all ended up hanging out the whole night. We had a long talk about Jake Trout and the Flounders. We ended up taking a taxi back to the Mirage and playing a little blackjack before we went to bed. But it was good. We just had a real good chat. I guess that was probably when I started noticing the change in him.

But when we were together, there wasn't any of the star thing with me. There might have been *(laughing)* when he started talking about his schedule or something. But, not really. No, he always treated a few of us as just one of the guys, but guys he always wanted to beat, obviously. You'd hear that from Wiebe. He never really talked down to us that way.

Q: *When you became heavily involved in the push for a players' union in recent years, that was a controversial issue that many of the top stars like*

Payne discredited and steered clear of. Did Payne interact with you on that subject?

Rinker: Yes, he did. Payne didn't join the TPA [Tour Players Association], but he made it clear to me that he favored a lot of the stuff we were doing. He did sign the letter that went to the commissioner saying we wanted to inspect the books and the records. He said, "Larry, it is a star-based Tour." I agreed and said I realized that but there should be a minimum payment for every player in a tournament. He agreed with that. Not long before the tragedy, he told one of the TPA attorneys the players needed a bigger voice in what is going on with our tour.

Q: *When did you first realize the "new" Payne might be a result of his increased spirituality?*

Rinker: I remember being with him at Memphis the week before he won the Open at Pinehurst last summer. He sits down and he's got this WWJD bracelet on. Me, personally, if my son walked up and handed it to me and asked me to wear it, I'd probably wear it. But I always thought I wasn't a good enough Christian to wear it. If I wore that and said or did the wrong thing, what would somebody think? Yet, here was Payne with it on! And I'm, like, wow!

Q: *What was your last discussion with Payne?*

Rinker: The last time was Wednesday at the father-child tournament just before the start of the Disney World Classic. I had played with all three of my kids and Payne was just starting on the first hole with Aaron. My wife had a camcorder, shooting everything, including them, and Payne was laughing and saying, "Get that out of here!" Then Aaron teed off and away they went. I never got to see him again.

chapter 4

The Rascal

B ee Payne-Stewart could tell very early that her only son was going
to be free-spirited. She remembers having to go to the door to calm
passersby, who were angry that their cars had come under a killer
pebble attack from her little blue-eyed, towheaded tyke.

"People would stop and they'd be mad as the dickens," she recalls with
a laugh. "Payne was very little then, preschool. He couldn't really hurt a car,
he was so little. Then, when he got barely old enough to caddie for his dad,
Bill would let him use a pull cart. But Payne would pull it right through
the sand traps and tell his dad, 'Why not? That's the shortest way.' He was
maybe seven at the time. He was always up to something like that."

Though most people know her only by her married name, this spunky,
eighty-one-year-old matriarch of the Springfield, Missouri, Stewart clan
insists you get her handle correct. She painstakingly explains that it is
"B-double-E—like the queen bee," which she still is on South Link Street
in Springfield.

"Payne was my maiden name and I connected it to Stewart with a
hyphen. You might say I'm a hyphenated lady," she said, chuckling at her
little joke. "I purposely didn't give the two girls middle names, so they could
keep the Stewart part when they got married. Now, they are Lora Stewart
Thomas and Susan Stewart Daniel. But you can give a boy a middle name.
So when we had one, we named him William Payne Stewart."

The way she recalled his mischievous youth, she could have named
him Rascal. He wore a constant cookie-jar smile—for good reason. In high
school, he was always hiding other students' padlocks, or slipping mentho-
lated ointment into the athletic supporters of unsuspecting teammates to
watch them hop around, trying to catch their breath.

"But it was never anything serious or bad. Usually just in fun," Bee
promised. "When he was in college, he would always bring some little
funny thing home for me. Once it was a little sign that said, 'Notice: I don't

do floors or windows —The Housekeeper.' He was always doing something to get me to laugh."

Payne Stewart would spend most of his forty-two years doing just that, often through design, but sometimes through his propensity to play the unwitting court jester. And even when the yuks came via that latter avenue, Payne had the wonderful gift of being able to join in the laughter at his own expense.

Perhaps his most famous foible is the one Paul Azinger trotted out to add a salving and germane touch of Payne-styled levity to the memorial service just four days after the crash. Explaining that Payne was never very mechanically inclined, Azinger revealed Payne's confession that he had cranked up his new bass boat while it was still on its trailer in his garage.

It seems Payne was so proud of his new toy that he climbed in and turned over the ignition. Liking the roar it made there in the enclosed garage, he began revving the engine, blissfully oblivious to the fact that outboard engines depend on the lake water flowing through them for cooling. Azinger did an imitation of Payne behind the wheel of the boat, grinning and pumping the throttle. And he added an equally believable impersonation of Payne flinching at the explosion and watching in horror at the flames shooting up. Zinger's hands mimicked the flames fanning to each side as they hit the garage ceiling.

The congregation roared with laughter.

Fortunately, fireman Stewart frantically managed to get this four-alarm blaze under control before it burned down his house.

"Then he made the mistake of telling me about it," Azinger mused impishly, "and I told *everybody* I knew."

At their next tournament together, Azinger left a reminder of the gaffe taped to Payne's locker. It was a huge magazine ad for an outboard motor over which Azinger had scrawled the notation "Just add water."

The common knowledge in the locker room that Payne was a mechanical klutz—the very last person you'd find landscaping his yard—made his brief commercial endorsement of a lawn trimmer all the more comical. It was a contraption called the Weed Terminator, and Payne attracted waves of ribbing for the TV spots.

The commercials had been appearing for months when the 1996 Open was staged at Oakland Hills outside Detroit. "At the entrance to the Oakland Hills locker room," recalls Lee Janzen, "there was a picture of a golfer digging in the weeds, looking for his ball. So I put up a sign saying, 'This wouldn't happen to you if you used the Weed Whacker —Payne Stewart.' Payne went up and changed it to 'Weed Terminator' and left the sign up. That was a good example that he could have a good laugh at himself, too."

SOME OF PAYNE'S AMUSING MISADVENTURES were born in the overestimation of his skills in other sporting pursuits. Granted, he *was* a three-sport letterman in high school, and anyone who can putt well enough to make a living on the PGA Tour could be excused for thinking their hand-eye coordination qualifies them for most any other sporting discipline.

Among those was billiards.

When Payne joined several Orlando buddies on bird-hunting junkets to south Georgia, he landed in the company of some good ol' boys, cold beer, and green felt off more than he could *cue*.

One of the regulars on the annual junkets was an Orlando car dealer and former college halfback during Georgia Tech's golden days under the legendary Bobby Dodd. But by this time, stumpy Ben Smith had filled out to the point that he measured roughly the same in any direction you'd care to measure him. A single-digit golfer around that huge bay window, Smith is a raucous, fun-loving sort who spits out funny lines the way a Xerox machine churns out copies. He once closed the sale of a small pickup truck with a pitch you're not likely to find in the General Motors sales manual. The potential buyer was a woman who worried whether the tiny truck was strong enough to pull her boat and trailer. "Ma'am," Smith snorted indignantly, "that truck can pull a fat lady out of a donut shop!" When the woman managed to stop laughing, she yanked the papers out of Smith's hands and signed on the dotted line.

Payne loved to be around Ben Smith and may have joined the bird-hunting junkets to south Georgia—where Smith had been a high school football hero—not so much to fill the air with shotgun pellets as to fill the air with laughter. But Payne's laughter died one evening in a roadhouse outside Valdosta.

The gifted and cagey football coach at Valdosta State was an old friend of Smith's, former University of Georgia player and assistant coach Mike Cavan. Smith gave him a call, and Cavan joined the group at their motel for a round of beers and tall tales after their long day of saving the world from an overpopulation of quail.

As Cavan recalls it, he was about to head home when Payne announced that he was ready, instead, to check out one of the local joints. "Payne, it's eleven o'clock and this is *Valdosta, Georgia*," Cavan said. Payne persisted, however, until Cavan said he did know of a beer stop a few miles out on Quitman Road that stayed open late. But, the coach explained, "The only way I can get out this late is for you to come by the house first and meet my wife and kids." Payne agreed.

The group paused at the Cavan household just long enough to spring the coach. In a flash, they pulled up to the New Knights, a rural gentlemen's establishment where the beer is cold, the two pool tables are busy, and every pickup truck in the gravel parking lot is equipped with a gun rack and a Confederate flag decal. Fortunately, Payne wasn't wearing his bright knickers and jaunty cap, or—to borrow from an old Lewis Grizzard Georgia-ism—the locals might have held him down and sprayed him with roach spray until he stopped wiggling.

Instead, Payne parked his designer hunting ensemble on a barstool and scouted out a couple of the good ol' boys playing eight-ball. He leaned close to Cavan. "Coach," he said in a near whisper, "I think we can take those guys."

Cavan, himself regarded as something of a lovable rogue back then, had spent several years traveling the Georgia backroads in pursuit of potential Bulldog all-Americans (he is the one who lured Herschel Walker to the University of Georgia). "I had learned that when you go in one of those places in a small town like that to shoot pool, you better bring your 'A' game. That night, I thought, 'I'm a fair shot, but these guys—holy mackerel!—some of them probably do that for a living.'"

Payne hadn't learned that lesson. But he was about to.

The match was on, five bucks a game. In this corner, the superstar golfer and the head football coach. In that corner, two old boys in overalls with Caterpillar hats, huge chaws, and the inner satisfaction that they were about to come into some money. Not surprisingly, if you know how these things work, the golfer-coach team won two of the first three games, and Team Overalls, the hook set just right, suggested raising the stakes.

After several rounds of beers, when the stakes had reached fifty dollars a game, Team Overalls' balls starting streaking into the pockets as if they were frightened field mice.

At about three in the morning Payne and Cavan finally ran up the white flag—and only then on Cavan's whispered insistence: "Payne, we can't beat these guys. We got to get outta here."

Leave it to Ben Smith to put the proper perspective on the billiards lesson. "When Payne left that place," chortles the portly car dealer, "his wallet looked like an elephant had stepped on it."

Years later, when Cavan had become head football coach at Payne's SMU alma mater, they were at a school fund-raising event and Payne thought the new Mustangs coach looked hauntingly familiar. "Let me remind you," Cavan said, grinning. "Valdosta, Georgia. Roadhouse. All-night pool game."

A combination grimace and grin spread across Payne's face as he cupped his hands on top of his head and groaned, "Oh, Lord!" The two laughed openly at the painful memory.

John Shelton, Payne's Realtor pal and one of the courageous bird hunters, laughed softly when recalling the day he pulled up in front of the Stewart house to fetch Payne for his rookie hunting trip. The adventurous young golf pro bounded out with a bright smile, carrying a new 12-gauge shotgun and only about three-quarters of a box of shells.

"Payne, I've got some shells you can have, because you don't have enough."

"Shelton, maybe I'm a better shot than you are," he playfully fired back, "and I don't need as many shells."

The old coach smiled knowingly.

"The next day, in the first twenty minutes he had used all of his shells and I don't think he had hit a single bird," Shelton muses in reflection. "That night, we had to go into Albany and, between the four of us, bought a case of shells for the next two days of hunting."

Shelton also can second Azinger's testimony that Payne Stewart with a casting rod in his hand could be equally scatterbrained. In his alternately moving and uproarious eulogy, Zinger recounted how Payne used to try to lift his friend's spirits between chemotherapy treatments by going fishing with him. Azinger said that, indeed, Payne's wild casting could certainly take one's mind off of anything—even cancer.

Bald as a cue ball from the treatments, Azinger had the good judgment to wear a floppy fishing hat to protect him from the harsh Florida sun *and,* as it turned out, from Payne. "I had learned to watch him very close," said Zinger. "But I took my eye off him for just a moment and—*whop!*—his lure hit me flush in the side of my head. All nine hooks of his lure buried in my hat."

The next time Payne returned to cheer up his pal, Azinger was ready. When the foursome reached the desired fishing hole, each began pulling out everything he needed to start casting. Payne, who had positioned himself at one end of the boat, looked around to discover Azinger and the other two trying to keep a straight face under football helmets. They all broke out laughing, including Payne.

Shelton and former Louisiana State University football coach Charlie McClendon also discovered that Payne's flying lures were first cousins to a Scud missile. "I had an eighteen-and-a-half-foot bass boat, which is rather roomy," Shelton recounts, grinning. "When we reached our spot, I was casting from one end, Charlie Mac was in the middle, and Payne at the far end. But after a few minutes, I looked around and discovered Mac had worked right up next to me. A few close calls from Payne's lure drove him down to my end. But Payne really enjoyed that trip and really let his hair down."

PAYNE'S EXUBERANCE AS A SPORTS SPECTATOR—once he learned to tone it down a notch—made for some amusing moments. He got it honestly from Bill Stewart, who could sometimes be perhaps not quite the Little League father from hell, but somewhere in that neighborhood.

A high-strung former three-sport letterman at Southwest Missouri State, Bill once became so verbally abusive shouting from the stands at a junior high basketball game that the refs hit Payne's team with a technical foul. "That was over in the little town of Lockwood and it was a Saturday morning game," coach Paul Mullins remembered with a laugh. "After they gave us the 'T,' they warned Bill that if he kept it up they would have the sheriff haul him off."

Matty Guokas, the first coach of the NBA-expansion Orlando Magic, no doubt would love to have seen the gendarmes haul off Payne from some of those inaugural games. Payne's season tickets were for seats just a few rows up behind the Magic bench, and he was often so loudly abusive toward Guokas and the refs, players, ball boys, popcorn vendors, *anybody,* that friends became too embarrassed to sit with him.

Fellow Orlando Tour pro David Peoples recalls playing a social round with Guokas, during which the coach brought up the nonstop harangues from Stewart. "Matty noted that he had played and coached for years in Philadelphia, where fans are known as some of the toughest in sports," Peoples said. "But Matty said Payne was tougher."

Magic General Manager Pat Williams chuckled as he recalled Payne's behavior those first couple of seasons: "He got into this basketball thing pretty early. And we describe him as rabid and unruly. He was incredible. I've never seen anything like it. As the years went on, he kinda settled down. But in the early seasons, it was staggering to me that he cared that much or was having that much fun or whatever his schtick was."

What seemed such a paradox to Guokas and Williams and others was that this was a professional golfer, many of whom are known to come unglued if a fan so much as clears his throat or crinkles a potato-chip bag from three fairways away. "Here was a guy who was in the business, so to speak," says Williams. "You'd have thought he would have understood and exercised some professional courtesy on his part."

After two screaming seasons, the club moved Payne's seats to the opposite side of the O-rena, getting him out from behind the Magic bench. And once he started moderating his demeanor at games, his act became more amusing than obnoxious. Payne's shouted taunts began to lean more toward gag lines that made those around him laugh, and less toward mean-spirited barbs that made them cringe.

When Payne's daughter, Chelsea, and son, Aaron, began to participate on youth sports teams, Payne was right there in the stands, as vocally supportive as ever, but not as biting as he had been in the early Magic seasons. Still, fellow parents found ways to gag him, particularly at Aaron's Little

League baseball games. Each team was required to supply a first- or third-base volunteer umpire, and the other parents often prodded Payne into that duty. With a purpose that Payne fully understood.

"They knew I couldn't scream at the umpires," Payne explained with a giggle, "if I *was* one!"

At The First Academy, where Payne's kids began playing on the school's various teams, headmaster Ed Gamble said he was drawn to sitting in the stands with Payne, often helping him cheer for their sons on the same team. "We have a lot of celebrity parents at the school and I don't make it a habit to cozy up to them," says Gamble. "But I did often sit with Payne because he was fun. I would have done that whether he was a golf star or a house painter. He was the type who drew people to him, and people enjoyed being around him. He was fun and always lighthearted. But always bordering on cutting up."

Much like Little League, the policy at First Academy sports events was for parents to serve as volunteers in various capacities. Brian Bowen, one of the FA coaches, vividly recalls Tracey working the concession stand and Payne, unpretentious and enthusiastic, selling tickets in the lobby for one of Chelsea's J.V. basketball games during a Christmas tournament. The game started and, from his post in the lobby, the famous ticket seller could hear the excitement spilling out of the gym. "Whoever mans the gate is supposed to stay there through the third quarter," Bowen explained. "But the game was getting too good for Payne as the second half started, so he put up a sign that said, 'Everybody come on in and I'll pay for the rest of you—Payne Stewart.'"

The second game that evening involved a team from Georgia that was broadcasting on a radio station back home. The announcers made the mistake of inviting Payne to the table for a halftime interview, and it was well into the second half before they recaptured their microphones. Payne "Costas" Stewart took over the play-by-play, giving the folks back in Georgia a dose of amateur but passionate descriptions of the game.

WHEN IT WASN'T A REF OR COACH getting playfully tweaked by Payne, it was one of his famous buddies from other sports. Sometimes intentionally, sometimes by accident.

For comic relief following Payne's memorial service, pitcher Orel Hershiser shared with Tracey and other friends the embarrassing thing that happened when he drove over from Atlanta to attend one round of the 1990 PGA at Shoal Creek in Birmingham. Payne was already on the course when Hershiser arrived. When he caught up, Hershiser was asked to do a brief interview with TV commentator Jerry Pate, who was walking along with Payne's group. After that was completed, Payne walked over and leaned across the gallery rope to embrace his baseball buddy.

But as they hugged, they both tilted their heads to the same side and accidentally kissed right on the lips. They recoiled in reflex, blinking and looked around quickly in the hope that Pate's cameraman hadn't caught them smooching on national TV. Luckily, he hadn't.

It was a hot day and Payne had applied a heavy coating of Chap Stick, much of it now transferred to the pitcher. Hershiser and Payne didn't talk about it for years, although their agent, Robert Fraley, often kidded them about it. "I wondered about you baseball guys," Payne would say, feigning dark suspicions.

It was not an accident, though, when Payne good-naturedly taunted friend and Isleworth resident Ken Griffey Jr. one night in the Tropicana Dome in St. Petersburg. Griffey's Seattle Mariners were playing the Tampa Bay Devil Rays, and golf pals Payne and Mark O'Meara made the short jaunt over to see their friend in action. They sat in the first row in center field to be near Ken when the Mariners were on the field.

At one point in the game, Griffey was caught in a rundown between bases and was tagged for the final out of the inning. As he strolled out to his position, embarrassed and frustrated, he heard Payne's familiar voice ringing out from the bleachers. "Hey, Junior! Hey, Junior!" Payne kept calling out. When Griffey looked up, Payne shouted, "Does this look familiar?!" and began frantically running back and forth in the walk space in front of his seat in a mocking imitation of the rundown.

Griffey had to hold his glove over his face to hide his laughter.

Frank Viola is another big-league pal who discovered he was not exempt from Payne's needle. Viola, also an Orlando resident, struck up a friendship with Payne, who began attending baseball games anytime the PGA Tour was playing in the same city where Viola was pitching. On one such occasion, Viola was facing the Texas Rangers. He left box seats right behind home plate for Payne, who was playing in the Colonial Invitational at nearby Fort Worth.

"I pitched a complete game that night, but lost 2–1 because I gave up two home runs that, together, must have traveled about nine hundred feet," Viola recalled. "The next day, I went out to the Colonial to follow Payne and there must have been about five hundred people around the first tee box when he teed off. I was in shades and a cap, trying to be inconspicuous. He hits his drive right down the middle, so we're all clapping. He turned around and saw me and got that big smirk across his face and yelled out, 'Hey, Viola! *Man,* you gave up some *total yardage* last night!' He broke out laughing and the gallery laughed with him.

"Here I was trying to keep it low-key and he singled me out and embarrassed me in front of all those people. But that's the way he was. You couldn't get mad at him."

Even the tallest of Payne's friends weren't exempt. He became pals with basketball stars Charles Barkley and Michael Jordan, sharing almost daily golf rounds with them during the Barcelona Olympics. Sir Charles and M.J. were there to win gold as part of the so-called U.S. Dream Team, and Payne was there to take in the Olympic scene and tweak these two famous but frustrated golfers. Boston columnist and NBC commentator Will McDonough arranged event tickets for Payne and received daily updates on golf matches in which Payne was spotting Michael eight shots—based on M.J.'s alleged golf handicap of 6.

Stewart let McDonough know that Jordan really couldn't play to that handicap, but pride wouldn't let Michael ask for more strokes, even though he shot in the mid-80s most days.

"He did, however, play pretty good today and shot 76," Payne reported one evening.

"I guess he clipped you for a little money, then?" McDonough wondered aloud.

"Nope," said Payne, his face spreading into a wide grin as he reached in his pocket and produced a thick fold of Spanish currency. "I shot 64."

IN MORE RECENT YEARS, young players just starting out on the PGA Tour could quickly tell how they stood with Payne Stewart. If he liked them, they had to endure constant pranks.

Like when second-year Tour pro Robert Damron, who grew up at Bay Hill admiring the fluid Stewart swing, was approached by a puckish Payne in the clubhouse grill at the St. Jude Classic in Memphis last year. "He was standing there with one of the lady volunteers and said, 'Hey, Robert, give me five bucks.' I thought he was going to do a trick and or show the lady something on it. But he handed it to the lady and walked off without saying a word."

That left young Damron standing there, suddenly realizing he'd been had. "Obviously, I couldn't ask the lady for my five bucks back." She smiled sweetly and thanked Damron, who could do no more than blink and smile back.

But while Payne loved to yank the chain of the young guys, he would also give them little lessons in the importance of pulling their weight if they wanted to run with the big dogs.

Damron was the recipient of one of those lessons, which cost him far more than five bucks. Self-sponsored as a rookie, Damron was particularly conscious of expenses. Because he had failed to enter the approaching tournament at Milwaukee, he suddenly found himself facing the expensive proposition of reworking his plane ticket from Vancouver, British Columbia, where he had just completed play, all the way home to Orlando. Without the benefit of a seven-day advance purchase or a Saturday night stayover, Damron was reeling at the fares he was hearing over the locker-room phone. Plus, with limited connections, he'd have to layover someplace that night and wouldn't be able to reach Orlando until the next day.

Fellow Orlandoan Lee Janzen overheard the conversation and advised Damron that Payne, who also had just finished, was about to dart home to Orlando in his rented jet. "Why don't you ask him for a ride?" Janzen asked.

"So I did," Damron recounted, "and Payne said, 'Sure.'"

Young Robert was delighted to arrive home late that Sunday night, having crossed the continent in grand style and comfort. However, a couple of days later he was startled to receive in the mail a bill from Stewart for his share of the flight—$2,600.

"It was the kind of thing that first took me by surprise," Damron sheepishly recalled. "But I understood what he was doing and it really was fine. And I do fully understand. It was funny, really, to him just a little barb. Fortunately, I had won a little money by that time. And he's been generous with me over the years. So I wrote a nice thank-you note and put the check in and sent it."

One thing bugged Damron, though. Payne had beaten him out of about one hundred dollars playing gin rummy on the flight home that night. "And he didn't even deduct that from the bill," Damron recounts, laughing.

Payne rarely asked for extra privilege, and he won other pros over to that thinking. When Rinker mentioned that he was seeking a discounted deal on a family membership at posh Interlachen Country Club, near his home in Winter Park, Payne had a better idea. "Aw, you don't want a deal," he told Rinker. "You want to be treated just like one of the other members out there."

Rinker took the advice and joined at the regular fee. "And it's just been wonderful," he said. "Payne was so right. It was one of his little things."

And he practiced what he preached. When Payne opened the 1999 season with no equipment-endorsement contract, he needed a golf bag to reflect that. Others on Tour were surprised and amused when he showed up with a dinky, plain black bag. His bridled ego no longer needed one of those fancy Tour bags half the size of Rhode Island. "Well, it's a funny story," Payne enjoyed explaining. "I got it at Edwin Watts, fifty-two dollars. I walked in, picked out the bag, and paid fifty-two dollars for it. The guy behind the counter almost fell over dead. The look on his face was priceless."

So was the victory celebration on the eighteenth green at Pebble Beach. If you look real close, you'll notice that the knickered champion has a golf bag you'd more expect to see with the winner of the Ocala Muny Fourth Flight.

When Payne wasn't tricking rookies out of five bucks or stuffing banana chunks inside someone's street shoes, he was forever looking for another way to break the monotony on Tour. Tour official Mark Russell says legend has it that Payne once did a most unthinkable thing in a paper bag and placed the bag inside the Tour's traveling fitness trailer. Supposedly, he then waited outside, grinning broadly as he watched the madcap exodus of pros, all gagging and cursing and trying to get out the trailer's door at the same time.

Nobody would confirm the yarn. But then, nobody denied it, either.

AS DAMRON WOULD LEARN, Payne was often generous about giving guys rides in his rented jet—so long as it was *his* idea. Once it was the PGA Tour field staff official he most admired and respected, tournament director Arvin Ginn. A onetime club pro in Mississippi, Ginn lives in the south Mississippi hamlet of Tylertown, which was reasonably close to the cross-country route Payne's pilots would be taking from San Diego to Orlando. Knowing Ginn had been out on Tour five weeks, working through various perplexing weather problems at several West Coast tournaments, Payne offered him a ride home. Or at least to whatever airport was closest to Tylertown and capable of receiving and refueling a Learjet. That turned out to be Hattiesburg.

Something of an Alec Baldwin lookalike, Ginn is a charismatic and stately sort who, until his semiretirement at the end of 1999, managed PGA events with a friendly but efficient no-nonsense style that Payne keenly appreciated. Ginn's staff officials honored him with the respectful nickname "Daddy."

Ginn has a passion for the finer things in life, and Payne, an amateur backyard chef, loved to talk cooking with Ginn, whose culinary skills ran the gamut from barbecue to exotic gourmet dishes. Each time the Tour was in Orlando, for the Bay Hill and Disney World stops, Payne invited Ginn to his house for an early-week dinner that he typically prepared with coaching tips from Chef Arvin.

"It was foolish for me to consider paying him for my half of that flight from San Diego," Ginn recalls, "considering my means and his. But I broached the subject, saying how much I appreciated being dropped off. I told him if there was some way, I would like to pay, but didn't know how, knowing the cost of all that. He just looked at me and said, 'Don't be foolish.'"

Then the grin came out and Payne blurted: "But you *do* owe me! Why don't you send me something you think I'd like to have."

At home that week, Ginn stirred up a fresh batch of the special barbecue sauce he'd been making from his own recipe for twenty years and sent Payne a large jar. The next time they were together at a tournament, Payne made a beeline for the Tour office and raved to Ginn about the succulent sauce.

Another Tour official overheard the conversation and said, "Barbecue sauce? Hey, Daddy, you never told me you made barbecue sauce. I want some."

Payne jumped between them like a mock sentinel and issued a stern advisory: "Oh, no! You have to go through *me* for the Arvin sauce!"

Ginn also raised Payne's standards for choosing Scotch whisky. Bypassing the more familiar brands, Ginn preferred the single-malt Macallan Scotch, which likely isn't available at the New Knights on Quitman Road or, for that matter, at a lot of other pedestrian American watering holes. He told Payne all about the heavenly wonders of Macallan. So on his birthday (January 30), Payne decided to treat himself to this marvelous elixir at the lobby bar of the Inn on Spanish Bay. It was on the eve of the AT&T Invitational and Payne was on his way to an informal players' meeting just down the hall.

"Yes, sir," responded the bartender. "You want twelve-, eighteen-, or twenty-five-year-old Macallan?"

Payne blinked and chuckled, admitting he didn't know he had all those choices. "What the heck. Make it twenty-five," he said, adding with a swagger, "And since it's my birthday, make it a double."

"He said he threw a twenty on the bar, thinking that would include a generous tip," mused Ginn, picking up the story. "The bartender poured, set the glass in front of Payne, and said, 'That'll be sixty-six dollars.' As Payne told me about it, he kinda jerked his head back and got that silly little smile of his. It was so funny the way he told it on himself. He said he sort of stammered and told the bartender, 'W-well, maybe you'd better put that on my *bill!*'"

With that, Payne padded off toward the meeting with a fine Scotch in his hand. And a fine layer of egg on his chin.

chapter 5

The Knickers

The marketing masterstroke of Payne Stewart's signature knickers outfit very nearly debuted and died on the same day. He first wore the jaunty getup during a tournament in his initial full season on the PGA Tour, at the 1982 Atlanta Classic. Fate would deal the ploy a tricky litmus test by landing Payne in the same pairing that day with outspoken veteran Lee Trevino, who shook his head gravely on the practice tee at first sight of the unseemly, look-at-me costume.

Oklahoma! and *Guys and Dolls* had to survive only fickle New York critics. Payne's fashion statement had to step across the white-hot coals of Trevino's cynicism. And it almost didn't.

The Merry Mex hammered the needle so deep during their round that Payne—ordinarily unabashed—began feeling self-conscious and more than a bit foolish. "I bet you thought you were coming to a golf tournament," Stewart later recalled Trevino wisecracking loudly to the gallery around one tee, "not a kindergarten fashion show!"

But immediately after the round, the knickers received gushing compliments from a lady volunteer in the scoring tent. And more from a sportswriter for the *Atlanta Journal-Constitution*. In the locker room, a couple of other pros added their approval, and the golf world's budding court jester was encouraged to consider staying the course—but not again during that Atlanta tournament, lest he have to endure another eighteen holes of abuse from the relentless Trevino.

Over the years, the upbeat reaction of golf galleries around the world helped affirm Payne's unorthodox uniform. The mere first sight of Payne's familiar knickers and jaunty cap bouncing into view invariably produced an epidemic of smiles in the grandstands scattered about tournament courses. His bold outfits, as well as the Aoki-in-reverse putting style that he employed during much of his career, were distinctive calling cards whose inspiration could be traced back to his father.

William Louis Stewart, a two-time Missouri amateur champion, was a furniture salesman best known for his outrageously garish sports coats and for holding his putter unusually erect, so that only the toe of the blade rested on the green. "My father was more up on the toe that I am," Payne said in the mid-1980s. "The way he taught me was that it was kind of like shooting pool. You always wanted the right hand going through down your line. I just seem to get in on the line better when I get my hands up real high and the club up on the toe. I can put a smoother roll on it that way. It's not a *hit* to it, but more of a *stroke*."

As a merchant, the elder Stewart knew the value of identity. Thus, the wild sports coats. Even if he had to take abuse from Payne and his two sisters, who would make the gag motion—poking one finger down their throats at the breakfast table—at their first sighting of each new, screaming jacket. *"Dad!! You're not really going out dressed like THAT, are you?!"*

"He always said if you stand out when you go in to sell somebody something, they'll remember who you are. If you come in dressed all in boring navy blue, you're just somebody else in the crowd," Payne recalled with a chuckle. "Sometimes he didn't even match. But you definitely knew when Bill Stewart was around. You could feel the radiation."

Soon Payne was the one radiating on the PGA Tour. He took a cue from his father's guidelines when, standing on a Tour practice tee early in the 1982 season, he was struck by what he saw around him. "I was wearing red golf slacks with a white shirt and white golf shoes. The guy practicing to my right had on red slacks with a white shirt and white shoes. The guy on my left was wearing red slacks with a white shirt and white shoes. I vowed right then I was not going to be another look-alike," said Payne, who began seriously pondering over the next few weeks what he might possibly do to create space between him and all the clones.

He recalled how nice he thought some of the players had looked in knickers on the Asian Tour and decided to give them a try in one round of the Atlanta tournament.

He wore the knickers throughout all four rounds for the first time a few weeks after the Trevino scare, in the Quad Cities tournament at Oakwood Country Club, in Coal Valley, Illinois. Because the tournament was within driving distance of his home in Missouri, his ailing father, Bill, was there to lend support to Payne's wardrobe and tag along in his gallery. The elder Stewart's early struggle with cancer was beginning to make it difficult for him to walk long distances. Young Tour rules official Mark Russell spotted him and gave him a ride in a golf cart as Payne played through the several holes under Russell's assigned jurisdiction. Russell would recall that the knickered Payne came to him later and expressed heartfelt appreciation for the gesture.

More significant that week, however, was that Payne, wearing the short pants every round, captured his first official Tour victory by two strokes over a pair of players who would later become special friends—fellow Orlando resident Brad "Dr. Dirt" Bryant and Pat "Magoo" McGowan. After putting out on the eighteenth green that day, Payne and his father promptly locked in a lingering embrace, tears of joy streaming down both faces.

Even after Payne later won a PGA and two U.S. Opens and guzzled celebratory champagne from the Ryder Cup, he held fast that the triumph at Quad Cities—the only one witnessed by his late father—remained his most cherished tournament experience. It also served to make the knickers a permanent part of his equipment.

Payne tried to work out a deal to represent the fledgling T. Barry Knicker Company of Palm Desert, California, makers of the bloomers he had selected to wear at Coal Valley. But Tim Barry, the firm's founder and president, was lukewarm at best.

"I had my manager call him and Tim kind of laughed and said, 'Who's Payne Stewart?' He wasn't interested in paying me or even giving me the knickers free. His best offer was to give me one free pair for every three I bought. I took it," Payne recalled.

Although Payne's rising visibility launched a mild revival of knickers and brought attention to T. Barry Knickers in particular, Barry saw no reason to sweeten the pot. Just before the start of the 1986 season, Head sportswear approached Payne with a lucrative offer to provide his plus fours and also make him the company's sole commercial spokesman for its men's and women's lines of golfwear. Payne tried Tim Barry one more time, willing to show his loyalty if Barry would spring for *any* kind of a contract—just something that would allow Payne to look in the mirror. No dice.

Interviewed by phone a dozen years later while Payne was leading the U.S. Open at the Olympic Club in San Francisco, Barry would sigh and lament the decision to forfeit that link with the golfer. "Who knows how that would have had an impact on my little company," he told the reporter. However, to suggest that the T. Barry Knicker Company would have double or tripled many times over would be folly. The knickers caught on for Payne's purposes but hardly became a sweeping fad in this country. Several golfwear companies took a flier on manufacturing and marketing the half-pants but in the process lost their knickers. So to speak.

The odd garment would, however, flourish in Payne's closet, which would become stuffed with a dazzling array of knickers in every imaginable color produced by Head and the other manufacturers that followed as his contracted suppliers. Plus one pair in the official Stewart family Scottish plaid that he broke out each year for the British Open.

Payne had refined the costume in 1984 by adding custom Italian-designed golf spikes that included a shiny metal toeplate. A Tampa-based shoe company, Fore-Limited, had provided a few pairs of its $300-to-$1,000 custom golf shoes to Tour pro Calvin Peete, who in turn had suggested Stewart as a showcase.

"The styling is exotic," Payne said of the shoes, "but the bonus was that they were soft and comfortable." Some thought the styling was out of sync with the rest of his G-rated outfit. A golf writer in Orlando, Payne's adopted hometown, often needled him in the locker room as Payne pulled on the garish spikes, saying things like, "Pardon me, sir, but I just noticed your unusual shoes. Are you a golf pro or a pimp?" He'd react with a pained expression that quickly turned into his trademark laugh and playfully throw something at the writer.

A year or so before he died, Payne had switched to more conventional golf shoes. But there can be no question that he had raised the bar for style among his peers.

"I don't know about trendsetting," he once reflected, "but I think that I kind of started fashion back into golf again. I'd like to be remembered for that. But more important, I want to be respected and have it known by the golfing public that Payne Stewart was a hell of a golfer. And that he was a champion."

Payne had explored that last credo with his new friend and colleague Peter Jacobsen.

"As for the knickers," says Jacobsen, "I had seen them on Rodger Davis, the pro from Australia, who was really Payne's inspiration. And I had seen them on Mike Ferguson, Payne's brother-in-law from the Australian Tour. When Payne was talking about going to the knickers, he told me he wanted to be more distinctive. I remember talking about that with him at the Buick Open in Flint. He said, 'I'm just tired of looking like everybody else. I want to be distinctive.' I thought it was a great idea. Obviously I fall in that same line of thinking. I've always tried to be distinctive and different. I've done crazy things, too."

Ironically, when Payne asked Jacobsen if he thought the world would take him seriously in the outfit, Jacobsen quoted Trevino, of all people.

"You know, I worried about the same thing when I started doing my impressions of Trevino and Palmer and Stadler," responded Jacobsen, who often enlivens golf clinics with his comic imitations of other pros. "I asked Lee if he thought people would think of me as just a clown. He said, 'Peter, as long as you win golf tournaments, you can do and act and say anything you want. Look at me. I love to laugh and joke and have a good time, but I win.' Lee told me if I could back it up with my game, people would think of me as a winner first and a guy who does impressions second. Payne, if you win golf tournaments, they'll say, 'There's the guy who won the U.S. Open and—man!—*look* at those clothes he's wearing! Look at 'em!'"

Mark Lye, the third member of Jacobsen and Payne's informal Tour rock band, was not as encouraging, initially. He advised Payne not to go there, warning that he'd "better have plenty of game to back up those things, because they look like crap."

Now admitting he was overlooking the big picture, Lye recalls thinking the outfit was totally ridiculous. First, he didn't think Payne had particularly attractive legs. He, too, had seen knickers on foreign pros Rodger Davis and Stewart Ginn and felt they had a place in Europe and Australia and a few other corners of the globe, but couldn't see the ploy ever being accepted in the more conservative United States.

"But when you're young and trying to make ten cents and survive for the next tournament, you never see that big picture," says Lye, a commentator on The Golf Channel since ending his eighteen-year Tour career. "Payne just wanted to be distinguishable from everybody else in the field, and nobody else had the balls to wear that kind of stuff. Except for Billy Casper, who *really did* look ridiculous."

But even Casper wore his plus fours (or, as goes the gag aimed at Billy's girth, plus *eights*) only about once a tournament, not every day like Payne. Lye reasoned that Payne looked terrific in regular clothes and looked really bad in the short pants and kiss-me-quick caps. Then Stewart took it another step by wearing lavender or pumpkin knickers or, worse, Tampa Bay Bucs colors. "That's when I really thought he was a whore," Lye said, "when he signed that deal with the NFL for all that money [three years, $600,000] to look like *that*!"

During the course of the contract, Payne's outfits would bear the NFL emblem, and he typically wore the colors of the franchise or franchises nearest to the tournament he happened to be playing. Although league marketing officials say they were very pleased with the association, the contract was not renewed because the renewal demands by Payne and his agent, Robert Fraley, were too rich even for the NFL. "That was Payne— always reaching for the highest plum," Lye mused.

Yet, Lye conceded, if Payne wanted to have some individuality, the route he took was one of the few ways to accomplish that during an era when "Aureus had thirty players on the tee, Izod had twenty players on the tee, and Munsingwear had a bunch of guys. It was just awful crap that we all wore. I mean, that stuff Larry Mize won the Masters in—just awful. But I wore it for four years. I guess I was a bigger whore because I did it for a lot less money."

During that era, Lye said, for Tour pros in his income range, if somebody offered you ten grand, you'd try to find something in their line that you would wear. Even if it meant you'd have trouble keeping your breakfast down when you looked in the mirror.

"But Payne's reason was not only the money," said Lye. "It was also the bigger reason of just being The Guy."

PAYNE'S CONTEMPORARIES WERE SHARPLY DIVIDED when recounting their initial reaction to the knickers ensembles he adopted as a personal statement.

Qualifying-school roommate Mark Wiebe said the rash move didn't surprise him at all, considering it was Payne the Vain. Plus, he felt it was an inspired tactic to accomplish what most every player wanted.

"I thought it was one of the best ways to get the deal done. As professional athletes, we play better when we're surrounded by people watching," Wiebe explained. "I know I play better when I have a gallery than when I don't. It puts more importance on it, or you're on stage, or whatever it is. And Payne came up with a way to get the people out to see him, so that he could show them what a good golfer he is. 'Let's go see the guy who had the guts to wear knickers.' It was one of the greatest marketing ploys I've ever seen.

"And I remember Payne going, 'Yeah, and I'm *paying* for it!' That was when he was buying them himself."

Said PGA Tour rules official Arvin Ginn, still a Mississippi club pro when Payne first established his personalized outfits: "Lots of people thought he was just trying to be cute, or smart. But I thought he was the nicest-looking guy on the golf course."

Hal Sutton admits he first thought Payne had lost his marbles. "Then I came to realize it was brilliant on his part to do that. Payne had the body type to get away with it." Sutton added through a smirk, "When we all wore knickers that day at the Tour Championship in his honor, I know he was looking down, laughing at us."

Fellow Orlando pro Scott Gump saw another reason behind the throwback duds: "That was Payne. That was perfect for him. I think he wanted to dress up as you would going out to a nice dinner. You don't go in shorts and T-shirts. You dress up for the occasion, and obviously he loved to do that and thought he played better for it."

Jacobsen continued that thread: "It was like he was putting on his battle gear, much like KISS doing a concert. When it was time to do battle or go play, it was like a ritual that got them into the proper frame of mind. Pick out his outfit, pick out the shoes—now, let's get it on."

Another Orlando pro, David Peoples, doubts that many other players would have pulled it off. "He was right at home in that outfit. And he looked great in it. He looked like he deserved the right to wear that and I thought he looked professional all the time."

But within the same town, at least one rising young Tour pro jokingly tweaked Payne about the garb. "I often kidded him," recounts Robert Damron, "that no matter how bad I was dressed, I'd always be better dressed than one guy on the Tour." Damron noted that a few of the bolder guys in the Tour locker rooms in more recent years labeled Payne with the moniker "Tinkerbelle," a nickname that stuck.

"Actually, I kind of liked him in knickers," Phil Mickelson insists. "When he first started wearing them, the Senior Tour was starting to become prevalent and some of the players on that Tour wore them—Jim Ferree and another player or two. I thought it was pretty cool. In fact, I went out and bought a pair once. I didn't quite have the courage to wear them in a tournament. But I actually bought a pair."

To Jay Williamson, a thirty-two-year-old rookie on the 1999 Tour, the unusual outfit gave Payne a surreal aura. Like Payne, Williamson is a Missouri native who moved to Orlando.

"So I've always known about Payne and his whole deal," said Williamson. But playing alongside him, Jay acknowledged, was much akin to cavorting with a live, breathing cartoon character—a fantasy figure. The temptation was to ask how Charlie Brown and Lucy were getting along, or what he'd heard lately from Bugs Bunny.

Payne and Williamson were in contention and paired in one of the final groups for a weekend round at the Air Canada Championship outside Vancouver in September 1999. Payne holed a long iron shot from the fairway, and Williamson, who had walked ahead fifty yards, remembers looking back and surveying the unlikely scene—a knickered golfer launching a smart bomb from 170 yards. "You just don't see that every day. It was absolutely like a fantasy. It was a real bizarre feeling that whole day playing with him."

An unexpected by-product of the jaunty, distinctive outfit was that it afforded Payne a certain anonymity when he was out among the masses in street clothes. Jacobsen noted that, just as few people would recognize the rockers of KISS without their dramatic stage persona, neither did many of the Great Unwashed realize when Stewart was walking among them.

"That's a huge bonus," Jacobsen said. "I've eaten a lot of meals with Greg Norman, and he can't go across the street or sit at a table in public without people all over him to sign things."

There was, however, one occasion when Payne was anonymous, even in those blazing bloomers. During the course of winning in 1983 at Disney World, where tournament workers are also outfitted in knickers, Payne strode triumphantly toward the media tent following one round. A dedicated minion on security detail at the entrance took one glance at Payne's knickers and stopped him in his tracks: "Sorry, but tournament workers aren't allowed in here."

Payne's pliable face quickly progressed from shock through indignation to an open-mouthed smile as someone identified the tournament leader for the overzealous guard, who apologized profusely. Payne signed the man's cap before proceeding inside to rap with the scribes.

Longtime Bay Hill pro Dick Tiddy witnessed a striking example of Payne's ability to blend in when "out of uniform." Tiddy was at the '96 Open at Oakland Hills, outside Detroit, tending to his student Steve Lowery, when Stewart, in khaki pants and a T-shirt, quietly sidled up next to him near the main scoreboard behind the clubhouse. The two old friends chatted idly and surveyed the numbers going up on the board for several long moments while frenetic autograph hounds swirled all about, virtually brushing past Payne, in futile search of any Tour pro.

Even winning his second Open at Pinehurst in the summer of 1999 didn't blow his cover. Just a few days after the victory, Payne drove his snappy little Porsche to a quick-change oil depot not far from his Orlando home. "At the oil-change place, those guys didn't know me in the least," yukked Stewart a day later. "When they were done, I said, 'You guys sure you can't find something else you can do to the car? This is a break for me, just being away from the phones.'"

The two mechanics looked at each other, obviously trying to figure out why anyone would be jangling this guy's phone.

The anonymity story Payne truly savored unfolded that same week at the nearby Wal-Mart, just up Sand Lake Road in southwest Orlando. A week after dear ol' dad's Pinehurst triumph, Chelsea and Aaron Stewart would be departing for summer camp. Clad in shorts and sneakers, Payne accompanied them to the big discount store to purchase some needed items for camp.

As they strolled down one aisle, past a middle-aged couple, the man gave Payne a double take. He overheard the man whisper to his wife: "Hey! Hey! I think that's Payne Stewart!"

Curious about how this scene might play out, Payne paused and tinkered with some item on a shelf as if it were something he was actually considering. Although pretending not to notice the couple, he could see, out of the corner of one eye, the woman giving him a serious once-over. Finally, she turned back to her husband with a sneer and Payne heard her rejoinder: "Nah! That's not Payne Stewart. No way!"

"I've got an identity which allows me to go out in public without my knickers and cap and not be recognized," Payne said, punctuating the Wal-Mart story. "A Tiger Woods can't do that."

But even when out of his golfing costume, Payne could be just as flamboyant. From the lectern at the memorial service for Payne, Pastor J. B. Collingsworth related that he and his close friend often drove the same route in the mornings, taking their children to school at The First Academy. Once when they were stopped at a red light on that same Sand Lake Road, it was clear that, even through tinted windows, Payne's choice of shirts that morning lurched out to grab other drivers.

"My daughter began shouting excitedly, 'Dad! Dad! Look at that *shirt* Mr. Stewart is wearing!' I looked over and had to laugh when I saw that Payne was wearing one of those 1970s-style tie-dyed shirts." The pastor tooted his horn, and the Collingsworths' morning was kick-started with one of Payne's megawatt impish grins.

The golf teacher Chuck Cook testifies that Payne's fashion taste for the distinctive also runs to formal wear. They once attended a gala dinner in Monte Carlo, where Payne met Princess Stephanie of Monaco. Naturally, even Payne's tuxedo was a bold departure from the norm. Cook recounted that the princess watched Payne from a distance for a long moment, then turned to her friends and offered in royal tones: "That Payne Stewart is quite the cat's meow!"

Indeed.

chapter 6

Jake Trout and the Flounders

Hardly anything in Payne Stewart's eventful life served to under-score both his fun-loving spirit and his uncompromising focus on becoming a top-rung champion golfer more than the madcap phe-nomenon of Jake Trout and the Flounders. Payne dearly loved playing his harmonica and singing in the Tour's jocular rock band, which sprouted from an offhand suggestion from then-commissioner Deane Beman to guitar-playing pro Larry Rinker during the Tour's West Coast swing in January 1988.

The band progressed from its first, skitlike performance at a pros-and-wives gathering at the Players Championship to parody songwriting, a cassette tape, a compact disc, and invitations to perform at pro-am dinners and other affairs. Payne relished the diversion, although he never let it compromise his family time or, especially, his golf game.

Mark Lye, one of Payne's fellow Flounders, recalled Stewart laying down the law at one band meeting: "Look, one thing for sure, boys. If this infringes on my golf ten cents' worth, I'm not gonna do it."

"He had his priorities straight," Lye reflected. "Let's face it. Back in the late '80s and early '90s, Payne was a completely different person then. He was much more selfish. He was not greedy, but felt his time was definitely worth something. He probably thought it was worth more than it actually was."

In fact, it was Payne's devotion to Job One and his reluctance to log too much Flounder time that eventually curbed the band's activities after EMI-Capitol produced the band's first-rate CD in 1997 and took an option for four more. The music company had hoped that the primary band members—Stewart, Lye, and lead singer Peter Jacobsen—would help promote sales with signings and show appearances.

"Payne was busy doing his stuff and he really didn't want to take part in any of the shows," Lye recounts. "First, we couldn't handle his appearance fee. Peter would do it for ten grand and jet fuel. Payne wouldn't even think of it. It takes work to put on a show, and Payne would play with us only when it was convenient."

EMI-Capitol had sunk some $500,000 into producing and marketing the enhanced CD, which had its own Web page, a lavish jacket with a twelve-page pamphlet featuring photos of the band members, and the uproarious lyrics they had adapted from various pop songs. The company chose not to exercise its options on additional CDs.

Lye shrugged. "They got tired of Payne saying no."

Payne even missed the Flounders' final performance, a stage show at the swank Ritz-Carlton hotel in Naples, Florida, presented in conjunction with the opening of the Tiburon golf resort designed by Greg Norman. That was in 1998, just about a year before Payne died. Lye and Jacobsen performed with a musician friend, legendary bassist Donald "Duck" Dunn.

"But Payne brought a lot to the band," says Lye, "because when he was there, he was pumped about doing it and he was a big draw for us."

"And Payne was actually a pretty good showman," Jacobsen chimed in. "He would always rise to the occasion. The thing is, when you're a pro golfer and you're up there on stage trying to sing or play guitar or harmonica, if you don't buy into it yourself, the crowd won't buy into it. And Payne would always put on his sunglasses and turn a hat around backward and he'd get into it. That was the one thing I always appreciated in Payne's performances with us."

No one is suggesting that Payne was anything close to an accomplished musician. Far from it. He could handle blowing a harmonica solo for a few bars within each song, singing backup to Jacobsen, and lending his amusing presence on stage. But when the task was serious music that would blend with the other instruments, Lye says with a chuckle, Payne became a distinct liability.

After the Players Championship debut, the group decided to write some parody lyrics and record the songs just for kicks. At the first recording session that year in Memphis, they began laying down the tracks, blowing and picking up a storm, with Dunn and two other real musicians backing them up. After a few minutes, the technicians in the sound booth signaled Rinker to step inside for a moment. They played it back, and the group in the soundproof room suddenly resembled a team of concerned doctors stroking their chins and reviewing the disturbing charts of a dying patient.

Rinker emerged with a sick grin and pulled Lye aside. "The harmonica just ain't happening," he confided. Rinker told Jacobsen and Payne to take five, then brought Lye into the sound booth to listen for himself. After a few moments, Lye blinked in astonishment and blurted, "Oh, my God!"

"Basically, we had to shut him out," Lye remembers. "We could let him do solos and he was okay on a solo. He was weak, but at least it was palatable. It was like getting a 30-handicapper who can hit a tee shot every once in a while. But Payne—God bless him—he blew his ass off. He blew hard on that thing. Unfortunately, it was in Chinese instead of English."

OF THE ORIGINAL FIVE, only Rinker and John Inman (who played keyboards but dropped out of the Flounders that first year) could truly read music. Jacobsen, who had messed around with a guitar since junior high school, could read a little music. Ditto for Lye. But to Payne, all those dots and stems and little flags and squiggles might as well have been hieroglyphics.

"Now, there's nothing wrong with that," Lye added. "I can't really read music and neither can a lot of excellent musicians. Duck Dunn never read a stitch of music in his life and he's one of the best—played with [guitarist Eric] Clapton and all those guys."

Jacobsen said Payne had good timing and knew when to jump in. "But a lot of times, he didn't really know when to finish," Jake mused. "I think Payne would get into it and start blowing a solo and he'd get on a roll. Then somebody would have to tug him away from the microphone."

Because three of them played guitar and Payne's was the only different instrument, they made sure he had a couple of solos during each song. Jacobsen and Stewart were the front men, Jake doing all the vocals with Payne singing backup and jumping in with his harp, as serious musicians prefer to call it.

After handpicking the original group, Rinker invited Jacobsen to his house while the Tour was in central Florida for the Bay Hill Classic. They'd play something together, record it, then play it back and laugh at one another. They exchanged a few ideas, settling on the makeup of the group, then scheduled a rehearsal early the next week when the Tour moved just up the road for the Players Championship at Ponte Vedra. The players-and-wives' clambake was set for that Wednesday evening. Rinker was part of the main entertainment and played a few songs before summoning his new compatriots to the stage. Ready or not, the world would be introduced to Jake Trout and the Flounders.

The name had evolved from a brainstorming session during their only rehearsal, the previous evening. They knew Jacobsen would be the lead ham and lead singer. An incurable shower singer, Jake is one of those guys who knows the words to just about every song written. Although he had already notched three of his six PGA Tour victories by that time, Jacobsen's fame was more as a funnyman impersonator than a true golf star. So his nickname, Jake, was a natural starting point. Some bawdy old boys in the locker room had added "Trout" to the moniker, using Jacobsen's playful euphemism for the male sex organ—as in "one-eyed trouser trout."

The rest gets a little sketchy, but what Jacobsen recalls is that they were shooting for something like the lead name "and the *somethings*. Sort of like in Huey Lewis and the News. Or Hootie and the Blowfish." Jake said he thinks Payne then chimed in with, "Well, if you're a trout, then the rest of us are just floundering around!"

"Jake Trout and the Flounders!" Lye supposedly blurted, wide-eyed.

At first blush, Jacobsen didn't like it, but the others quickly voted him down, and the name was etched in fish scales. It struck the perfect tone of silliness and double entendre, reflecting the boys-will-be-boys nature of the whole venture.

The evening before their debut, the group rehearsed in a large banquet room of the Sawgrass Marriott, next to The Players Club. One of the songs they would perform was a rewritten version of "La Bamba."

"We basically just sang all of the Latin and Spanish players' names," says Jacobsen. "La Bamba became Lee Trevino, and we added Chi Chi Rodriguez and Seve Ballesteros, and so forth. Everybody got a kick out of it. I guess to the politically correct, today that would be considered racist. But because 'La Bamba' was a Hispanic song, we thought that was a way to celebrate the Hispanic players throughout golf's history. Our friends. And a bunch of them were there at the dinner and thought it was great."

That inaugural performance consisted of just two other songs, played to the accompaniment of hoots, laughs, and whistles from colleagues in the audience. They concluded with Lye's rewrite of the lyrics to the pop song "Cocaine" into a raucous commentary on slow play.

You know it's a joke when you're stuck with a slowpoke
I'm wearin' a frown 'cause I'm paired with this clown
We don't like, we don't like, we don't like slow play!

They left the stage to a cheering, whistling, standing ovation.

One of the officials from the Memphis Tour stop practically booked them for his pro-am dinner before the applause died. Then the Tour asked them to fire it up again for the annual awards dinner at the Tournament of Champions at La Costa the next January, to start the 1989 season.

They wrote more parodies and began to record an album, on cassette, in the fall of 1988. The Flounders were flying.

But after La Costa, they pared down to just three. Rinker, who wanted to hire a manager and start booking serious gigs, left the group because Payne and Mark Lye weren't as keen on Rinker's idea. Neither was Jacobsen, who, as Rinker noted, tends to just take over when he gets involved in something.

Said Jacobsen, "Larry wanted us to play some real gigs. He had a friend he wanted to hire as a manager, and said, 'We need to pay this guy fifteen percent of the gross and he will book gigs for us around the country at tournament sites and handle the business.' Payne and Mark and I just kinda looked at each other. Payne, especially, was very much against that. When you're on the Tour, besides trying to juggle a family, just trying to play golf was difficult.

"Larry was different. He could handle that. Larry was good at doing both. For some time before that, he would sit in with musical groups on the road. He would have no problems with that. But Payne and Mark and

I, we said no. So Larry did get upset at us, and said, 'If you're not going to hire the manager, then I'm out.' But we loved him and still do. And we all made sure we parted as friends. We really loved each other and loved the music, but just had a difference of opinion on how deep we wanted to go with it. We had thought we'd just hang out and do this for fun. Getting all four of us together was a lot of fun. We were reluctant to get up and perform in front of people because this was not our profession and we weren't really any good. We never shied away from getting together and practicing and just having fun by ourselves in a hotel room."

The remaining three completed their album in 1989, sold sixty thousand cassettes, then went into hibernation for a while. The production of the tape underscored their music-business naïveté. They had no CD, which had become the preferred medium for recorded music. They had no video, and they used their own label (Course Records) and their own money to record and to promote.

The group finally sought help from a California music producer–manager named John Baruck, who was asked to pull the album together. They had been writing and recording a number of the parody lyrics, with Dunn handling the arrangements. Jacobsen and Lye wrote most of the parody lyrics. Payne's main contribution in that department was his transformation of REO Speedwagon's "Time for Me to Fly" into "Time to Let It Fly."

I've had too much of my weakness in these situations
Too much of the lunacy of my hallucinations
My game makes you laugh, but it makes me cry
I think it's time to let it fly

It all seemed great fun until one day Baruck happened to ask to see copies of the releases for the songs. That may have produced one of the few times they were all in perfect harmony.

"Releases?"

Here they had spent a lot of money recording these songs without realizing they needed permissions. They had none. Zero.

Now came the mad scramble to mend fences with the original songwriters, not all of whom were cooperative or amused by these dizzy interlopers from the PGA Tour. Rinker says the code in the music industry is that if you use something first—especially if you *record* it first—and *then* ask for permission, the response is not likely to be good. Eventually, they managed to get releases on most of the songs, at least in time to use them in the 1997 CD. But several had to be replaced before the 1989 tape cassette could be distributed for sale.

They'd eventually be able to laugh at the faux pas, but at the time it wasn't so funny.

What *was* funny, however, was Payne's first experience with a real recording session. Typically, each member of the group is recorded separately in a sound studio, the master music fed through earphones while he adds his own vocals or instrumental work. When it came time for Payne to lay down his track for the cassette, he flew into Tallahassee and Jacobsen met him at midmorning.

"As he walked off the plane," Jacobsen recounted, "Payne had this big Cheshire grin on his face and comes up to me chuckling in that silly little laugh of his and says, 'What are we doing?' I said, 'Hey, we're making music.'"

They drove across town to a recording studio owned by a friend in the music business, arriving in time for Payne's scheduled 11:00 A.M. taping. He was introduced to the technicians and the producer and director, who set him up in a room to begin work. They explained that they would play the body of the song, that he would hear Jacobsen's vocals begin, and that when that ended it would be time for Payne to come in with his part.

It was a bit like taking a postman and plopping him down at the console of a space shot. There were dials and red lights and, besides, there was no audience and it was eleven o'clock in the *morning*, for Pete's sake. Until this defining moment, Payne's Flounder work had come in hotel rooms with only his buddies, or on stage in front of an encouraging crowd, and always at night when music is *supposed* to be made, right?

"Payne just couldn't get into it," Jacobsen says. "After nearly an hour, he asked for a break. He said, 'C'mon, let's get in the car.' We drove off to get something to eat and as we started back, he pointed to a convenience store and asked me to stop there for a minute. He walked in and came out with that big grin and a six-pack of beer."

They drove back to the studio and sat in the parking lot, where they consumed the entire six-pack in fifteen minutes. "Now I'm ready," Payne announced.

"And he was!" laughs Jacobsen. "He was great. He went in, kicked his chair back against the wall, put on his sunglasses, turned the lights almost off, and got into the music. He laid the tracks down in about two hours and then said, 'Now I need some coffee and a couple of sandwiches and I'll be ready to go home.'"

PAYNE HAD TROUBLE RECONCILING the musical foolishness with the respected legacy he wanted to leave as a golfer. In a rare serious moment, he broached the issue with Jacobson in the same manner that he had discussed the image he was creating with the knickers.

"I don't want anyone to think of me as a silly musician," he told Jacobsen. "I want people to think of me as a champion golfer."

Jacobsen responded: "Payne, they're going to think of you as a well-rounded, fun guy. People don't remember O. J. Simpson for what he did on the field. Athletes are always remembered for what they do off the field. It's amazing. People don't think of Arnold Palmer for winning all those tournaments. They think of his courage through prostate cancer, the Arnold Palmer Children and Women's Hospital. You go, 'Hey, this guy's a good guy.'"

Few moments with the group were that deep. Lye says he enjoyed occasional visits with Payne in his hotel suite on the road. He always had lots of CDs and a little stereo set up in his room. He'd blow his harmonica along with the CDs. "He was pretty good like that," Lye recalls with a laugh, "so long as he didn't have to play with anyone else."

Payne gave everyone he liked a nickname. Mark Lye became "Lofton Lye," as in the loft-and-lie machines used to measure the angles of a golf club.

Lye came to enjoy Payne even more after his hiatus from the Tour, a three-year span between the end of his playing career and the start of his tournament reporting work with The Golf Channel. In between had come Payne's personality transformation.

The Flounders were reunited to produce the CD and the spin-off appearances that resulted. That included a one-hour show on The Golf Channel and a video off the CD. Lye noticed the pleasant change in his formerly flippant friend, even if there was an ego leak every now and then. While working on the video in a Los Angeles studio, Payne caught a glimpse of himself in a mirror and decided he needed a hair trim. Everything came to a halt. The crew rounded up a barber to cut his hair on the spot while Jacobsen and Lye cooled their heels and shook their heads.

"What made it really absurd," Lye laughed in the retelling, "was that he said, 'Okay, boys, I'm ready,' then put his goofy hat on. So it didn't matter. But I really enjoyed that time with Payne. He was really a nice guy to be around at that time."

Part of the shoot was in an industrial area outside Los Angeles and involved the camera crew floating by on a barge, shooting the Flounders making music. Back and forth the barge went, shooting take after take, until Payne's bladder demanded attention. He strolled into a nearby Shell service station, where the proprietor turned out to be a Japanese-American gent who had a framed photo of himself and Payne at some long-ago tournament. The man excitedly produced the photo and Payne signed it before ducking into the men's room.

When he emerged, the man had assembled several of his friends and relatives to meet Payne, who was only too happy to chitchat with the whole clan while Jacobsen was forced to watch impatiently from afar. Lye was silently amused by both scenes, Payne engulfed by the fawning Japanese-Americans and Jacobsen stewing "because that damned Payne had upstaged him. Peter has a big ego, too. And as far as the Flounders were concerned, believe me, Peter was the show."

Four months later, in April 1998, the CD and video were released, and Rinker sat in and played on two songs on the album. It was more than somewhat remarkable when you think about it featuring headliner performers like Crosby, Stills, and Nash singing backup for a former golf pro, Mark Lye, and a pair of Tour superstars, Peter Jacobsen and U.S. Open champion Payne Stewart.

Between the songs on the CD are facetious snippets from other famed musicians and golf pros, including this from Arnold Palmer: "Well, I don't want to take all the credit for talent, but first I had to teach them to play golf. Then I had to teach them to sing. And then I taught them to play various instruments—none of which they do very well."

The comment followed the Flounders' rendition of "Love the One You Whiff" (a takeoff on Stills's hit "Love the One You're With") and served to introduce their parody of Steppenwolf's "Magic Carpet Ride." Jacobsen recrafted that one into "Play the Senior Tour" with lyrics that included:

We're not young like we once were
Why don't you come along, old girl
Gonna play the Senior Tour (well)
This place is just right for me
Probably can't compete with Lee
But I think I can take Chi Chi

As best as he can estimate, Lye said they each went $10,000 into the hole on the cassette tape but made about $15,000 apiece on the CD. They decided to put the roughly $25,000 in residuals that eventually accrued from the video into more copies of the CD to sell at pro-ams for charitable causes. They also kept a few copies for their home libraries.

It was in early January 2000, almost three months after Payne died, when Lye was interviewed for this book. He closed the session by telling of the moving and vivid dream he had had the previous night.

"I dreamed Peter and I were at the Buick Open," he said. "I dreamed we went there and the people at the tournament had set up a room for us to see videos of the shows we had done. I kept looking at Payne on the screen and after about ten minutes, I had to leave and go out in a hallway and bawl my eyes out.

"I woke up crying."

chapter 7

The Mayor of Waterville

In the days and months following his death, there was considerable focus on Payne's spiritual blossoming as the sole reason he had become such an embraceable human. But insiders knew that the transformation had begun in earnest at least two or three years before he began to step up his faith significantly. And when that happened, it simply completed the process.

In truth, the turnaround likely began as an emergence of the exemplary values and decency instilled in him long ago by Bee and Bill Stewart. They raised their children to exercise the kind of respect and thoughtfulness toward others that often goes dormant during an athlete's head-turning rise to stardom.

It was Bee who gave Payne the most grief, even after he became a global celebrity, when she saw him disrespect others or violate the simple tenets of civility. After she'd watched him stalk off in frustration after a disappointing round at a U.S. Open a few years ago and blow off fans thrusting pairing sheets at him, Bee nearly took him over her knee. "I told him, 'You're being rude to people. That's not the way life is to be lived,'" recalls Bee. "Tracey told him the same thing."

Frank Viola, the pitcher, could relate. Viola and Stewart developed a friendship in the 1990s, primarily after Payne began to turn the corner, and Frankie was intimately familiar with some of the ingrained traits he saw in his new pal.

"We had similar upbringing and values from our parents, and I think that's why we hit it off so well," he said. "There was the attitude that we were very fortunate to be in the big leagues of sports and do what we do. As I heard stories about Payne and his father and mother, I know he learned right from wrong in no uncertain manner. That's the way it was in my own family coming up. We were taught not to walk around thinking we were better than others—that we were just people. And he was that way—no pretentiousness. And that's what his connection was to a lot of people."

Mark Lye and Peter Jacobsen, Payne's musical "Troutmates," knew that wasn't always the case. They felt their knickered friend had simply been too selective in earlier years about who would be recipients of his considerable charm.

"To be in the arena we were in all that time and have the cojones to win a major tournament," says Lye, "you have to be a little self-centered. Somebody has to pay, and it wasn't going to be Payne. It was going to be the others around him."

Like many pros and even a few members of the media, Jacobsen enjoyed a relationship based on fun with Stewart, but he also knew that Payne often didn't have time for "outsiders." "He was sometimes more into what *he* wanted to do," says Jake. "But when we started recording the second album, Payne and I talked. He said, 'I'm tired of trying to be somebody I'm not. I'm tired of being a golf champion and I'm tired of being a superstar trying to win tournaments. I'm just gonna be the person I am.'

"I would say to him, 'Payne, when we're together we have so much fun. And when you're with your close friends you're that way. You need to be that way with your not-so-close friends. Let people see who you are.' And he did that. He kind of expanded his scope of family, in his mind, from just his close friends to include virtually everybody in the world.

"I'm not gonna mention any names, but you know some players today act like they have to be cool or act like they're above everybody else. And Payne said he wasn't going to do that anymore."

Lye's Tour-playing career ended after the 1994 season and he missed some of the transformation over the next few years. When he joined The Golf Channel as an announcer and spent some time around Payne at the '98 Open at Olympic, Lye was jolted by the change.

"I hadn't paid much attention to it, but all of a sudden, I was, like, Wow! He . . . has . . . become . . . a . . . *nice* . . . guy!" Lye spoke slowly for emphasis. "And that's what's so tragic about his death. He had found out what was really important."

When that change of attitude came, says Lee Janzen, Payne's bond to the masses strengthened quickly. "It got to where he was always happy to see everyone and made everybody feel so good to be around him. Whatever he was doing and whoever he was with, he always made them think, 'This is special and I'm his best buddy.'"

Phil Mickelson saw the same pleasing turn. "Over the last few years, he had become much more caring about others. He was more accommodating of people, whether they were members of the media or fans in general or even other players," said Mickelson. "And even when he could not be accommodating, I noticed that he would say no much more politely. And I just thought, as an overall person, he became so much more enjoyable to be around. I gained a lot of respect for him, respect that grew over time."

Payne's old Q-school roomie Mark Wiebe credits the turnaround to a simple adjustment in his goals. For years, he felt, Payne worshiped only the first-place trophy as the Holy Grail in his life. "But I got the impression that through all of his titles he saw that victories are great and so cool— win a major title and people would be proud of you. But he discovered that wasn't everything, after all."

Payne began telling friends that even after major triumphs, there would be another winner the next week and the experience was something of a vapor—and it didn't offer the end-all gratification he had expected.

"And he was right," said Wiebe. "As soon as Monday comes around, we're writing other stories and reading other stories. We're talking about other tournaments. And I think that maybe he realized that. He wanted to take time to smell the roses and make an impact. He wanted to be more than just a good golfer."

Payne's more passionate embrace of the "little people" began with small hugs.

There was a female food-and-beverage staffer at Isleworth Country Club who discovered Payne wandering around the cart-storage area down in the bowels of the rambling clubhouse, trying to deliver his initiation check upon first joining the club. The woman stopped what she was doing and escorted him up a level and into the membership office. Taken by her thoughtfulness, he made a point of later introducing Tracey and his children to her and routinely paused to strike up a conversation about their respective families when he encountered her at the club.

That fall, she summoned up the courage to tell him about the Halloween costume party she and her husband were giving their children. Noting that his children were of similar ages, she invited him to drop them off for a while. He jotted down the address and thanked her. Overcome by misgivings, the woman wondered if she had overstepped her station with not only one of the club's members but one of its most famous.

Halloween night she answered one of the many knocks on the door of her modest home to find not only the Stewart children but also Payne in a silly Halloween costume. He frolicked right in behind a wide smile and took over the party, entertaining all the children for the better part of two hours.

That sort of unpretentiousness paved the way for a special act of self-less charity in 1990 involving Worth Dalton, a competitive blind golfer. Then forty-three, Dalton had been blind for a decade, having lost his sight to retinitis pigmentosa. Dalton stumped for the R.P. Foundation and had tried to find a pro golfer willing to help bring exposure to the research effort. A mutual friend, Disney World club pro Jon Brendle, introduced him to Payne, who instantly displayed an empathy for Dalton and his cause.

"How can I help?" he said.

"Why don't you play me a nine-hole match, blindfolded," Dalton said, harboring little hope that Payne would actually accept. After all, he had made the same suggestion to several other Tour pros, each of whom was fearful that such a stunt might dent their exalted self-image.

"I could give you some big names, before and since. But I won't," says Dalton. "When I made that playful dare to Payne, he just sort of laughed that laugh of his and said, 'Well, you know, I've never tried it. I've hit a lot of balls with my eyes shut, but never played a match that way. Hey, let's do it!'"

So here was the reigning PGA champion, pulling on a blindfold a few weeks later in front of a media throng, to play a forty-three-year-old blind man. After warm-ups on the range, he called out to Dalton and asked if he would be allowed, during the match, to remove the blindfold between shots.

"I said, 'Well, hell, I can't!'" Dalton recalls. "Payne got a big kick out of that and said he'd leave it on."

With Brendle guiding him around Disney's Lake Buena Vista course and lining up his shots, Payne not only fell hopelessly behind in the match but grew queasy from moving about sightless.

After three holes, Dalton told him, "Look, we've made our point and you've been more than gracious to do this. Why don't you go ahead and take that thing off and let's not keep score." Payne declined, saying he had promised to keep the blindfold on and, besides, he wanted to see what he *could* shoot for nine holes. So the match continued, Payne laughing in good humor at his clunkers and finishing with a 63 to Dalton's 47. When he pulled off the blindfold leaving the ninth green, his first comment to the media was, "I can't believe I took my eyesight so much for granted."

Payne sat around talking to the media about the match for almost two hours, then later overwhelmed Dalton with the announcement that he would make the R.P. Foundation his designated charity for a portion of his Skins Game winnings that year. He continued that for three years, creating a six-figure windfall for R.P. research.

"I became his number one fan for what he did," gushes Dalton, "which was valuable not just for the money but for the tremendous exposure he brought us. But the thing I love most about Payne was that he was one of the few pro athletes where what you see is what you get."

That from a man who can't see, one might say. But then, Worth Dalton and other sightless people often can "see" more accurately than the rest of us see one another.

CLEARLY, PAYNE BEGAN TO PEEL OFF the cloak of arrogance and self-importance that was leading so many other famous Tour pros and other marquee athletes around him to dig a moat between themselves and the common folk.

Tiger Woods developed hives if a fan walked up and said hello at an Orlando Magic game; Payne would often ask the person to sit down or would at least carry on a lighthearted conversation with the person.

Mark O'Meara openly railed about the public boat ramp across from the main entrance to the gated and high-walled Isleworth enclave that allowed just anybody to put in and putter around on the pristine chain of lakes behind his mansion. Payne occasionally stopped at the ramp to swap fish stories with these perfect strangers, or chat about their boat if it caught his eye.

Said the golf shrink Dick Coop: "He learned to talk about a lot of things other than golf. He had reached a point that he could ask about the person he was talking to and really mean it. He could listen and show genuine concern."

Larry Rinker has a gem of a story illustrating the way Payne began to reach out to embrace most any John Doe. It was Super Bowl Sunday 1999, and they were clearing out their lockers after completing play in the Phoenix Open early that afternoon. This was after Stewart had reached out to pull the journeyman Rinker back into his inner circle.

"He asked me to fly with him from Phoenix to Pebble Beach," Rinker recounts, adding with a grin, "Scott Hoch overheard and told me, 'Well, you better ask him how much he's gonna charge.' So I did and he gets this big wounded grin and goes, 'Bud, I'm not going to charge *you!*'"

They whisked off to Pebble Beach and landed in midafternoon, in time to watch the telecast of the Denver-Atlanta Super Bowl in the home of a mutual friend, Monterey Peninsula beer distributor Jeff Couch. Rinker was again staying at Couch's house, as he typically did during the AT&T. Couch had stepped out when they arrived, and the two golfers made themselves at home. Moments later, Couch rang his house to see if Rinker had arrived.

"Who is this?" Payne playfully demanded, answering the phone.

"Well, who is *this*?!" Couch shot back.

"This is Payne Stewart and I'm smoking your cigars and drinking your beer! So you better get over here!"

After watching John Elway and the Broncos finish off the Falcons, Stewart, Rinker, and Couch headed for the Inn at Spanish Bay, where Payne would check in and they would share dinner at Roy's in the hotel. While checking in, Payne struck up a casual conversation with a gentleman also checking in. He asked the man if he was alone. The man nodded.

"No, you're not. You're with us now," Payne declared.

Somewhere is a traveling businessman with a golden story of sharing a delightful dinner with *the* Payne Stewart, who, of course, went on to win the AT&T Invitational at Pebble Beach that week. Not that anyone would really believe the guy.

"An act like that was not typical of the early Payne," says Jacobsen. "But that's typical of the late Payne. I think it was about the end of 1997 and the start of 1998 when Payne just simply had a dawning."

He flashed back to the '98 GTE Byron Nelson in Dallas when he and Payne were to make the first of some promotional appearances at tournaments for their new Jake Trout and the Flounders compact disc.

"That sort of thing was always difficult for Payne some years earlier, when we did the cassette. He didn't want to spend much time with the people," Jacobsen said. "But this time around, we set up this little booth at the tournament and we'd stop by after our rounds to sign CDs. The 'new' Payne was always the first one there. He's signing the CDs, shouting out to people, 'C'mon over here! You need this CD! This is great stuff—Jake Trout and the Flounders, with Peter singing, Mark playing guitar, and me on the harmonica.' He'd open the case and sign the CD and tell them, 'Okay, give this young lady sixteen dollars. Let's go, let's see the color of your money, get it out!' He got so animated that the hour we would sit there seemed to go by in two minutes. And Payne would say, 'Let's do this again tomorrow.' Because he was now connecting with the golf fans.

"I think he actually got to the point that he liked strangers better than acquaintances. Because when you meet strangers, it opens up another part of the world to you. So I just loved doing all the promotional stuff with Payne in 1998. Mark and I just kinda saw him blossoming. And it was wonderful."

Payne had often displayed those "sideshow barker" talents before, but usually in more private settings. He took over the show as star auctioneer at a fund-raiser in O'Meara's spacious garage and had the elite audience laughing and writing out huge checks for assorted golf memorabilia. He did the same at one of Magic coach Brian Hill's annual Cystic Fibrosis Foundation fund-raisers at Isleworth, going the extra mile by inventing on the spot auction items that would require a commitment of his own time.

Recalls former Magic exec Alex Martins, "At Brian's affair, Payne gave away a dinner with himself and rounds of golf with him. He ended up raising in excess of $20,000 just in items he donated on the spot, then sat around and chewed the fat with all of us for more than an hour afterward."

Payne's strong charitable impulse didn't need a stage, however. He could embrace the joy of giving on a modest, personal level, as well. While playing in the 1998 Michelob Championship in Virginia, he and Tracey visited the nearby amusement park at Kingsmill, frolicking through the facility one evening like two teenagers. Payne won two large stuffed animals on the midway by knocking over Coke bottles or some such. At first, he intended to drag the big, furry toys back home to Orlando, for Chelsea and Aaron. But as they departed the park, Payne impulsively gave the stuffed animals to a random pair of children.

"The look on their faces made it worthwhile," he said, recounting the story just days before his death. "It excites me almost as much as winning a golf tournament to help people and see their faces."

When the Stewarts put their lakefront mansion up for sale in early 1998—in part because Payne felt it was simply too pretentious—he was accorded a peek at just how far removed from the mainstream a celebrity can become. The experience made a deep impression. One of the prospective buyers was pop singer Michael Jackson, who dropped in with a real estate agent late that summer. That was Home Run Derby summer, when the nation was enraptured by Mark McGwire and Sammy Sosa's race to surpass Babe Ruth and Roger Maris.

While Jackson was being given a tour of the home, Payne and the agent gushed about the big news of the day—Sosa had hit his sixtieth home run to reach Ruth's legendary plateau. Overhearing the conversation, Jackson asked who this Sosa person was and what was so special about sixty home runs.

"It was sad, really," Payne said later, "to think that someone can allow themselves to live in such a cocoon." During the visit, Jackson remarked on how cordial and friendly the Stewarts were to him. When the agent called a few weeks later with the pop star's request for a second visit, Payne was skeptical. "Is Michael seriously thinking about buying the house, or does he want to come back just because we were nice to him?" Payne asked. The agent confessed it was probably the latter. Payne politely declined.

He said the encounter caused him to look around at how some of his fellow Tour stars and other high-profile athletes were similarly walling themselves away from society. He vowed not to let that happen to him.

At the time of Payne's death, the mansion was still on the market—asking price: $7 million—though he and Tracey had launched design plans for a less-gaudy home nearby. "A lot of rooms in this house won't exist in the new house. A formal living room, a formal dining room," he said, naming two. "We're not formal people. We've used the formal dining room twice. We're casual people. The new house will also be elegant and nice, but it won't have a formal feeling."

PERHAPS THE MOST GRAPHIC EXAMPLE of Payne's connecting with everyday folk was his pre–British Open junkets the last two years to Waterville, a picturesque village of 450 residents on the craggy southwestern coast of Ireland. He joined colleagues Tiger Woods and Mark O'Meara and friends in his initial visit to Waterville in 1998, for what was a combination vacation and casual Open tune-up on a seaside links course.

Enthralled by the locale and the warmth of its residents, Payne returned just before the '99 British Open, this time with Lee Janzen, David Duval, and Stuart Appleby added to the roster. Also on hand were numerous friends and a small cordon of reporters attracted by the glitzy lineup. While the other pros made a minor attempt at protecting their privacy, Payne was everywhere, visiting the townsfolk in their shops, interacting with stroll-along members during social rounds at the Waterville Golf Club, taking Tracey to Mass at St. Finian's Catholic Church, and holding court until the wee hours in the High Bar at the Butler Arms Hotel. He sang with the locals, blew on his harmonica, and even tended bar.

Noted golf reporter Jeff Williams researched the Waterville junkets and penned this conclusion: "Payne Stewart became part of Waterville in those two visits. He reached out to the people, who in the abiding nature of the Irish, reached back. His warmth matched theirs. His depth of feeling matched theirs. His spirit matched theirs."

What amazed the villagers was not only that Payne interacted so completely with them during his four-day visit in 1998 but that he remembered all their names and their personal stories when he returned in '99. He revisited Sheila-Ann and Padraig Fogarty and their paraplegic son Patrick, and was clearly delighted that Patrick was now pursuing college studies, as Payne had urged the previous summer. "Payne was so supportive of him, so caring, so genuine about it all," Sheila-Ann told Williams.

"All the other players were very nice, but Payne was different. Payne didn't seem like an outsider."

Payne had met the Fogartys when he popped into their little ice-cream shop in the heart of the village.

Waterville Golf Club member Maura O'Neill connected with Payne as he walked along during one of his rounds that first visit. They exchanged good-natured patter. She even playfully tweaked him about losing to Janzen in the U.S. Open just weeks earlier at Olympic. As she nervously watched on television while Payne lined up the final putt that would give him the Open title at Pinehurst the next summer, O'Neill lurched toward the TV set and made the sign of the cross over it, trying to provide spiritual support. When the putt went in, the roar of approval at Pinehurst probably included O'Neill's whoops of joy all the way from Waterville.

"I have his autograph on my [golf] handicap card I carry in my wallet," she says proudly. "I will probably always carry it."

Chuck Cook, Payne's coach, was part of the 1999 entourage that observed this love affair between the little Irish hamlet and Cook's gregarious student.

"We started calling him the mayor of Waterville," Cook reflected, "because he was entertaining everyone in the pub every night. I mean, the pub was just full of people. He was there playing his harmonica, singing, and drinking Guinness with them and staying up to three o'clock in the morning. I could tell in a hurry this wasn't going to be a working trip.

"So after he got that 'mayor' nickname in the press, the townsfolk called him up and said, 'We don't really have a mayor of Waterville. The most important position you can have is to be captain of the Waterville Golf Club. So we've made you our honorary captain for next year.'"

In a little ceremony during the Ryder Cup matches in Boston in the fall of 1999, they made it official.

part three

PAYNE
THE PLAYER

Q&A

with Chuck Cook

Through most of the last decade of Payne Stewart's life, Chuck Cook, a kindly munchkin of a golf teacher based outside of Austin, Texas, served as something of a surrogate father. After growing up around various Air Force bases, this son of a military pilot attended Tulsa University, served a hitch in Vietnam, and was discharged in Indiana, where he started a career in golf as an assistant club pro and golf teacher. He molded a couple of champion juniors, then moved to Texas and joined the instructional staff of *Golf Digest*'s Golf Academy. He branched out on his own as an independent teacher in 1991, continuing to work with Tour pros such as Tom Kite, Corey Pavin, Bob Estes, and the one he calls his most rewarding challenge, Payne Stewart.

Cook's assigned task was to maintain that fluid swing with the silky tempo that Payne had developed under the tutelage of his late father, Bill Stewart, a Missouri state amateur champ. But as Payne worked with this diminutive gent some thirteen years his elder, he grew to trust not only Cook's instincts about the golf swing and the mentality needed to become a champion on the course, but also his instincts and philosophies about becoming a champion in life. Particularly after the working relationship was resumed following a brief interruption in 1995, caused by the kind of impetuous snit that later all but disappeared from Payne's modus operandi.

Cook became a virtual member of the family, often staying overnight in Payne's lavish lakefront home during practice sessions in Orlando. He traveled as a special guest with Payne to tournaments and on more informal junkets—like that stopover in Ireland before the British Open. One of the speakers at Payne's memorial, Cook sweetly shared his memories of the special trip to Pebble Beach when Payne had invited him to tag along for the defending champ's Media Day appearance a few weeks before the '92 U.S. Open.

Following afternoon activities, dinner, and an extended nightcap in the bar at the storied Del Monte Lodge, Payne and Cook ventured out to the famous eighteenth green accompanied only by the U.S. Open trophy Payne had won at Hazeltine the previous summer. On a perfect starlit night with the Pacific crashing onto the rocks below, the two of them sat on the concrete seawall adjacent to the green, the trophy perched between them, and talked about life until three o'clock in the morning. A month after offering his own touching eulogy at Payne's memorial service—including references to the seawall heart-to-heart—Cook spent another two hours discussing the friend and pupil he dearly misses . . .

Question: *You started working with Payne in 1989. How did the relationship come about?*
Chuck Cook: Payne had hired Dick Coop, the North Carolina–based sports psychologist who works with a number of pros. Dick and I had done a lot of work together. He felt like Payne needed someone who was up to date, so to speak, with the golf instruction that was going on and to keep an eye on his physical work. Payne had been working with Harvie Ward, and Dick recommended me after Payne stopped seeing Harvie. So I went to work with him in January 1989. We worked together until 1995, broke up about a year and a half and then got back together again for the rest of his career.

Q: *From the first few sessions, what was your impression of Payne the person and Payne the player?*
Cook: Well, as a person, I liked him. Payne always loved to be around people and be the center of attention. He liked his notoriety. He was always comfortable that way. And because he liked people so much he was also fun to be around. We always had a good time together. I immediately enjoyed him as a person.

As far as his golf swing, I thought what everybody else thought. I thought he had a beautiful, graceful movement to his golf swing. But I also always thought it was kind of complicated. And not orthodox. His position was always sort of a shut clubface going back, and he always overswung a little bit. Things like that.

Q: *Harvie said the main thing he did while working with Payne was simply to get him to trust his swing, rather than change it. Did you depart from that plan?*

Cook: No. What he had asked of me when we first started working together was not to try to change his swing materially. His father had told him never to change his swing. And he didn't really want to change his swing. So what we did at first was I filmed him—not for him, for me—to sort of know what he did when he was doing well. So when he wasn't doing well, I could see what he was doing differently. I still have films from back at that time.

If he would get off, I'd film him again and then compare it to the earlier film. By the time we had worked together a few years, I didn't need the films. I could just see what he was doing differently. When Payne had trouble, the majority of time his alignment would get off. That was the main thing, just to get him realigned. Then sometimes it was his takeaway and he would tend to take it too straight back. When he played his best, the club came inside a little bit with his turn. We worked an awful lot on those things.

Q: *Don't I recall your saying once a change in equipment set Payne's swing back a few years?*

Cook: That's right. When he changed from Wilson to Spalding, his swing changed dramatically because of the new clubs. The year before he switched to Spalding, he didn't win but he had finished in the top three seven times. So he just had this great year. After he switched, it was probably three years before Spalding could come up with equipment that was suited to his swing. They started off with offset irons with square grooves and high-spin ball. He lost yardage. The ball would spin so much it wouldn't go anywhere.

His best swing was when he sort of looped it inside on the downswing and hit a draw. But when he got those clubs and the ball wouldn't go anywhere, he started to get on top of the ball more, trying to trap it. His swing got real steep. So the last few years, we mostly worked on trying to shallow out his downswing and get back to his old swing so he could hit the ball more with a draw—as opposed to swinging so steep that he would pull the ball or slice it.

Q: *When that Spalding contract expired at the end of the 1998 Tour season, Payne didn't sign on with another clubmaker at the start of '99. Phil Mickelson saw that as part of Payne's change in priorities and maybe even relating to his increased faith. In Phil's view, it was as if Payne was saying that just making money was no longer his life—that excelling and being happy had become more of a priority.*

Cook: I don't think it related to faith. Two things happened with the club deal. There weren't a lot of substantial offers from club companies at the end of '98. Many of those companies were struggling at the time. Payne's Spalding contract was just coming to an end. Several companies came to Payne, but he had such a terrible taste in his mouth about what had happened with Spalding that he just didn't want to do that anymore. So he wasn't going to sign just to be with some club company.

Golfsmith [Lynx] approached him and offered some real good incentives—win a tournament and get a big bonus. If you win a major, bigger bonus. *And* you don't have to play our clubs. We want you to try to. We want you to try them out and tell us what you want and we'll try to build exactly what you want. But you don't have to use any of them if they don't work for you. So when Payne won the AT&T, he still hadn't signed with anyone. Then he finished second at the Honda and Golfsmith came back at him, saying they'd not only give him the contract but also the retroactive bonus for AT&T. That's when he signed with them. One of the comments he did make that was in keeping with the way he had come to view things was that the family that owns the company were such nice people and family-oriented people, that they had everybody in the family working in the business. He felt comfortable with them. Trusted them. After he won the Open at Pinehurst, he told them he would change to their clubs, but not until after the Ryder Cup. True to his word, after the Ryder Cup, he took some Lynx irons with him to use in the Dunhill Cup. He also used them in the Disney Classic, just before he died, and missed the cut.

Q: *Didn't you also work to improve his practice approach and his confidence?*
Cook: Oh, yes. And Payne trusted me implicitly on that. I was very honest with him. And he would pretty much do what I told him. If I felt like he needed to spend more time practicing, he'd do that. We had a series of exercises and drills we did in the short game that were sort of "end result" drills, not how to chip or anything like that. I'd make him chip and make him putt a lot. And he would believe in me when I'd tell him, "Your swing has gotten too much that way or this way and you need to practice this." And he would do it. I think that was a real comfort to him—that he knew I was being totally honest with him and not sugarcoating anything or just agreeing with him to pick up his business.

Q: *Where did you usually work with him?*
Cook: I'd go out on Tour maybe eight or nine tournaments a year where he was playing. I'd go to Orlando about four times a year and he'd come to Austin maybe twice a year.

Q: *What was the usual routine when you got together?*
Cook: If I came to Orlando, I'd usually fly in the night before and stay at his house. Payne always had family things to do—take kids to schools, have back exercises to do, and so forth. So we'd generally get out to the Isleworth practice tee about ten o'clock, practice a couple of hours, usually half the time on the full swing, half on the short game. Then we'd go in and have lunch and then go play eighteen holes. In the evening, we'd sit and talk an awful lot. We became good friends and shared a lot of our personal lives. We'd

Q&A with Chuck Cook

have Scotch-tasting contests or sit and drink beer. Payne wasn't one to sit still for very long. He loved stimulation. When I was there in his home, he'd have the TV on, have music on, everybody would be running around doing something. He'd be cooking or something. Something would always be going on at Payne's house.

Q: *What caused the eighteen-month hiatus in your working relationship?*

Cook: It started with an incident at Shinnecock, at the 1995 Open. He had made an appointment on Monday of that week. I had gone to Kemper to work with him and Corey and Tom Kite the week before and they all played well—finished in the top ten. So I had set appointments to give each of them a day at Shinnecock. I told Payne I would just meet with him on Monday and then Tuesday I would give to Corey and Wednesday to Tom. So I went up to Shinnecock on Monday and Payne wasn't there. He didn't show up until five o'clock and I had already gone by then.

He came out the next day and said, "Can you watch me?" I said, "Well, I'm with Corey today. We had already made the plan, you know, to work with you yesterday." He said, "Yeah, well, I just didn't feel like practicing. I just couldn't do it." So I said I could give him some time, but I'd primarily be with Corey and out on the course with him. I said, "You're welcome to play along if you want and I'll watch you some." Well, he played along with Corey, but I could tell he was really mad with me. And then he got real mad when Corey won the tournament. Payne said, "Of course he won. He finished second last week and you spend all day Tuesday with him. I just can't count on you. I'm just not gonna work with you anymore." I told him that was okay, if that's the way he felt.

Earlier that year, he had asked me to come down to New Orleans to work with him the week before the Masters. We had to really work hard just to get him to keep the ball in play. This was during that time he was struggling with the Spalding irons. He had gotten very steep [in his backswing] and we were working to put the loop back in his swing. He'd hit it great for nine holes, then awful for nine holes. So finally he started goofing around. He'd aim it way out over the water and slice it back. And then hook one back. He basically had quit playing and was goofing around. I walked off the golf course and left him a note at the hotel and I said you don't need me here if that's what you're gonna do. During that particular time, that was the way Payne's history was. He would be very petulant and moody and pouty about a lot of stuff.

There was the Tour Championship at Hilton Head when he wouldn't even shake Tom Kite's hand after Tom beat him in a playoff. And you remember, of course, how he acted at the PGA in Chicago—laughing in the scorer's tent while poor Mike Reid was giving him the tournament by bogeying the last several holes. It was awful. That's just sort of the way he was.

Q: *When the two of you resumed working in 1997, did you notice a dramatic change?*

Cook: Well, there was definitely a change. In 1996, he changed all of that. And I never saw him revert back. Once he made up his mind to change his attitude, he never reverted. But even during the time we weren't working together, if I was at a tournament working with one of my other players, I'd always come over and watch him swing and make suggestions. So we weren't really out of touch and he could see I wasn't bitter.

I was very proud of him for simply deciding he was going to have a good attitude no matter how he played. He had said some things at different times and he and Tracey had talked about how he just needed to change his attitude—or quit. That's what Tracey told him. So he made an effort to change. I think Robert [Fraley, Payne's agent] had him go to a media consultant, and he learned how to handle the press better. I know with his golf, his attitude changed with just the way he approached it. That year, he played with smoke and mirrors and still had a good year, a reasonable year. He couldn't hit his ball at all, but still played well just because of his attitude. He wasn't going to let himself play poorly. He'd make a miraculous up-and-down. It was unbelievable, really.

Q: *What was he now doing that affirmed to you he had, indeed, upgraded his attitude?*

Cook: On the course, it was real obvious. He was always upbeat, never hung his head, never got down on himself. He'd come in and if he had a good round he'd talk about that. If he had a bad round, he'd say, "I'm going to do better tomorrow. I gotta go hit some balls." He'd be upbeat that way. Off the course, the way he started acting toward people changed a lot. He started reaching out to people and became much more gracious with people. His humor was still the same—he liked to tease and liked to dig. That didn't change, except that it wasn't as harsh or as cruel as it had been. The tone of it changed dramatically.

I'm sure you remember how classy he was after Lee Janzen beat him at Olympic for the '98 Open, with Payne losing a four-shot lead on the last day. I'm going in the press room afterward thinking, "Oh, my gosh, how's he gonna possibly handle this?" Yet, he was perfect. He talked about how he didn't play well enough to win and Lee played a great round, and how you have to give him all the credit in the world. If you compared tapes of Payne at the '89 PGA and Payne at the '98 Open, you wouldn't believe it was the same person.

Q: *Did his treatment of you also change?*

Cook: He always did great things for me, before and after the change. He always treated me so well. That was what was different with him in comparison to some of the other guys I work with. With Payne, it was a lot more than just a business relationship. There were things I would never have experienced if not for Payne's thoughtfulness and kindness toward me. He took me to Augusta the week before the Masters one year to work, but also because he knew I wanted to go and play there. After he won the

Open in '91, he took Coop and myself and Hicksie [caddie Mike Hicks] and we all went to Scotland the week before the British Open and had a wonderful time. We still talk about it. He took me with him to the Super Bowl in Tampa, the one the Giants won. He always included me. Last summer he took me along on that trip to Ireland the week before the British Open. We played with Tiger Woods and David Duval and Mark O'Meara. There were a lot of stories in the British papers about that trip, including Payne staying up all hours singing and playing his harmonica with the locals in the pubs.

Q: *When he took you along for the U.S. Open Media Day at Pebble Beach, and the two of you sat up talking half the night on the seawall next to the eighteenth green at Pebble Beach, that has to be among your most cherished memories of Payne. Your telling of that story was certainly one of the special moments of the memorial service.*
Cook: It was very special. The weather was beautiful that night. I've got a picture right over my desk of Payne and me holding the trophy during one of the functions that day. The weather was beautiful. It's amazing to me how many people have asked about that story since the memorial service. Tom Kite asked, Byron Nelson asked, lots of others. One person even wanted to arrange it for me to go out to Pebble Beach and re-create that scene on tape. The guy said, "I'll arrange that for your birthday." But I explained that was sort of a private thing.

Q: *That said, were there parts of that seawall talk that you can share? That would have come during a period in Payne's life before he began reexamining his own spirituality. Is it safe to assume that he didn't launch a discussion about faith that night at Pebble Beach?*
Cook: Actually *(laughing)*, we were pretty pie-eyed when we first went out there. But I do remember that we talked about how insignificant it seemed to him right after he had won the trophy the year before. And the trophy was sitting right there on the wall between us. He had brought it with him to leave with the USGA

at that time. He was saying things like, "I worked all my life for that trophy and that was the tournament I always wanted to win. And there was a lot of to-do made. But then all of a sudden everybody was gone and I'm just there. And it doesn't mean that much." He talked about how he hoped that at some time he would look back and see his name on that trophy and realize it was an important thing. But it didn't seem that important to him at that time in his life.

Trouble on Sunday

When the first of the PGA Tour's then-semiannual qualifying tournaments opened at Walt Disney World in the spring of 1981, the gregarious former all-American out of Southern Methodist University was touted as one of the potential stars to watch. Although he had failed in his first attempt at Q-school, adventurous Payne Stewart had gone off to sharpen his game that winter on the mystical Asian Tour.

There he had managed to wrap his arms around some trophies. And there he met his future wife, Tracey. He won the Indian Open and Indonesian Open en route to finishing third on the Asian Tour's order of merit. There seemed little doubt—least of all in Payne's mind—that he would splash onto the glitzy American Tour.

"Quite simply, the plan was that he was going to make the Tour and then he and Tracey would get married, which they did that November down in Australia," recalls fellow pro Mark Wiebe, who shared a hotel room with Stewart during that Q-school. Wiebe was a husky Californian whom Payne had met and befriended at various amateur events in which they competed as teenagers. They clicked, though Wiebe had reservations.

"He was arrogant as all get-out," Wiebe recalls. "It was one of those deals where I really liked this guy—but *should* I like this guy? I didn't know him all that much, but, man, he was really cocky. At that time, all the guys I knew and had met, we all felt we could go on the Tour and win. But we weren't willing to tell people that. Payne had a willingness to say that he wanted to go out on the Tour and kick some butt. There would be some raised eyebrows. But he had so many other great qualities and was such a likable guy that you couldn't help but like him."

William Payne Stewart was held in much the same regard at Springfield, Missouri's Greenwood High School, where he was the Big Man on Campus—quarterback on the football team and guard on the basketball team. He deftly ran the pattern offense of the Greenwood basketball team and averaged almost twelve points a game in his senior season. His signature moment in football came when he triggered a trick play to surprise the heavily favored defending state champions from nearby Jasper. With the ball positioned on the right hash mark following a short kickoff return, the Greenwood offense paused near the left hash mark entering the field. Only Payne drifted over, nonchalantly, to where the ball and the unsuspecting Jasper defense were located. Acting as the center on the trick play, Payne whipped an underhanded pass across the field to running back Tom Martin, who scooted down the left sideline for a sixty-five-yard touchdown. The play gave Greenwood a shocking 20–20 tie that was nearly as sweet as an outright victory.

Everyone knew, however, that golf was Payne's special gift. Perry Leslie, a club professional then at Hickory Hills Country Club, where Payne and his father played, says that Payne had the same fluid swing now familiar to millions when he was a junior-high tyke. And the rich golf heritage in Springfield—and at venerable Hickory Hills, in particular—fostered high goals for the youngster. Horton Smith, the very first Masters champion, was from Springfield. Fabled hustler Titanic Thompson allegedly pulled his first golf con there. In addition to Bill and Payne, Hickory Hills produced four other state amateur champions and was the springboard for assorted other significant cup winners. One sleeve of windbreakers sold today at the club's pro shop proudly boasts this list of the glamorous titles won by former and current Hickory Hills members: U.S. Open, Masters, PGA, PGA Tour events, LPGA Tour events, Missouri Amateur, Missouri Senior Amateur, Missouri Women's Amateur, Missouri Women's Senior Amateur.

Golf came so easily and naturally to Payne that when Leslie gave group junior lessons, his star pupil would hit three or four perfect shots, then run off to the swimming pool.

"His dad would have to go get him, drag him back, and tell him to hit balls and practice," muses Leslie, now the golf director at a new Tom

Fazio–designed club at nearby Branson, Missouri. "Payne wasn't much on practicing. He could already do what we were teaching."

Leslie recalls that Bill loved to play for money and introduced Payne to that at an early age in the interest of teaching him to play under pressure. "He liked that. 'Cocky' probably comes closer than 'confident' in describing Payne at that time, so he was pretty good at playing for a few bucks. As a result, he usually had plenty of spending money."

While Leslie took a brief, undistinguished stab at the PGA Tour, Payne was becoming an all-American at Southern Methodist University, tying for the Southwest Conference individual title as a senior with a laid-back University of Houston star named Freddy Couples.

Payne won the Missouri Amateur in 1979 just weeks after finishing at SMU. It was his farewell to amateur golf, as he turned pro that summer and promptly won a pro-am at Carthage, Missouri, the victory worth $1,000.

But he failed to land his Tour card in the November 1979 Q-school at Waterwood National Country Club, outside Houston. Payne missed the early cut and gave up his condo room to a promising Wake Forest hotshot named Scott Hoch. He would later become close friends with Hoch when they were reunited on the PGA Tour, and after the Hochs moved to Orlando, Payne and Tracey would be drawn there by their tight friendship, staying with them while house hunting. Sally Hoch once had to tone down Payne's extrovert nature by curtailing his habit of walking around the Hoch house in his skivvies.

After Payne missed the Waterwood Q-school, his father and Leslie, back from his PGA Tour attempt, discussed the golfer's options. Leslie advised him to go play a southern California mini-tour that had tournaments in sets of four. Payne made a small check in the first one, then finished 1–2–1 in the closing three. The manager of the mini-tour had a working relationship with the Asian Tour and made arrangements for Payne to sharpen his game further in a short season that winter in the South Pacific.

Emboldened by his successes there, he returned to the States fully confident that his second crack at Q-school that spring at Disney World would land him in the Big Show. Payne was ready for the Tour. The bigger question was whether the Tour was ready for him.

MARK WIEBE HAS A PRESSING MEMORY of that Disney Q-school. The room they shared was on an upper floor in one of the Disney hotels. It was high enough that they had a clear view over the pines of central Florida's notorious late-spring thunderstorms rolling across the peninsula. One was particularly nasty and headed right at them.

"We were out on our little balcony and lightning was flashing everywhere," Wiebe recounts. "All of a sudden, there was one of those flash-boom things. I told Payne, 'Well, that's about enough for me,' and headed back inside the room. The sliding door stayed open and he kind of looked in and said, 'Hey, Bud, if it's your time to go, it's your time to go.' And I said, 'Yeah, but, you know, I don't have to push it. I don't want to go out there and have people read about a golfer struck down by some freak lightning accident.'"

Payne's face twisted into a quizzical expression as he thought about what Mark was saying. "You know what? You're right," he said, stepping inside and closing the door. The pair would look back often over the years and laugh about that moment.

Wiebe thought that was quintessential Payne Stewart.

"Usually, if it was his way it was the right way. But if you ever said something that caught him, he would stop—like right now—and think about what you said, lay it out, figure it out, and go with it or not go with it."

Wiebe would have to endure two more Q-schools before earning his Tour playing card, but Payne breezed in with three strokes to spare. Wiebe remembers Payne calling Tracey in Australia that night to spread the good news trans-Pacific, but also remembers Payne being sympathetic toward him.

"He asked me all about how I had played. I remember being sad, but I also remember being happy for him and seeing the joy that he had. I knew I would be there eventually and he knew that too."

After Wiebe played his way onto the Tour, in 1983, the two rekindled their friendship, often playing practice rounds or sharing dinner—the burly rookie from California and the rising star who already had two U.S. victories. "The thing that was very cool was when we talked—and here's a guy who already had won and would win majors and was always way higher on the money list than I was—it was just two buds hitting balls together. Payne never talked to me like he was looking down on me or I was looking up to him. But I *did* look up to him."

Payne had nicknames for everyone he liked. His name for this author was "Scoop." He had two names for Mark: "Webber," which was a play on Mark's last name, and "Luker," its origin unknown to Mark. But Wiebe can still hear the latter one echoing from the time they were together in the 1985 Anheuser-Busch Classic, shortly after Wiebe had posted the first of his two Tour victories. "I hear this 'Luker' yelled from, like, the next county, and anytime I heard that I knew exactly who it was. I looked around and here comes Payne with the biggest smile on his face. He came over and gave me a big hug and handshake. He was genuinely happy for me and my first win."

THERE WAS ANOTHER PLAYER who missed his card at that Disney Q-school who would become a key player in Payne's life. Payne and Mitch Kemper, another free spirit with musical inclinations, had become tight friends during that California mini-tour series the previous year. Kemper's dream of playing on the PGA Tour was never fulfilled, but he did join the circuit briefly in another capacity. When Payne needed a fill-in caddie late in his first full season, he asked Kemper if he was interested. Mitch jumped at the chance and Payne finished third that week in the Buick Open at Flint, Michigan. The $18,200 check was his second-largest of the year, so he was happy to have Kemper stay on the bag. Kemper was delighted, too. He was enjoying the glitter of PGA Tour life, even if in a caddie bib. Besides, he could supplement his meager caddie pay with his uncommon gift for playing the stock market.

So when Payne embarked on the 1983 season, grinning there on his bag was old pal Kemper, who could play a guitar and the Big Board with equal skill. The Stewart-Kemper team bolted from the blocks with a Tucson top-ten finish and was in position to make a huge statement the next week at a Los Angeles Open that aging Arnold Palmer very nearly made legendary. The fifty-three-year-old Palmer rocked the golf world by making a serious and sustained run at what would have been his first regular-Tour victory in ten years. The popular icon turned back the calendar with an opening 66 there at Rancho Park, then added a 69 to lurk just two shots off the thirty-six-hole lead. That forced tournament officials to print extra tickets and landed Palmer a third-round pairing with a rising star named Payne Stewart, whose youthful cockiness would dissolve that Saturday in the pulsing presence of the King.

"That's the only time I ever saw Payne intimidated," Kemper recalls. "But that was the first time he had played with Arnie and, with all the excitement of him being in contention and the enormous gallery that followed us that day, Payne forgot about his own game and got swept up watching Arnie." Palmer delighted the masses with a 68 to charge one shot closer to the lead; Payne sputtered to a 73 and faded from view. But the experience became a preamble to a catchphrase that would live as the special bond between Payne and Mitch.

Three weeks later, they were on the famed eighteenth at Pebble Beach, where Payne hit a big drive that placed him in go or no-go territory on the par-5 hole that runs alongside the Pacific Ocean. If he boldly tried to reach the green, he'd run the risk of his ball later washing up in Honolulu.

"What have we got?" Payne asked, surveying the possibilities.

"Two thirty-five to the green. Two fifty-two to the pin. Three-wood."

"Do you think I can get it there?"

"Yeah."

Payne grinned impishly and asked: "What would *Arnie* do?"

"Arnie would *go for it!*" Kemper blurted without hesitation, heavy on the last three words.

"Well then, let's effing *go for it!*" declared Payne, who did just that, sending a 3-wood laser to within twenty feet of the pin. The resulting eagle 3 punctuated a fine round of 68.

The battle cry of "go for it," though popularized by Palmer, also became the catchphrase that defined the relationship between Stewart and Kemper. The photos and notes and everything else they would exchange over the next sixteen years would invariably contain that inscription as a guideline not just for golf but for the way each of them would play life.

That relationship took a drastic turn a few weeks later, when Payne fired Kemper for his own good.

"I'm firing you today, not as my friend, but as my caddie," said Payne, who went on to say that Kemper was wasting his time carrying a golf bag when he should be pursuing his unique investment talents.

Deflated and angered, Kemper nevertheless followed Payne's advice. With Payne helping to open doors, Kemper reluctantly took a job as a stockbroker and, as Payne suspected it would, his career took off like that three-wood at Pebble. Today, he is one of Oppenheimer's top twenty-five worldwide producers, working out of the firm's Los Angeles offices with an elite client list that includes Bill Gates, Gateway founder Ted Waite, musician Stephen Stills, and the Wynn family of Las Vegas hotel fame. The original $5,000 that opened Payne's account with Kemper multiplied deep into seven figures as Payne kept adding to the pile and actively working "very hands-on" with Kemper on buy and sell decisions. They talked regularly, exchanged cards, and got together three or four times a year to laugh about those early years.

"While I didn't see him every day, I regarded him as my best friend," says Kemper. "He set my life straight. When he died, I was devastated."

The impact of his personal loss even edged over into the surreal.

"I've had experiences where I felt I've been in contact with Payne. I haven't told many people that, knowing they'd think I'm nuts or something. But either he was speaking to me, or it was my mind thinking that this is what he would be saying," Kemper confided. One experience came when he was overcome with grief over his lost friend, crying as he took an early morning shower several days after Payne died.

"I didn't feel I could even get out of there and go to work. And he said, 'You gotta get your ass out of that shower and go to work. I don't want to see you moping around.' He was just *talking* to me, I felt. You never know if it's really him or something going on in your mind."

Kemper worked even harder on Payne's account, which had become his last tangible link to his dear friend. Suddenly and unexpectedly, even that tether would be snipped. In February 2000, he received a form letter from Tracey, instructing him to liquidate the account and send her the proceeds. He complied, but anxiously called her, three times, just wanting to be sure she was acting prudently. After all, he felt more than a pride of authorship in that money; it represented the very bond he and Payne had so joyously shared over all those years.

Sadly, he says, the calls were never returned.

PAYNE'S FIRST FORAY onto a Tour leaderboard had come pre-Mitch, at the 1981 Southern Open outside Columbus, Georgia. Orlando-based Tour official Mark Russell recalls seeing Payne's name go up during the closing round. All he knew about him was that Payne had won the two Asian events.

"I had a ruling with him on the eighteenth hole that day," Russell recalls. "I didn't even know which one he was. He had longer hair then and I remember some metal studs in his ears. Several of them. I would later find out they were acupuncture needles for concentration or something. In the ruling, his demeanor was good. He carried himself with a lot of class. We became friends then and have been friends ever since."

Payne posted his first top-ten finish on the PGA Tour that tournament, winning $5,200 and whooshing away to Australia to take his bride.

The next April, he still had the acupuncture studs in his ears on the putting green at the Magnolia Classic in Hattiesburg, Mississippi. A Tour rookie named Paul Azinger mistook them for earrings and wondered what sort of character this was.

"He won the tournament," Azinger would recount seventeen years later during his roller-coaster, keynote eulogy at Payne's memorial service. "And he said, 'What the world needs is another blue-eyed blond!' I thought, 'Who is *this* guy?'"

Three months later, former Tour regular Wally Armstrong, hanging on near the end of his career, was paired with Stewart in the Monday qualifier before the Quad Cities Open and figured it didn't matter who he was. "I thought, 'This guy's got no chance on the Tour.' I had never seen a guy with such perfect tempo, but he was all over the world. I don't think he hit more than two or three fairways. He had a little Bullseye putter and held it real upright," Armstrong recalls. "But he made everything. He had about twenty-one putts and I think he shot 68 to get in the tournament."

And then won.

It was Payne's first official Tour win—the earlier Hattiesburg tournament had no exempt status at the time—and Armstrong made it his point to get to know this wild *wunderkind*. "He was fun, easygoing. The thing he really cherished was his love of a good time and his relationships with people."

The '82 Quad Cities was Payne's first of eleven official Tour victories and the first of some five hundred tournaments where he wore his trademark knickers outfit every round. On the eighteenth green that day, the guy who became to short pants what Tammy Faye was to mascara collapsed sobbing in the arms of the guy who had inspired both the silky swing and the Great Gatsby duds. His coach and best friend. His father, William Louis Stewart, who would soon begin his losing battle with cancer.

PAYNE'S KNICKERS ENSEMBLE had been firmly established by the time he and Tracey arrived at the Disney World Classic the next year, a young couple in the midst of a living fantasy. Years later, at a banquet where he was being honored, he would offer a misty-eyed observation that the "good thing about dreams is that sometimes you get to live them out." Payne and Tracey were already on that thrill ride that was about to hit warp speed.

Clad in the same sort of outfit many of the Disney entertainers wear, here was a contemporary Doug Sanders in bright red knickers over long white stockings with a red-and-white striped shirt and the jaunty white cap. Each time he walked onto a green, the gallery giggled, seemingly unsure whether Payne was in search of a birdie or a banjo. For that final round, he even added a Mickey Mouse pin to his knickers, a good-luck charm he had bought while frolicking through the Magic Kingdom with Tracey the previous evening.

When his two-shot triumph over Nick Faldo and Mark McCumber had been completed, he seemed perfectly at home with Chip 'n' Dale, Minnie, Mickey, and the other Disney characters in the usual Disney Classic awards ceremonies on the eighteenth green.

Off to one side, Tracey hoisted a bottle of champagne in salute—and relief. It had been an unnerving day. She had spent it trapped in a nearby Polynesian Hotel room, where she followed her husband's progress through printed updates on the Disney World information TV channel. She told reporters she was too emotional to follow Payne on the course, a barrier she later conquered.

"She saw me four-putt in the Southern Open," Payne mused, "and became so upset I told her she had to control herself or stay away."

Just a few days short of their second wedding anniversary at the time, Tracey was asked to assess her high-profile husband. "He's definitely different," she said, laughing. "He's too extravagant for me sometimes. I'm the one that has to tone him down. If he had a choice, he might wear a purple and green outfit to the course one day."

They couldn't have imagined on that giddy Sunday afternoon that they would not have another chance to taste the sweet spoils of victory again for more than three years.

One of his closest pursuers that day had been Scott Hoch. The two made up the final pairing, tied for the lead at the start and at the end of the front nine. Payne eagled the par-5 tenth and never looked back. Hoch and his wife, Sally, a pair of North Carolinians who had just made Orlando their home, had become close friends of the Stewarts and were pushing them to also drop anchor in the golf-rich central-Florida city.

Tracey was only too happy to make the move. Following their marriage in November 1981, Payne and Tracey had lived in an apartment in Springfield. Life in a small city in the Ozarks was not an easy transition for Tracey. "It just wasn't a good fit for a headstrong foreigner," Payne's mother, Bee, candidly recalled.

A few weeks after the Disney victory, Payne and Tracey bought a golf villa in a complex bordering Arnold Palmer's Bay Hill Club, the first of their three Orlando residences. Two years later, they would move to a larger villa in the complex, the one made famous by Payne kissing fifteen-month-old Chelsea through the fence just after his tee shot on the adjacent twelfth tee each day en route to winning the 1987 Bay Hill Classic.

But the forty months between dancing with Minnie on the Disney eighteenth green and accepting a trophy sword from Arnie Palmer on the Bay Hill eighteenth would become the most trying period of Payne's life.

He would lose his father to cancer. He would lose the respect of many fellow pros and most of the golf media. He would lose his desire to continue his Tour career. He would lose and lose and lose.

In Payne's next 109 Tour starts, he was unable to grab the brass ring again. He couldn't shake the collar even in foreign tournaments. He had always seemed to be able to grab a trophy in Australia or Europe or *somewhere*.

Now it wasn't happening *anywhere* and Payne was increasingly flustered about what to do.

There were some close calls, but something always seemed to happen. In the '84 Colonial, he bogeyed the seventy-second hole, then lost in a playoff to his friend Peter Jacobsen. He played his way into contention through fifty-four holes of two other tournaments only to have the final rounds and his would-be closing charges washed out. He played his way into the lead of the '86 Open with just six holes to go, only to become mesmerized by playing partner and eventual winner Ray Floyd's glassy-eyed stare. Payne faded to sixth. And to that point of his career, his 0–3 record in playoffs hardly conjured an image of a gritty closer.

Payne was having so many problems losing leads down the stretch that the media he so often treated curtly saddled him with the nickname "Avis." After all, in 1984 he had raised the Tour record for earnings by a nonwinner to $288,795, then blew that away two years later with $535,389, all as an also-ran, to finish, remarkably, number three on the official money list. No player before or since has finished that high on the money list without a tournament victory.

But where the fates dealt him his cruelest blow was in his old college town, Dallas, in the 1985 Byron Nelson Classic at Las Colinas Sports Club.

THE INDELIBLE AND PAINFULLY GRAPHIC IMAGE of his agonizing failure down the stretch of the '85 Nelson Classic was the closing TV shot and still photo in the next day's Dallas papers. The picture captured Payne and Tracey somberly drifting away through a field of wildflowers, hand in hand, taking the most direct escape to the sanctuary of their hotel room just off the course.

"It just killed him," Jacobsen recounted. "I'll never forget him and Tracey walking off through that field. It broke my heart."

Payne had stood on the eighteenth tee that day with a comfortable three-shot cushion. Up ahead, journeyman Bob Eastwood would run in the long birdie putt that cut Payne's lead to two. Still comfortable, right? Payne needed only a bogey 5 on the final hole, a long, spacious par 4. He could probably score bogey or better on the hole forty-nine times out of fifty. Alas, this was number fifty.

He bunkered his tee shot and could have simply laid up short, wedged onto the green for a two-putt bogey and the victory. Instead, he chose to go for the green with a long iron and plopped that one into the deep bunker guarding the front left corner of the green. From there, Payne would blade his bunker shot to the far side of the green and three-putt coming back to create the playoff.

Payne took a two-handed grip on his composure, calmly signing his scorecard and nodding at the Tour officials' instructions with an admirable air of nonchalance, then climbing into a waiting automobile for the trip back out to the first playoff hole. In the car with Stewart were his caddie, PGA Tour official Mike Shea, and a lady volunteer driver. As the foursome bumped along a maintenance road through a remote part of the course, the frustration chewing on Payne's lower colon became too much to bear. He leaned forward, tapped the woman on the shoulder and said evenly, "Ma'am, can you stop here for just a minute?"

"Sure,'" she said, and brought the car to a stop.

Payne stepped out of the rear door, closed it gently, walked around to the back of the car, and shouted a raw obscenity in a volume he later said caused sharp pain in his vocal chords.

Sketchy reports have it that several nearby mesquite trees were instantly charred and mother gophers frantically covered the tender ears of baby gophers in case more was to come. It wasn't. Payne returned to the car, his face tranquil, gently opened the door, eased onto the rear seat, and pulled the door to. "Thank you, ma'am," he said politely. "We can go ahead now."

Jacobsen laughed knowingly when told the story. "That's perfect," he said. "Controlled rage."

Payne followed the double-bogey at eighteen with another double-bogey on the first playoff hole to gift-wrap the title for Eastwood. He was devastated by the loss, which had come in front of so many of his old college friends. It was one of his newer friends, Rinker, who provided the only meaningful salve for the wounds.

The Tour shifted to nearby Fort Worth for the Colonial Invitational the next week. Just two days after the Disaster in Dallas, Rinker encountered Payne in the Colonial locker room.

"I knew he had just gotten a Porsche convertible," recounted Rinker. "And he made about $50,000 for second place at the Byron Nelson [$54,000, to be precise]. So I told him, 'Hey, you just paid for that car, Bud.' I remember he looked at me a moment and sort of blinked and brightened up with a smile and said, 'Hey, you're right. I did.' He was really crushed by the loss, but that seemed to help him get over it a little."

THE 1986 TOUR SEASON brought more of the same—solid play soiled by Sunday failures—but proved to be the watershed year for Payne Stewart. He would have a half dozen top-five finishes, but still no victories. The excruciating pattern finally exhausted his commendable patience and poise at ancient Shinnecock that summer when the U.S. Open slipped through his fingers.

Fate was particularly cruel to him that Sunday at the tony old club on Long Island immediately after he had surged into sole possession of the lead with a birdie on the twelfth hole. He had a short birdie chip from the fringe at the thirteenth that looked perfect as it approached the hole. They call it a "power lip"—no relation to Dick Vitale—when a ball dips into the high side of a cup and spins out in slingshot fashion, skittering away from the hole. When this one stopped, Payne had a full six feet left for his saving par. He missed it. And zombie-eyed playing partner Ray Floyd made birdie to vault into the lead past Payne, who would also bogey the next three holes while gawking at Floyd's trancelike march to the title.

Afterward, he told Tracey he just sort of stepped back and watched Floyd. "He got caught up in awe of Raymond and forgot about what he was doing," she sighed to a hometown writer.

In the locker room, Payne slipped out of the snakeskin shoes he had added to his bold outfits and shook his head. "I thought this was my day for a while. I was in good position. But when I made the second bogey coming in, that kind of took the steam out of me."

Over the coming weeks, Tracey had to pull him out of a post-Open depression that had him seriously discussing an alternative line of work. He became so distraught with his hated bridesmaid role on the Tour that he vowed to make a career change or at least take an extended sabbatical from tournament golf.

"The Open took a lot out of me," he would recount weeks later. "My next tournament was the Canadian Open and I just didn't care about being out there. The U.S. Open was one of those tournaments where I felt like I let it get away from me. I beat myself. Nobody beat me. I was leading the tournament and if I par in, I win. It's Payne Stewart's Open. At the twelfth, I'm two under par and one under wins the tournament."

On the first tee at the Canadian, Payne had a hollow feeling he couldn't explain. "It's the worst I've ever been. I turned to my caddie, Rob Kay, and said, 'Bud, I don't know what's gonna happen today.'"

He snap-hooked his opening drive into a parking lot, three-putted the first green, and a few holes later, skulled a wedge over the green. From that point on, he had totally lost interest. He'd grab a club, take a quick swat, and giggle at the result. At the turn, he was confronted by Tracey, her face stern and foreboding. "Look," she scolded, "if you don't want to be out here, just quit and let's go home."

Payne completed the first two rounds but missed the cut badly, and the Stewarts shared a gloomy flight home to Orlando. "I might just take the rest of the year off and get a job," he announced, breaking the silence.

"Oh, yeah?" Tracey replied, skeptically. "What would you do?"

Yeah, Payne. What *would* you do?

In an interview in his kitchen—with Tracey typically sitting in and frequently interjecting her own thoughts—Payne noted that his business degree at SMU had included mostly real estate courses. He ventured that he might do well in some real estate pursuit in a booming area like Orlando.

Unconvinced, the reporter turned to Payne's wife. "Tracey, what *could* he do?"

"Nothing," she blurted, laughing.

But in her mind, she was already formulating a plan to pull her husband's golf career out of that agonizing pattern.

chapter 9

A Taste of Victory

E. Harvie Ward is something of a senior version of Payne Stewart. A gregarious, fun-loving man, he had been a world-class amateur of 1950s fame and was a free-spirited celebrity in his own right. As a former U.S. Amateur champion, he was respected as an accomplished ball-striker and serious teacher, but did little to erase his reputation as a lovable rogue. Armed with the gift of self-deprecation, this engaging leprechaun can openly laugh at himself through the retelling of tales from his high-octane youth.

That would include the time someone had to awaken young Harvie from his slumber on the carpet the morning after a particularly raucous Masters-week party. They were shaking him to deliver the jolting advisory that he was scheduled on the tee at Augusta National within the hour. Wearing stubble on his chin and a golf shirt tucked into the wrinkled dress slacks from the night before, this particular Masters competitor made his tee time and smacked the first drive square down the fairway, smiling brightly to acknowledge the applause.

By the mid-1980s, he had become a dapper and popular icon within the golf business, the first director of golf at the posh new Grand Cypress Resort just down the road from where Payne lived at Bay Hill Village. In fact, Ward had become a neighbor of Payne's, having bought one of the golf villas nearby in the gated complex that ran along the par-5 twelfth hole at Bay Hill Club.

Ward's top assistant, Paul Celano, had become close to the Stewarts, often socializing with them and sharing practice rounds with Payne when he showed up to work on his game at Grand Cypress, where Celano had just moved up to the top job. Ward had made the crosstown move to become head pro at an upscale club, Interlachen, created by the vibrant area's *nouveau riche* interminably stuck on the Country Club of Orlando's waiting list. Now they had their own opulent club, and even a famous head pro to thumb their noses at the old money.

In that summer of discontent, Tracey Stewart pulled Celano aside and asked if he thought his old boss, Ward, would consider working with Payne. Payne knew and liked Ward. And he knew of his reputation as one of the best teachers in the country.

In short order, Payne had the first serious golf coach of his life who was not named William Louis Stewart.

Payne and Bill, who had died of cancer shortly before this, shared a bond that goes beyond the usual father-son relationship. Bill was Payne's coach and, more often than not, his best friend. The elder Stewart passed on to his son the fierce competitiveness he used to win two Missouri amateur titles, a state senior title, and to excel as a furniture salesman. Payne's first taste of tournament victory came when he was just four years old while teamed with Bill to win a three-hole, father-son event at their home Hickory Hills Country Club.

When Payne first made the golf team at Greenwood High, the football coach, Paul "Moon" Mullins, was in charge. Bill showed up in Mullins's office the first day to lay down the law: The coach was free to discipline Payne in any way he thought necessary and to require anything of the lad he wanted. "But I don't want you to screw with his golf swing."

"Actually, I think he used a word much stronger than 'screw,'" Mullins recalls fondly. When the first team match came, Mullins had to lay down the law to the elder Stewart. Galleries were not allowed at Missouri high school golf matches, but one of the opposing coaches serving as a marshal reported a problem in mid-match. It seems that Bill Stewart was driving along a perimeter road skirting the golf course and jumping out at various holes to shout instructions and encouragement to Payne. "When I confronted him after the match," recalls Mullins, "Bill began crying and promised it would never happen again."

During Payne's first few years on the PGA Tour, any flaw in his game was treated by an emergency call to Springfield, and Bill came running with the cure. For example, when Payne missed the cut in the '84 Bay Hill

Classic, he dialed 1-800-DAD-HELP! Bill was on the next flight to Orlando and while the tournament rocked along during the final two rounds, the two Stewarts were just down the road on the Grand Cypress putting green working on Payne's stroke. He didn't miss another cut in his next nine tournaments, and posted a second at Colonial and a third at Memorial. But Bill was gone and now Payne needed a new tutor.

"I went to Harvie and hit some balls," Payne said, looking back on their first, informal session. "I noticed right off that he sounded just like my father. He wasn't there to change my swing. He was there to help rebuild confidence in my ability. He helped me understand that you have these letdown periods and that you can't play awesome golf all the time; that you have to be able to deal with the bad aspects as well as the good and not let the bad affect you. He helped put my attitude back together."

Ward modestly explained that he just mainly reminded Payne what a good player he was and related that he, Harvie, had first played in the U.S. Amateur in 1947, but didn't win it until eight years later, in 1955. "I was just getting beat by good players—Charlie Coe and Gene Littler and Billy Maxwell," he told Payne. "And there are even more good players out there on the Tour today."

He stressed that Payne was a terrific player, but just *among* the best. He reassured Payne that he would win again and often. Ward liked his temperament for golf, liked his attitude. He understood that all the near misses were warping the gyros between Payne's ears, but promised they would work through that.

Looking back at the association more than a decade later, Ward said: "Payne was stubborn. From what I'm told, his dad was stubborn. But we got along fine. From a personality standpoint, we got along fine. It was a great fit and we had a lot of fun."

Ward refused to accept a fee from Payne, insisting on working only for expenses. When Payne wanted Ward to work with him at a Tour site, he would spring for Ward's airfare, hotel room, and meals.

As for Payne's game, Ward said the task was obvious.

"His swing was light-years ahead of his thinking," says Ward, who later moved on to teach golf in the Pinehurst, North Carolina, area. "That early problem of not winning all those years was a simple matter that he was not mature enough. At that juncture, he just wasn't as mature as a guy like Tiger Woods at the same age. He didn't know how to be loose and tenacious at the same time. He was immature and often acted immaturely."

Perry Leslie, that hometown club pro back in Missouri, has a theory about Payne's inability to close tournaments early in his career: "Payne had a golf swing that was like playing with a piece of spaghetti. So his success depended on total relaxation. He was actually the classical golf machine. So anytime any tension would get in that swing, it wouldn't perform properly. The thing he fought, early on, was to get into contention and then get distracted—thinking ahead, or having other outside thoughts to add to that tension. Once that happened, his swing was gone. The problem was to get past that somehow, to the point that he wouldn't worry about losing or think about what the win would mean to him, and just go ahead and let his great swing get the job done."

"That's a very good analysis," said Ward. "You tighten a screw or two on a swing like that and it's going awry."

With Ward's mental massaging taking root, Payne would finish the 1986 season back on the leaderboard. After missing the cut in four of his six starts following that U.S. Open downer, he closed the season under Ward's watchful eye with a fourth and a second in his final two appearances and expectantly looked to 1987 as a new dawning.

PAYNE HAD A GREAT CHANCE to part those lingering clouds in his third start of the year, at Pebble Beach. But after a trio of 69s, he once again failed to mount a charge over the final round, slogging along to an even-par 72 and losing touch with Fuzzy Zoeller, who won by five shots. He blew off the usual runner-up's expected debriefing in the press room and stalked off to the parking lot, ignoring the several reporters trotting along, trying to keep up.

Watching the scene and shaking his head a few yards away was Peter Jacobsen. "I was thinking, 'Talk to them, Payne. Don't do this to yourself. Talk to them.' He didn't, but he would learn that later. He learned to talk, no matter how disappointed."

Back home at Bay Hill, Arnold Palmer had watched the Pebble finish on television and empathized with Payne's nagging habit of falling short on Sundays. "As much as I would like to see him win," the famed proprietor told friends, "I can see what he was doing. He was decelerating on his swing the last few holes. He's scared. We've all gone through that, and it becomes a problem that is strictly mechanical. He's a good player, and he deserves to be winning."

A month later Payne would finish second again, at the Honda Classic outside Fort Lauderdale, but this time it was due more to three-stroke winner Mark Calcavecchia's stellar play down the stretch, not faltering by Payne. He drove up the Florida Turnpike that evening to Orlando with a better feeling about himself to carry into that next week's Tour event, which would be held literally in his backyard.

Paired for the first two rounds with Jacobsen and close-pal-to-be Paul Azinger, Payne was right back on the leaderboard with a 69–67 start on Arnie's demanding playground, which usually supplies several holes for the toughest-on-Tour stats each year. Payne caught a buried lie in a greenside bunker at the fourteenth and seemingly had little hope of saving the par he needed to hold his position just behind the leader, grim-faced South African David Frost.

Payne blasted creditably to twenty feet from the cup and, as he settled in over the par putt, Jacobsen prophetically whispered to Azinger: "If he makes this, I think they can go ahead and engrave the trophy." Payne's putt disappeared into the heart of the cup, yanking a roar of approval from a gallery of friends, family, and neighbors.

Payne was still a stroke off Frost's pace at the end of the day, but Jacobsen had seen enough of Payne's action over the first two rounds to project victory. "I think this is his week," Jacobsen said outside the scorer's trailer. "There's no weakness in his game right now. He hit five chips that should have gone in. When he did make a mistake and hit it in jail, he got it up and down to save par. Those are the things you do when you win."

In the press tent, Payne declared that he was comfortable on this particular course, having played from about every spot on it either in past tournaments or the fabled daily "Bay Hill Shootouts" with other pros and members. "So I can deal with whatever presents itself. It would be something really special to win here at home. Of course," he added wistfully, "it would be great to win—period."

By that point of the tournament he had established the daily good-luck ritual of kissing baby daughter Chelsea through the fence as he passed his home off the twelfth tee. "That's automatic. Every time I see her, I give her a kiss," Payne said. "After I got my kiss today, I made a birdie and all pars. So maybe it's working."

It worked even better the next day. Payne vaulted past Frost to take the fifty-four-hole lead by blistering Arnie's immaculately conditioned layout with an eight-under-par 63, just one stroke off the course record. Leading a garrison charge of red numbers on an idyllic spring day in central Florida, he shot 30 on the front, kissed Chelsea again during a 33 on the back nine, and inspired yours truly to file this report in the next morning's Sunday edition of the *Orlando Sentinel:*

As a dues-paying member of Arnie Palmer's Bay Hill Club, I want to lodge an inquiry with the Metropolitan Bureau of Investigation, or the Truth-in-Advertising watchdogs. Maybe even the Tower Commission.

There's an army of pro golfers and their hired officials who are claiming a batch of 65s and 66s and nine-hole scores of 30 and 31 and the like Saturday at Bay Hill Club. I smell a scam. Thirty isn't a nine-hole score at Bay Hill. It isn't even a pants size around there. Surely, the guys slipped over to scruffy little Alhambra for Saturday's third round. The Dubsdread muny, maybe. David Frost shoot 65? Hal Sutton and Davis Love with 31s on the front? Tom Watson 33 on the back, even with a double bogey?

C'mon, who are they kidding? They're calling in those scores from par-64 Cannongate, right? You don't shoot 31 at Bay Hill; you shoot your three-wood and two-iron when they go lame from overuse. I mean, this is the course Steve Melnyk snidely calls "Bay Long." Short-driving Calvin Peete won't even fly over it anymore after he staggered off after the 36-hole cut the last two times he tried it. And now we're supposed to believe a guy in short pants shot 63 there yesterday?

Well, if true, the reports have it that Payne Stewart carded a 30-33, pausing only for an emergency dash to the locker room between nines. Understandable. If I ever shoot 30 for nine holes, I'll have to change a certain unmentionable item of apparel.

There's one round to go in the Classic and no matter where they play it, the story line focuses on young Mr. Stewart, a local resident known for his golfing bloomers, sunny disposition and nagging near-misses.

Only in golf can a guy earn $800,000 and everybody's sympathy at the same time. But it seems the fates are devilishly conspiring to keep Payne from his appointment with superstardom. Nineteen times in the past fourteen months he has finished in the top ten without snapping a three-year victory drought. There is strong suspicion by certain trained observers this streak will mercifully end today. "There's not a lot that impresses me. But Payne impressed me with both his game and the way he's handling himself," declared Paul Azinger.

Indeed, Stewart has maintained a bounce in his step and stiff upper lip under the circumstances. He has been exemplary in coping with the frustrations of listening to a lot of eighteenth-hole acceptance speeches while standing there with the runner-up check and loads of anguish chewing at his innards.

There have been only brief exceptions. There was the time last summer when he sank into such a funk he considered a real-estate license.

And there was the moment two weeks ago that he had the blues after missing the cut in Miami. A couple days later, he was on the practice tee across town at Interlachen Country Club with his new mentor, Harvie Ward. Payne went through the motions of hitting a few balls, then chucked the routine. Riding Payne back to the clubhouse in his golf cart, Ward stopped for a moment behind one of his members hitting practice shots. The man had one arm. Ward's unspoken message sank in.

"His attitude was bad and he was in a bad mood," Ward recalled. "He watched the one-armed man hit balls and said, 'Here I am worrying and thinking I've got troubles. This puts things into perspective.'"

Just to be sure, Ward hammered home the message. "You're acting like a kid in high school," he scolded. "You're supposed to be a professional. If this is the way you're going to act, I think we should end our association right now. I don't need this."

That night, Stewart phoned Ward to apologize.

No one was prouder of Payne's heroics Saturday than Ward, though he stayed away and watched on TV because he thinks he would be a distraction or bad luck. The wonder to Harvie is that Stewart has but a one-shot lead.

"Why does this happen to Payne?" Ward sighed. "Any other time you shoot 63 you run away and hide. But God love him, that's a super round. His good attitude has returned. I love the kid. He's got a lot of heart.

"He's going to win. And once he does, they're going to have trouble getting him stopped."

Payne will be working on that today at Bay Hill. Or at Winter Park Pines, or the Disney Wee Links. Wherever it is they're putting up all those suspect numbers this week.

Sensing the historic breakthrough moment at hand for his famous pupil, Harvie Ward could no longer stay away from that final round of the 1987 Hertz Bay Hill Classic. So there was Ward's chipmunk grin— sparkling out from under a large, floppy hat and the 1980s-style, oversize sunglasses—bobbing along behind the ropes. He struck an amusing sight in that altogether unfamiliar and uncomfortable role of spectator. For much of his life, when a tournament was on the line, Ward was accustomed to walking down the middle of the fairway with a golf club in his hands so he could do something about it. But now he was a helpless bundle of nerves, agonizing over every shot.

"This is too much for me," he told a nosy columnist strolling along with him. "This is like walking around in the maternity ward! I've finished my fingernails and now I'm starting on my fingers!" He was joined by a huge throng seemingly trying to *will* this long-elusive victory for the flamboyant guy in knickers.

Even the other pros wanted Payne's misadventures with first place to stop. "We need a guy like him to win—personable, nice-looking, and can play like hell," said, of all people, Ray Floyd, who had played a role in sending Payne into a deep funk that previous summer. "People said Watson couldn't win. Then he broke through and became the best player out here. Payne can be an even stronger force."

Bay Hill neighbor and friend Greg Norman put it more succinctly in a note he had attached to Payne's locker that morning. "I know you can do it," the Shark penned. "Go kick ass!"

In a sense, he did, closing his statement week with a 65 to shatter the tournament record with a 20-under-par virtuoso performance. But Frost was as persistent as chiggers, answering each of Payne's sensational shots with one of his own. Except for Frost, Payne would have headed into Bay Hill's difficult four closing holes with an eleven-shot lead. Instead, he would gingerly clutch a slippery, two-shot cushion as he strode to the eighteenth, a hole no more dangerous than roller-skating into a railroad tunnel.

Like the true champion he would become, Payne tamed it with a birdie, and the long pent-up anxieties in the Stewart camp exploded in relief, joy, and tears. Payne and caddie Rob Kay embraced. Tracey let out a long breath. Chelsea squealed. Arnie Palmer charged down the hill to the lake-guarded green to present the tournament's unique sword trophy.

The color even returned to the face of Harvie Ward, who put the whole occasion in perspective. "Ain't nothing like winning," he chirped through a smile wide enough for an extra row of teeth.

Following the perfunctory media debriefings, Payne posed for an official portrait photo in his new gray Bay Hill champ's blazer and shared an unofficial shot and beer with Arnie. The celebration then shifted to Payne's home by the twelfth tee, where the final-round, Chelsea-kissing ritual that afternoon had attracted a forest of TV and print photographers and golf fans. Payne had to fight his way through the crowd to buss his infant daughter through the wrought-iron fence, but it all worked out just peachy, and now he was on the other side of that barrier basking in it all.

It was enough to make a guy feel he could walk on water. So he did. So to speak.

His back patio, now crowded with friends and well-wishers, was built around a small lap pool, a narrow, three-lane model perhaps fifteen yards long. It had a canvas cover that unrolled from one end and was in place for the victory party. At some point during the evening, someone suggested it looked almost as if a person could just walk across the canvas the length of the pool. Payne, now in casual attire and perhaps on his third or fourth Scotch, cocked his head curiously at the observation. His face slowly spread into a mischievous smile.

"Well, let's just see," he said, stepping off one end of the pool onto the canvas and churning forward, Scotch aloft and his expensive Gucci loafers disappearing in each indentation into the canvas until he stepped onto the deck at the far end to a rousing cheer. He responded by holding high the tumbler of Scotch, not a drop of which had been spilled during the feat.

The phone jangled constantly as far-flung family and friends responded to Payne's win. One call came from just across town, from a special colleague, fellow pro Larry Rinker.

"Man! I'm having a party! Get your skinny little rump over here!" Payne demanded.

A half hour later, Rinker walked through the front door to discover Bruce Springsteen blaring from the stereo and Payne grinning over a refreshed tumbler of Scotch. The two old friends embraced and Payne pulled him into the privacy of his office, just off the kitchen.

They talked about the clutch, final approach Payne had struck to the eighteenth green to seal his victory. Rinker knew well the treachery of that long iron shot across water to Bay Hill's usual Sunday pin placement, tucked fiendishly on the far-right finger of the green. With Frost having fired to within twenty feet of the cup just before him, the two-shot cushion meant little until that final, demanding approach had tested Payne's resolve.

"He said, 'Bud, I just hit it.'" Rinker recounted. "He said, 'I didn't know what to do, so I just hit it. And it came off gooooood!' In retrospect—and taking what I've been told by a lot of sports psychologists—he did just what he needed to do: not think, trust his swing, and stand up and hit it like every other time."

Rinker had been working at the time with sports psychologist Fred Shoemaker, author of the book *Extraordinary Golf*. They talked about the patter that goes on inside the heads of golfers trying to make crucial shots. "It could be, 'This is for the championship.' 'If I don't hit this, my wife's gonna hate me.' 'I'm gonna die if I don't hit this right.' Things like that.

Fred and I worked on just saying, 'Thank you,' when your caddie hands you the club, and then hit the shot," said Rinker.

"So looking back, and having Payne say that to me—'I just hit it!'—says there were no conversations going on in his head. There was no 'I've had thirty top tens without a win. Can I hit this shot?' It was kinda like, 'Hey, let's just hit it!'"

He did. He won.

Years later, after winning three majors, Payne would acknowledge that the PGA and the two Opens were very, very important. And that first official win at Quad Cities in the presence of his father remained his most cherished. But the '87 Bay Hill breakout was the crossroads of his career, the glorious juncture he would use as a launching pad in his journey from a knickered curiosity with potential to a respected champion of a gentleman's game.

The salving victory in what was then the Hertz Bay Hill Classic would yield one sweet extra that was sealed the next afternoon. With the previous evening's Scotch pulsing at his temples, he sat in that same office with another old friend, Terry Anton, a former pro out of the University of Florida who had been Payne's principal sidekick when they'd played the Asian Tour nearly seven years earlier. Anton was there at the Malaysian Open when Payne and Tracey first met, and he was supposed to return as best man for the wedding later that year. However, Anton didn't make the long trip.

Nevertheless, they remained fast friends and now were sharing a laugh over the headline in that morning's paper: AVIS WINS HERTZ.

Payne also shared his intention of donating a portion of his $108,000 first-place check to a charitable endeavor in the name of his late father. The question was how much of the check he should give.

"Give it all," said Anton. "It'll come back to you many times over."

Anton remembers Stewart shooting back a long, thoughtful gaze before breaking into that silly smile of his. "That's a *great* idea!" he declared, wide-eyed.

A few days later, the world was startled by his generosity when it was announced that Payne was giving his entire winner's check to charity, in honor of his late father. The money would fund a small home adjacent to

Florida Hospital, just north of Orlando, to be used by the families of patients being treated at the facility. In the years since, the tidy, five-bedroom William Louis Stewart Home has been a blessing to hundreds in their time of need. In turn, it proved an endless source of pride to Payne, who loved reading and rereading the growing stack of appreciative letters from those whose lives had been touched by his generous spirit.

There is no charge for its use, though most who stay there make a donation toward the upkeep and operation of the home.

"They've written that it is awfully nice to be able to be with their families, all together in the house, at such a trying time," Payne said on the occasion of the home's first anniversary. "I read the letters and I appreciate the people writing. It makes me feel good because of what I've done and that people are getting a benefit from it. I think I got satisfaction out of just doing it and having my father being remembered by more people than just my family."

Payne's original concept for the facility was for it to be used by families of cancer patients undergoing treatments at the hospital. But it is occasionally utilized for others' needs. For example, a Korean deckhand lost part of a hand in an accident aboard a freighter off the coast of Florida. After his initial hospitalization, the victim, who could speak no English, needed follow-up treatment as an outpatient, but had no place to stay and couldn't afford a hotel room.

Thank you, Payne Stewart.

chapter 10

Finding the "Zone"

The salving effects of the Bay Hill win and the inroads that Harvie Ward was making on Payne Stewart's character and competitiveness were just that—inroads; the process was far from complete. Payne would not score another victory during the next two years. And his bouts of immaturity would end his working relationship with Ward and plummet him to a new low in the eyes of many colleagues and others in the world golf community.

Though the Bay Hill triumph didn't set off the expected string of Stewart victories, he stopped beating himself on Sundays when in contention. He simply fell victim to a closing hot hand by others, a circumstance that he could more easily accept. He would finish third in Houston the next month, but closed with a spiffy 67. He was fourth early the next year in the '88 Bob Hope Chrysler, but finished bravely with a 65. A runner-up spot at Honda was punctuated by a 67. Another second at the Provident Classic was closed out with a 65.

The only glaring departure came in the '88 Memorial, where Payne ballooned to 75 on the final day, fading out of contention to a disappointing sixth. Otherwise, Payne was serenely confident that the victories would start coming again as long as he continued to knock on the door and put up good numbers in the final rounds.

Ward noticed that he was perhaps becoming too confident.

"As Payne got better and felt more comfortable with what was happening, he decided he wanted to fade and draw like Seve," Ward recalls, alluding to the imaginative Spaniard Seve Ballesteros. Ward walked up behind Payne on the range one day late in 1988 and was stunned to see him alternately hooking and fading tee shots.

"What the hell are you doing!!??" Ward demanded, alarm in his tones. Payne explained his new approach.

"Well, it's nice to know how to do those things, but the great players— the Hogans, Sneads—all groove the ball one way," Ward said. "You keep fooling around like this and you get on the eighteenth tee one day, you won't know what direction the ball's going."

Looking back on that conversation as the beginning of the end of their working arrangement, Ward reflected, "Payne didn't like me being that blunt with him and started looking around for another coach. I wasn't aware of that and didn't know he had hired [Chuck] Cook as his new coach until I read it in *Sports Illustrated*. That really disappointed me in him, and our relationship was never the same again."

The two rarely spoke during the remaining decade of Payne's life.

The final exchange would come in the summer of 1999, moments before the final round of the Open at Pinehurst. Ward lived just a few minutes' walk from the Pinehurst clubhouse and he had wandered over to the club during the closing round that Sunday. He walked down the row of contenders warming up on the range and arrived at Payne's location just as he yanked a practice shot dead left.

"I never taught you to hit 'em like that!" he said playfully.

Recognizing the voice instantly, Payne turned and flashed a big smile at his former coach. He suspended his rehearsals for a moment to exchange pleasantries. It would turn out to be, Ward noted wistfully, the last time they talked.

In mid-January, Ward would discover for the first time that it was his good friend Dr. Richard Coop, the sports psychologist, who had urged Payne to replace Ward with Chuck Cook. During their two-year stint, Ward urged Payne to try a few sessions with Coop, who already had an informal, tag-team relationship with Cook.

"He didn't want to come see me at first. Harvie pushed him," Coop wrote in *Golf Magazine*. "I told him pretty bluntly about some things I had heard about him—that he was prickly, arrogant, cocky, and brash."

When Coop finished, Payne asked to borrow his phone. He dialed Tracey and told her what Coop had said, adding, "What do you think?" From what Coop could tell of Payne's half of the conversation, Tracey apparently felt that the assessment was on the money. Payne agreed to work with Coop, and the two developed a trusting relationship. So when Payne began to express some irritation with Ward late in the 1988 tour season, Coop recommended Cook, who officially became Payne's new coach in January 1989.

Although Ward had a major impact in getting Payne pointed in the right direction, it would be hard to argue that the revamped Team Stewart—with Cook coaching, Coop "shrinking," and agreeable caddie Mike Hicks newly on the bag—wasn't supremely successful in taking him to the next level.

Payne had connected with Hicks while both were in Japan for the Four Tours Challenge. "Payne had a caddie at the time he was giving a trial run," Hicks recounted in an interview a month after Payne's death. "I told him at the time that if the job ever opened up, I'd be interested. In May of '88 it did, and I went to work for him, sort of on an interim basis for four weeks. We had all top-ten finishes, and four weeks turned into twelve years."

Hicks compared the player-caddie relationship to that of a marriage. "Your personalities can't clash. You have to learn a guy's emotions—when to say things, when not to say things. Payne liked for me to talk to him. I was always talking to him on the course. We just hit it off. It was a great relationship."

PAYNE WOULD WIN TWICE IN '89, a year that featured the bittersweet occasion of his first major title. Sweet for the sensational golf he played down the stretch. Bitter because his lamentable attitude during the closing moments of the tournament only seemed to confirm to critics that Payne was, as they had suspected, a shallow show-off in silly clothes.

It was hardly the classic manner in which you win a major tournament. Payne opened the tournament at Kemper Lakes outside Chicago with a daunting 74 to promptly drop eight shots off the lead. Although he retreated in frustration at the end of that first round, he would later look back on it as a blessing. "It relaxed me and I was able to freewheel the rest of the way—even on the last day," Payne said the next week. Indeed, with the pressure off, he coasted through rounds of 66, 69, and 67, the last a dazzling shot-making clinic of 31 on the final nine when he was "hope-lessly" out of it. Or so he and most everyone else thought. Affable leader Mike Reid had made the final turn up by five shots and apparently would coast to a wire-to-wire win.

Although Reid had taken the lead on day one, the opening round be-longed to Payne's famed Bay Hill neighbor Arnold Palmer. Just a little more than a month short of his sixtieth birthday, Arnie had turned back the cal-endar with a 67, only one shot off Reid's opening pace. In the locker room before Friday's round, Payne kiddingly asked Arnie for mercy. "Why don't you go back to the Senior Tour and leave us alone?" he jabbed. "I probably will," Palmer countered. "Actually, I don't think you guys are worried much about me."

Indeed, Palmer faded in the second round, and the spindly Reid—known as "Radar" for his uncannily accurate iron shots—would dominate the story-line right up until the closing few holes on Sunday. Even after Payne reeled off birdies at the fourteenth, fifteenth, and sixteenth holes, Reid, playing three groups behind, held a three-shot lead. But Payne's birdie at the last hole while Reid was bogeying back at the sixteenth trimmed Reid's cush-ion to one stroke. Also seeking his first major win, Reid, who had been burdened with the lead for three days, was unraveling.

After signing his card, Payne lingered in the scorer's tent to watch Reid struggle through the final two holes. The television coverage alter-nated between Reid's anguished face out on the course and Payne laugh-ing away in the tent.

Reid doubled the seventeenth, allowing Payne to back into the lead, then missed a seven-foot birdie attempt on the final hole that handed the yuk-yukking Stewart his first major. The image was not a pretty one, and it was made worse by the crestfallen Reid's brave attempt to make light of his disaster in postmortems.

"I guess the Russians were transmitting, because my radar was zapped," Reid said, trying to mask his hurt with humor. Tears began welling in his eyes, then he added through a weak smile: "It's okay. I cry at supermarket openings. As disappointed as I am personally, I'm happy for Payne. Hey, it's only a game, right? Shucks, life goes on."

He stood and departed to a rare ovation from the world's golf press.

Reid had been classy in defeat, and he was promptly followed at the dais by the knickered guy who had displayed anything but class in the preceding hour.

Making matters worse, Payne revealed that he had, in effect, asked for divine assistance to scuttle the martyred Reid. "When I was in that scorer's tent," he told the scribes, "I said a little prayer: 'Lord, how about some good stuff for Payne Stewart this time?' He obliged and let it happen."

The temperature on that August afternoon in the press tent suddenly dropped to somewhere around freezing. The locker room, where many of the pros had lingered to watch the finish on a big-screen TV, was equally icy. In a moment that should have been a joyous celebration and affirmation of Payne's skills, most onlookers mainly hoped he'd drop the trophy on his toe.

He would finish the year number two on the money list and number one in the all-around category of that year's PGA Tour stats. But somewhere near the bottom in esteem.

And his stock wouldn't even be boosted in the eyes of friend and fellow "Flounder" musician Mark Lye the next year when he would get sweet redemption for his 1985 Disaster in Dallas. Payne's double-bogey, double-bogey collapse continued to chew at him, the bad vibes only heightened when he also faded from serious contention with a final-round 71 in the '86 Byron Nelson. He had had to settle for a fourth-place tie behind the winner, Andy Bean.

The Dallas payback would finally come when he won the fifty-four-hole, weather-shortened 1990 Byron Nelson. The final round was played on Monday, and Payne shared the final twosome with Lye. And while the turn of events settled a long-standing contretemps with the tournament for Payne, it provided a chilling perspective for Lye, who was taken aback by Payne's demeanor that day.

"We were friends because of the music thing, but I could just tell my intensity and his intensity weren't even on the same planet," Lye recalls. "He wanted to win at all costs. I mean at *all* costs. And I'm in the middle of this round and I wanted to win, too, but I thought to myself, 'I *never* want to become like that.' I just felt like that was just *waaaay* out of line."

Lye conceded that Payne's previous travails in a tournament so special to him likely increased his intensity when afforded a *third* chance to win it.

"Somebody was telling me the TV coverage went good and they said it was a good draw for him to be playing with me, but that the attention was on Payne. Well, at that point of his career, that's the way he would always want it to be. Forget about everybody else in the field—the attention should be on him."

THE OVERDUE TROPHY IN DALLAS came in the midst of what would stand as the hottest streak of Payne's career. A messy legal separation from his former managers at ProServ had been completed. He was in his second full year with caddie Hicks. And with the coaching of first Ward, then Cook now in full bloom—plus the work of the psychologist Coop beginning to take root—Payne reeled off a streak of six tournament appearances in which he had five top-ten finishes, including two seconds and two victories, at Harbour Town and Dallas. It might have been three were it not for a final-day rainout that forced the Memorial Tournament to make official its fifty-four-hole standing with Greg Norman one stroke in front of Payne.

The Memorial was another source of ongoing frustration for Payne, who would narrowly lose again at "Jack's Place" three years later when pal Paul Azinger holed out from a greenside bunker on the seventy-second hole for a birdie to Payne's bogey. Both had come to the final hole tied with Corey Pavin for the lead. (Although Payne would never win the Memorial, he earned the heartfelt admiration of Jack Nicklaus, who, after attending the moving services following Payne's death, swayed his tournament committee into declaring Payne their annual honoree for the 2000 Memorial.)

Even with the two near misses in the blistering 1990 streak, the surge suddenly ran Payne's official victory total to seven and earned him some of the respect denied him during the tainted PGA victory the previous year over Reid. And his triumph in the MCI Heritage Classic was his impressive second in a row at Harbour Town Links, where neither the faint-of-heart nor those lacking a shot-making magna-cum-laude degree need apply. The first of those two Heritage wins, in 1989, had come not only by an awesome five-stroke margin but also with a humorous story.

The outcome had golfniks thinking the newest formula for winning a golf tournament was to get very little sleep all week. Payne was sleep-deprived enough when he arrived at Harbour Town that year: William Aaron Stewart, offspring number two, had arrived just two weeks earlier to interrupt dad's sleep regularly. Tracey's parents, Norm and Shirley Ferguson, had flown in from Australia for the happy event and were still in town when time came for Payne to make some diaper money at Harbour Town. Because Tracey wasn't ready to travel, Norm pinch-hit as Payne's road companion for the entire week.

A friendly chap whose Aussie accent transforms his son-in-law's given name to "Pine," Norm is a retired Queensland policeman, avid fisherman, low-handicap amateur golfer, and world-champion snoring machine. It was that latter, nocturnal habit that would send Payne to the Harbour Town Links each morning with eyes too bloodshot to focus on an image of himself holding a trophy at the end of the week. So he focused on one tee shot after another, and the first thing you knew he was so far out in front of the field they needed binoculars to read the "Kangol" logo on the back of his tam-o'-shanter.

The townhouse that Payne and Norm shared that week featured one bed downstairs and another upstairs in a loft. Payne spent the week in the loft, catching catnaps jolted by the midnight buzz saw Norm was producing below.

"I spent the whole week dropping things down on Norm, trying to interrupt his snoring," Payne would recount with a grin in his high-pitched midwestern twang. "I threw some towels down on him and that didn't work, so I wet some washcloths and dropped those on him."

Reenacting both his and Norm's parts, Payne offered a dramatization of the nightly bombing raids—or what happened each time one of the soggy washcloths scored a direct hit on the Aussie conning tower.

Payne *(cupping his hands to shout down over an imaginary railing):* "Roll over, Norm!"

Norm *(jolted awake and peering groggily skyward through turkey-buzzard slits):* "Fraph, brawrff . . . was aye snoring?"

Payne *(shaking his head wistfully):* "Yeah, just a little. G'night, Norm."

Norm *(rolling over):* "G'night, Pine . . . fraph, brawrff . . ."

As Payne was replaying the scene in his living room for a local reporter, Norm Ferguson shook his head in amused dispute.

The victory had ended another drought, of a little more than two years' duration this time, and was credited to two factors. First, Payne forced himself into extra concentration on each tee shot, the crucial part of playing Harbour Town's eighteen bowling alleys. Second, he was rewarded for his long-resisted departure from the exaggerated upright putting stance his father had ingrained in him. That winter, Payne had adopted a more conventional putting style, and he'd made one final adjustment the previous week at Augusta—he'd moved the ball nearer the heel of his putter on address. Suddenly, Payne felt he'd make every putt he stood over, and he very nearly did at Harbour Town.

Ward had helped him make the physical transition and Dr. Coop helped him focus positively on the switch. Payne had been absorbing mental-focus strategies during this period from Coop's mind-over-bogeys tape *Golfing out of Your Mind.*

Now Payne began to talk as if he would string together tournament trophies like so many watch fobs. After the Bay Hill breakthrough two years earlier, he had made similar blasts. "That seemed the right thing to say at the time," Payne later reflected. "But I didn't really believe it inside like I do now. I'm excited about the rest of the year."

And he delivered. He would notch the first of his three major championships that summer at the PGA and finish the year number one in scoring average (69.48) and number two in official money ($1.2 million), behind relentless Tom Kite. (Or "The Ant," as Payne renamed Tom for his large-rimmed glasses and scarlet complexion.) The unanswered question was whether Payne went on that rampage motivated by Coop's incantations, or by a tape of Norm snoring.

WHEN PAYNE ADDED ANOTHER major title with his gritty defeat of steady Scott Simpson at Hazeltine in 1991, it was becoming obvious that he had overcome whatever it was that had caused him to wilt so many Sundays during his first decade as a tour pro.

Dr. Coop had sensed a difference at the start of the week, when Payne picked him up at the Minneapolis airport. "He and Tracey had talked about the fact that even if he never won another tournament, he'd still be a great person," Coop wrote in his *Golf Magazine* piece. "This seemed to have given him a great sense of serenity and perspective."

Whatever caused it, Payne displayed a steely win down the stretch of a week in which he was fighting a back problem. He wore a back brace beneath his trademark costume and slept most of the week in the small bed intended for son Aaron—then two years old—because it was firmer than the one in the master bedroom of the home rented for the week.

Coop shared the home all week with the Stewarts, steadily massaging Payne's focus on "playing in the present" while Aaron's bed soothed his back. Each round ended with Payne at his locker unlacing the girdle-type brace with a whoosh of relief. Not as much relief was required after his opening-round 67 gave him a share of the lead. "There's nothing like a 67 to make your back feel good," he mused.

The daily interviews would be followed by a ninety-minute regimen in the PGA Tour fitness trailer, a program designed to strengthen the muscles around three degenerated discs in Payne's lower back.

He would later reflect that the Hazeltine Open raised him to a new level of preparation and control during the week of a major tournament. Even during the practice rounds, when most other players signed autographs on the course, Payne politely declined all requests, promising he would be available behind the eighteenth green when his rehearsal round was over. And he delivered, lingering there for nearly an hour after each practice round to sign for all comers.

"On the course, I wanted to concentrate on what I was trying to accomplish with my golf game," he explained. "Things like that helped my mental awareness and attitude during the week. I think I was really prepared for what was coming off.

"I was very focused. Playing with Ian Woosnam and Greg Norman during the first two rounds, I never saw them hit a shot. I wasn't even watching what they were doing, I was so into doing what I had to do on that golf course."

Payne said at Hazeltine he entered that elusive "zone," that mystical mental state athletes would love to be able to switch on and off at will. "When I'm in it, I don't see anything else. All the colors and all the people are just a blur. All I'm seeing is the ball and the hole. It's like a horse with blinders on. You don't see anything on either side."

As the Open rocked down to a final lap on the course that outspoken Dave Hill had once assailed as a farm wasted, Stewart and Simpson were tied for the lead. That created something of an odd-couple pairing—the quiet, understated Simpson and the brash, flamboyant clotheshorse who was now into his $200,000-a-year clothing tie-in with the National Football League. For the record, Payne had been clad in the hometown Vikings' colors for the first round, was a red-and-white Buffalo Bills tout for round two, raised the candlepower considerably for the Saturday round in the aqua and orange of the Miami Dolphins, then gave in to the shouted wishes of the galleries to trot out the Vikings' colors again.

It was an easy sell because that's what he wore when carding that sizzling 67. Besides, it wouldn't be a bad idea to have all those Minnesota fans cheering you on in the last day of a U.S. Open. Certain USGA bluebloods were grumbling about the propriety of that latter competitive edge, though Payne insisted that was not part of his game plan.

Unshaken by several birdie putts that walked over the corners of cups on the final nine, Payne rammed a six-footer into the heart of the eighteenth hole to force a Monday play-off and further affirm the new, gritty version of William P. Stewart. "I was proud of the putt on eighteen," he said afterward. "That proved something to me—that I deserved to be there tomorrow."

He would prove even more in the Monday play-off, battling back from a two-shot deficit with just three holes remaining for the second day in a row. A determined par on the dreadfully long eighteenth gave him the victory and every right to claim the respect he had earned with this second major title. He and Tracey locked in a lingering embrace there alongside the green, savoring the end of a trying journey from frustration to fulfillment.

"The first one was sweet," he said of the '89 PGA. "But a lot of people say I backed into it. I didn't back into this one. I played my ass off and I never gave up."

Payne also made a stride that day toward mending some media fences. He dispatched two cases of bubbly to the press tent, inspiring a few "Cham-Payne" headlines the next morning. "I just wanted to show you that I'm a nice guy," he explained to the scribes. "In the past, I may have come off as arrogant at times. Maybe you caught me at the wrong time. I think when you get to know me, I'm a pretty nice guy."

For sure, he had convinced the press he could be a pretty focused guy, even if his penchant for jocular moments hadn't disappeared. Play-off. Third hole. Payne belted a perfect drive, ducked under the gallery rope, and strode briskly though startled fans to a row of Porta-Johns. His face twisted in concern when a quick check determined all six units were occupied. He waited impatiently for a moment until a middle-aged woman swung open one of the doors and was jolted to discover one of the day's principal performers standing there with a silly smile on his face.

"Hello," Payne Stewart said brightly, tipping his tam-o'-shanter as he succeeded her in the relief station for a lengthy pause. With a girdle brace, pit stops became an involved process. Somewhere in Minnesota is a woman no doubt often telling of her amusing rendezvous with a major golf champion.

While shot doctors like Perry Leslie and Harvie Ward and Chuck Cook proffered their technical analyses on what transformed Payne from a Sunday chump to a Sunday champ, there were other ingredients that brought this soup to a fine blend.

"I just think it was perseverance," insists longtime pal Mark Wiebe. "Payne was a guy who was going to persevere and get it done. When we look at guys like Tom Watson who had a similar reputation and then moved on to become one of the all-time greats, we get strength from that. Payne saw that and he knew it, way before anyone else.

"The relationship he had with his father and the way he was brought up let him know that he was going to do whatever it was he set out to do. You put that on a learning curve and he just finally figured it out—to hang in there and don't force things. Don't do this and next time I'm gonna remember to do that and, I'll be damned, the next time he remembered."

Peter Jacobsen also subscribed to the learning-curve theory. "I think it happens to everybody. It either happens for the better or happens for the worse," he said. "You can be in contention on Sunday a lot and either learn to break through, or you go away."

You'll recall Payne had thought about the latter just five years earlier. But Tracey refused to let it happen.

"The lady he married," says Wiebe, "was so perfect for Payne to keep up that drive and belief. It wasn't often that he didn't believe he would get it done, but when he had any dents at all, she would be right there to pound them out. What a great combo they were."

Adds Harvie Ward: "Payne never would have gotten there without her. She was really, really strong."

Chuck Cook agrees that Tracey played a positive role in Payne's becoming a confident champion, but recalls the times when her overbearing nature may have delayed the process.

"For the longest time, Tracey had been very hard on him," said Cook, who recalled a shattering moment in 1990 right after Payne had won at Hilton Head and Dallas, then finished second at the Memorial. Cook was reviewing the stunning skein with Payne at his house when Tracey interjected a snide, "Well, if you'd only won Memorial."

Cook could see the hurt on Payne's face.

"There was a lot of friction about her being on him so hard all the time," Cook added. "And then this huge change came. She would still ask him how his day went, but it was never like it had been. Obviously, she and Payne had had a talk about that."

But even when there had been momentary consternation, Payne made it clear he appreciated the constant prodding by his wife to reach higher. On a hunting trip to Arkansas in January 1999 with University of Central Florida president Dr. John Hitt, the subject somehow came up. Hitt said Payne told of driving home with Tracey after the Players Championship the previous year, expressing satisfaction about his closing 65 for an eighth-place finish. "Tracey said, 'Yeah, but you should be doing so much better.' And she was right. She wasn't going to let me settle for anything less than my very best," Payne told Hitt.

Payne was unfailingly protective of Tracey. In the course of kidding banter in the locker room one day, one of golf's ranking superstars crossed the line with an off-color remark about the ample size of Tracey's bustline. Payne's smile instantly vanished as he rose and challenged the famous player to a fight. Realizing that Payne was dead serious, the superstar quickly backed down, offering an apology. Payne nodded his acceptance, and walked away. The two didn't speak for months afterward.

THE NEXT SPRING WAS WHEN COOK was invited along on that poignant junket to the U.S. Open Media Day at Pebble Beach. That night they sat on the seawall by the eighteenth green and talked about life until three in the morning, the Open trophy perched between them.

The reason the trophy was out there in the predawn, as Cook related in his eulogy at Payne's memorial, was a boisterous guy in the bar who didn't believe that was really Payne Stewart sitting there. "Well, if I go get the U.S. Open trophy out of my room and bring it in here," Payne countered with a smirk, "will you keep it filled with whatever we want to drink?"

The guy agreed and Payne fetched the prestigious old silver cup. When that convinced the doubting Thomas, Payne called out to the bartender to start bringing bottles of Cristal champagne.

"Now, Cristal champagne is pretty expensive," Cook picks up the story. "But in the bar at Pebble Beach, it's *really* expensive. We had several bottles and I think that guy may be the only guy ever who was sorry he met Payne Stewart."

Two hours later, Payne and Chuck and the trophy ventured out to the seawall for that rambling heart-to-heart. "We were planning to have a redo of that this year when Payne went back to Pebble to defend his championship," Cook concluded his eulogy. "I'm gonna be there with some Cristal champagne on that seawall. And I'm gonna talk to my friend about life. I love Payne Stewart. And I miss him."

chapter 1 1

From Churl to Champ

Payne Stewart's perspectives began to change after that '91 Open conquest at Hazeltine. The shift was noticeable even the very next day. He had been scheduled to fly from Chicago to Dublin that Monday to play in the Irish Open at the end of the week. That plan was changed by the Monday play-off. Payne instead decided to charter a private jet very late that night to Orlando, then fly commercially to Ireland the next night on a red-eye. That would give him a day at home to savor the triumph with his family.

Aaron, two, and Chelsea, five, had little concern that their world-famous father was sleep-starved or even that he was the freshly minted, grand exalted U.S. Open champion. They were just happy to be back in their Orlando home where they could drag dear ol' dad into the swimming pool. It was a toss-up as to who enjoyed the splashing more—Payne or the kids.

The session reminded him what was really important as he braced to face a wave of determined competitors even more daunting than Scott Simpson: agents and corporate officials anxious to convert Payne's Open title into mounds of cash not even a show dog could leap. Vowing a departure from his experience following the '89 PGA victory, he insisted he wasn't going to chase the money at the expense of family time.

"I don't think you can put a price on what I did in the pool this morning," Payne said that afternoon, lounging in shorts, a U.S. Open T-shirt, and a Chicago Bulls championship cap. "Those other things are tempting. But you give up a day here and a week there and all of a sudden you don't have time for the things and the people that are important." He was determined not to let that revered old silver trophy sitting there on his kitchen counter, or the beckoning stack of greenbacks, take control of his life this time.

Helping him to that end, he felt, was his decision not to throw in with another large management company. After he departed Pro-Serv, Mark McCormack's global conglomerate International Management Group had pressured him to join its vast stable of superstars. Instead, Payne signed with Fraley, the Orlando sports lawyer and friend. "I got to the point I was fed up with large management companies. I found that they lie too much," Payne said with typical frankness. "When I turned down McCormack, he said, 'Well, before your career is over, you'll be with IMG.' When he said that, well . . ."

It was obvious that the old saw about a cold day in Honolulu applied.

"When you get to the Tour, you have dollars and dollars thrust upon you. But you have to remember what got you here. I've learned how to say no. I believe that if I play the way Payne Stewart should play, the money will take care of itself. I want to be around and play to my potential for a long time to come. I don't feel I'd be giving myself a chance to do that if I spent too much time on the other things. I'm pretty happy right now. I can do pretty much whatever I want. I enjoy my job. I make a nice living at it. How much money's enough?"

Then he said something that now takes on haunting overtones.

"I guess I could have more toys, but they can get very expensive and demanding. Airplanes, helicopters, boats. Let's go here, let's go there. There gets to be a lot of responsibility with each one. I lease a plane occasionally, but there are few times when it's really practical. Only if you're out to impress people do you need more things. But that's been something I've never been concerned with—impressing people with what I have."

Eventually—and tragically—he would soften his stance on chartering executive jets, but only because he saw that as a way to whisk home after tournaments and corporate obligations to maximize the time spent with his family. But it would be chasing the money in a low-rent jet—pursuing a course-design project in the Dallas area—that would end his life prematurely in October.

JUST WHEN IT SEEMED PAYNE STEWART had all of his golf stars in alignment and was turning the corner toward becoming a most admirable figure, he would follow that '91 Open victory with a bleak, six-year run in which he added just one lone win on the PGA Tour. And that trophy, at the '95 Shell Houston Open, came gift-wrapped from his old pal Scott Hoch.

Headed down the stretch at the TPC/Woodlands, Hoch had a five-shot cushion that he gave away in chunks to create a two-man play-off with his onetime houseguest. Hoch promptly bogeyed the first play-off hole, yanking his drive into the left rough on the eighteenth, then punching a low screamer across the guarding lake into an impossible lie on the back slope of a bunker behind the green. Payne's two-putt par—shaky in its own right with a three-and-a-half-foot comebacker—was enough for his first Tour win in almost four years.

"I just gave it to him. No other way around that," Hoch recalled. "I just flat choked."

For Payne, it was something of a replay of his '89 PGA victory when Mike Reid collapsed. Playing nearly an hour ahead of Hoch and seemingly out of reach, Payne freewheeled to a four-under-par 68 in difficult final-day winds and on parched, almost barren greens. Except this time he was more considerate to the victim. When it was over, he somberly gripped Hoch's hand and said, "Hey, I know how you feel."

Hoch recalled that Payne went out of his way to congratulate him for making birdie on the seventy-second hole to force a play-off when it had appeared that he had blown that, too. "When I told the media that I simply choked, Payne stood up in my defense. I appreciated that."

Although Payne had just the one official win during that 1992–98 span, it was hardly a bust. Aside from the 1994 season, when he was struggling to adapt to the Spalding irons and dropped to a career-low ranking of 123 on the PGA Tour money list, he didn't finish outside the top forty on the annual money list during that span or after any other full season throughout his career. (He was number 160 in his 1981 half season as a rookie.)

Also, he kept his acceptance speeches in tune with victories on foreign soil. He would win three times overseas during the 1990s, capturing the '91 Dutch Open and the lucrative Hassan II Trophy tournament in Morocco in both '92 and '93.

And despite the dearth of official Tour wins during that time, he continued to make headlines at the more important tournaments. He was third in the '95 Players Championship and was nudged twice in the Open by another tight friend, Lee Janzen. Janzen will go down in history as the man who deprived Payne of the right to etch his name among legends such as Bobby Jones, Ben Hogan, and Jack Nicklaus—four-time U.S. Open winners.

What hurt most during that period was not the two runner-up Open finishes to Janzen, in '93 and '98, but Payne's absence from the Ryder Cup team. After making the biennial squad four times in a row—1987 through 1993—he missed qualifying for the '95 and '97 teams. It thus became his most important golf goal during the second half of the '90s to reclaim a spot on the U.S. team.

When he did make the '99 team, Payne embraced it with a fervor. He would serve as a motivational team leader and beacon of good sportsmanship at Boston after first lending philosophical support to Captain Ben Crenshaw when some of the younger stars were disrespecting the Ryder Cup privilege.

"Payne was kinda the motivator and the intensity bringer," Phil Mickelson recounted. "He was the one who really invoked a lot of the intensity and focus among our players. I think that when we were down 6–10 going into the final day, everybody was talking about how we could do it.

"But Payne was really important in getting us really to believe that, and instill the confidence in the whole team that we were the better players."

And when the U.S. team rallied to win on the final day—touching off a controversy and bad vibes from across the Atlantic—it was Payne who earned the admiration of all continents with his show of sportsmanship toward fan-abused Scot Colin Montgomerie. Compounding three days of rough treatment for the Europeans from overzealous, often rowdy American galleries, most of the U.S. team—including, lamentably, a few of the pros' wives—stormed the seventeenth green to celebrate Justin Leonard's forty-five-foot smart bomb that completed the remarkable U.S. turnaround.

Spain's José María Olazábal was forced to blink in astonishment and irritation at the group gaffe in golf etiquette while he still had a tying putt to attempt. When his putt missed, the Cup was clinched.

Up ahead, on the eighteenth, Montgomerie had a birdie putt to seal an inconsequential one-up victory over Stewart. But before Colin could settle over the ball, Payne picked it up and conceded the match, apologizing to

Monty for the rude treatment he had received from fans. "He doesn't deserve what he went through out there [from hecklers]. It's not fair. That's not what this sport is about," Payne said that day. "As he was getting ready to putt, I said to my caddie, 'He doesn't deserve to have to make this putt. I'm not going to put him through that [if he misses].'"

So in high-impact golf competitions, Payne will be remembered for two heroic and exemplary moments in the final year of his life. There was the clutch, fifteen-foot putt to win the Open at Pinehurst, instantly followed by his thoughtfulness to expectant father Phil Mickelson. Then came his act of conceding a putt to defeat himself in the classiest act of a feud-besmirched Ryder Cup.

"To pick my ball up in those circumstances was the gesture of a pure sportsman," Montgomerie wrote in *Golf World* after Payne's death. What Montgomerie hadn't realized at the time, as jubilant U.S. fans ran onto the green, was that Payne picked his way through the milling throng to find Montgomerie's wife, Eimear. He hugged her and said, "I just want you to know that what went on here should never have happened. I apologize for the fans' behavior."

"When I heard that story from my wife, Payne leaped in our estimation," Monty later reflected. "I have always respected Payne for his golfing ability, and no one will ever forget the courageous way in which he won all three of his majors. Above all, I respected his approach to the game and none more so than at Brookline."

Brian Bowen, golf coach at First Academy, where Payne's children attend, and a member of an informal men's fellowship group that included Payne, was there in Boston and couldn't have been prouder of his famous friend's actions that day.

"What he did with Colin on the last hole was great," said Bowen. "But also, on number five, when a guy was screaming and hollering at Colin, Payne stopped what he was doing to go over and admonish the heckler, then asked the police to take the guy away.

"In our fellowship meetings back home, he had told us all year long, 'All I want to do is play in the Ryder Cup. I don't care if I win a tournament. I just want the points to make the Ryder Cup team and restore the Cup to America.' He did that, and with ultimate class."

While Phil Mickelson was reflecting on those matches, he laughed sweetly, looking at a photo on his wall taken hours after the Ryder Cup triumph. It was snapped in the "squad room" suite in the U.S. team's Boston hotel.

"Payne has a bottle of wine in one hand and a big cigar in the other," Mickelson said as he began describing the photo. "He's in sweats and a T-shirt. I thought that was very typical of Payne—that he could be very serious and intent on the course, but let loose off the course. The PGA sent that out to everyone on the team. It's really funny. And it's pure Payne."

LEE JANZEN ACQUIRED NOT ONLY his first major title by nipping Payne in the '93 Open at Baltusrol, but a heightened respect for his friend and fellow Orlando resident. Comprising the Sunday final twosome, they found themselves in a virtual match-play scrum for the championship as the tournament clattered down to a pulsing finish.

Payne had bravely hung on over the front nine when his driver developed some serious rudder problems. Reporters with red media armbands padding along just inside the ropes were impressed that Payne had carved a one-over-par 36 on the front, considering all the places he had sprayed his tee shots.

"Somebody needs to give Payne a red armband and tell him he can play inside the ropes!" someone said.

Janzen finally seized the lead with a chip-in birdie from the fringe late in the round and carried a one-stroke lead to the par-5 eighteenth. There, Janzen pushed his drive into a dicey lie a few feet off the fairway and chopped the ball out with an iron short of the large pond fronting the green. He wedged on and, needing only a two-putt from ten feet to seal the prize, was surprised to hear Payne openly pulling for Janzen to finish it off in style with a birdie. Janzen obliged, thus winning by two shots.

"I was almost stunned," Janzen recalled. "I thought he'd just come over and shake my hand and walk off. But he really wanted to talk to me. He was smiling, and probably had a bigger smile than I did because he was genuinely happy for me."

As Janzen smooched the trophy at the behest of photographers, runner-up Payne laughed and shouted: "C'mon! You're using frog lips. Kiss that thing like you mean it!"

Janzen said Stewart had coped so well with the narrow loss, in fact, that he remained playful enough to pull a prank on the man who had just beaten him. Janzen knew that two weeks earlier, after Paul Azinger holed a bunker shot to beat Payne on the last hole of the Memorial tournament, Payne had put banana chunks in Azinger's street shoes.

"So before the last round at Baltusrol, I put a note on top of my [street] shoes saying 'No Bananas,' just in case," Janzen recounted, chuckling. "I got back to my locker after all the press conferences and ceremonies about ten o'clock that night and I noticed the note was missing. I started to put my shoes on, but something told me I needed to check my shoes. So I looked in there and, sure enough, there were bananas down in the toes."

When Janzen again nudged him for the Open title five years later, the loss was even tougher for Payne. Another of those winless streaks had stretched beyond its third year and he had had a four-stroke cushion when final-round play had begun that 1998 June morning at San Francisco's demanding Olympic Club. No Open competitor had lost a larger final-round lead. But Janzen was doubly impressed with the stand-up way Payne acted immediately after the round.

"He handled it like the true champion he was. With a lot of class," said Janzen.

In a Kodak moment witnessed by only a handful, when Payne and Janzen were virtually alone in one of the Olympic Club's locker-room alcoves, they hugged again for an extended moment.

STEWART WAS EQUALLY MAGNANIMOUS about the buzzards' luck he was dealt that Sunday by the usually wacky USGA course setup and by a USGA rules official. His lead dwindled to one, Payne caught a terrible break when his perfect tee shot on twelve came to rest in a sand-filled divot. While pondering the tricky shot, a USGA official hit him with a slow-play warning—seen as nonsensical, since Payne was playing in the final twosome and, thus, unable to hold up anyone behind him.

Distracted, Payne left his approach from the sand divot in a bunker fronting the green and took bogey 5. That dropped him into a tie with Janzen, playing in the twosome just ahead. Then on the par-3 thirteenth, Payne hit what appeared to be a perfect five-iron that landed just a few yards onto the front of what had become one of the USGA's trademark marble greens. The ball bounded like a lovesick rabbit into the long, gnarly collar rough just beyond the green. Though only about twenty feet from the cup, Payne had to chop it aggressively out of the tangled grass, the ball squirting well left of the pin. He made bogey 4 and fell a stroke behind Janzen, never to lead again.

At Olympic's dramatic amphitheater eighteenth green, Payne would make a nice run at a twenty-foot downhill and sidehill birdie putt to push Janzen to overtime. But the ball slid by on the low side. Payne turned to caddie Mike Hicks, smiled, and said, "Well, we're back in the Masters." Augusta National extends invitations to the top sixteen players in the U.S. Open, if not otherwise qualified; Payne had failed to make the previous two Masters fields.

Once again, he had played well enough in the final round of a major to win, but had suffered a bad break or two while Janzen played bravely and had an assist from that signature moment when his pushed tee shot belatedly tumbled out of a tree alongside the fifth fairway. A Pacific breeze jostled the ball out of the tree just as Janzen had given up and was returning to the tee to play a second ball. He made 4 instead of a likely double-bogey 6 and later that day beat Payne for the trophy by just one stroke. (During a long layover at the San Francisco airport en route to Asia several months later, Janzen and a buddy hopped a cab and revisited the scene. They walked down to the fifth fairway so Janzen could point out the tree that helped him win the Open. "Thank you, tree," he said to his towering accomplice.)

Although Payne didn't win at Olympic, the week remained special to him because it was one of those occasional tournaments when Tracey and the kids were at home in Orlando and his mother, Bee, then a still-spry seventy-nine, pinch-hit as his traveling companion. As Payne played his way into the forefront, Bee became an integral part of the storyline, charming members of the media. By day, she joined her son at the golf course, following him a few holes at a time, then holing up in the clubhouse in front of a TV set. "He kept telling me not to walk too much and find a good place in the clubhouse to watch," Bee recalled. "I kept telling him I would be just fine."

By night, in their shared suite at the Airport Marriott, Payne and Bee ordered room service, watched in-room movies, and just talked. Early in the week, they even took in a Giants baseball game together as guests of Payne's friend and fellow Orlando resident, pitcher Orel Hershiser. It was a week of quality time that both of them would openly cherish.

"I would often go with him if he was alone," said Bee. "Once it was to Morocco. I wasn't too hip on that, but he said, 'Mom, if you would just go with me to Morocco, I'll take you to Japan, too.' So I did that with him. It was very dear to me because we could bond. Not that he didn't love his wife and children, but it was special with us."

And what did they gab about at night?

"Well, we didn't talk about golf," she laughed in recollection. "We just talked about our family. He brought me up to date on all the things his kids were doing. He was so proud of how Chelsea was doing in her school-work and proud that she knew, even at that age [twelve], that she wanted to be a lawyer.

"One night there was a funny incident," she continued with a twinkle. "Payne's coach, Chuck Cook, was staying at the same hotel and we were all going up on the elevator with some other people. As Chuck and his wife got off at their floor, he said loud enough for the other people to hear, 'I wonder how long he's been dating that older woman?' Chuck is so funny like that."

Bee and Payne simply camped out in the suite one evening, yukking through a movie with a title appropriate for their charmed week: *As Good as It Gets*.

The week was something of a sweet flashback for Bee, who similarly had traveled to San Francisco and the Olympic Club with Bill Stewart, when Payne's father had qualified as an amateur to play in the 1955 U.S. Open, two years before Payne was born. The difference was that Bill flamed out with 83–88 in the first two rounds and no doubt went to his grave without fond thoughts for the Olympic course. "But I think he's got a big ol' smile now, looking down on what I'm doing here," Payne said moments after completing three rounds with a four-shot lead and the only sub-par total in the field.

Although he was on the verge of a wire-to-wire major victory at Olympic—one of the most demanding shot-making crucibles in golf—

many skeptics clung to his outdated reputation for coming unraveled down the stretch. Even the official player guide prepared for the media by the USGA that week contained this passage in Payne's bio: "He became known on Tour for wearing plus twos and a habit of choking in the closing stages of a tournament."

When shown the bio, Payne masked his irritation behind a chuckle and a glib remark. Later, he assailed a USGA official, who apologized for the unflattering, though not altogether inaccurate, portrait.

Sensing the lasting imprint that the outcome might leave on his close pal's career, Azinger taped a note of encouragement onto Payne's locker, using the nickname that was their private joke. "Smoker: Stay in the present and enjoy the walk—Zinger." The message boils down the prevalent theme of golf shrinks, who urge players to forget bad shots and avoid projecting through the remaining holes. Azinger could have helped more by lending Payne a few birdies; Zinger, playing far back in the pack, had eight of them that day in a tournament-low 65. Payne would manage just one as his lead oozed away.

When it was over, he was classy and disarming in front of the world golf media. He offered smiles and philosophical takes and gracious salutes to Janzen—now validated as his official U.S. Open nemesis—for once again being a tenacious bulldog with a tournament on the line. Payne's demeanor that day helped further dissolve years of accumulated acrimony with many in the press corps. During the week, an on-line service had informally polled golf writers on which pros they'd least like to see win a tournament they're covering and Payne had finished third, behind media-hostile Vijay Singh and misunderstood Scott Hoch.

"I didn't play good enough to win today," Payne shrugged. "And I got beat by an outstanding round of golf. A 68 under these conditions and in this pressure—that's a great round of golf. But I'm gonna hold my head up. I never gave up. I'm proud of that. I'll still be Payne Stewart when I walk out this door and I'll sleep just fine tonight."

Payne and Bee walked out of the media tent arm in arm and in jaunty determination not to let another close Open loss dampen their golden week.

But he would be unable to maintain that composure when one of his harsher critics, *Palm Beach Post* columnist Craig Dolch, appeared on a cable-

TV golf talk show shortly after the Open at Olympic. Dolch had written a biting piece about Payne's loss and now here he was on The Golf Channel.

Payne picked up the phone and called in, questioning the writer's logic and crudely accusing Dolch—on the air—of having a "hard-on" for him.

"I always wanted to talk to this guy," Payne explained later, "and all of a sudden he was on *Viewers' Forum*. I said, 'Gimme the phone.'" Payne confirmed suspicions that he was into his cups that evening at home. Otherwise he might not have made the call. He definitely wouldn't have used the off-color metaphor, he asserted. "As soon as I said that, I thought, 'Whoops!' But that was how I was feeling."

The incident inspired Payne to cut back on his imbibing, even though there was no indication that he had become a problem drinker. He reminded himself that his mother, Bee, was a recovering alcoholic, and he blanched at the notion that one of his own children might one day be moved to take him to a dry-out clinic, as he had taken Bee to a St. Louis facility several years earlier. He was thankful she hadn't had a relapse during the intervening years.

Payne urged Dolch to introduce himself the next time he was at a tournament where Payne was playing so they could talk and let bygones be bygones. "But I also told him I didn't do anything that [Open] week to justify him writing that article the way he did."

At his very next U.S. Open, he would back up those words.

SETTING THE 1999 U.S. OPEN at venerable Pinehurst No. 2, with its Donald Ross–designed convex greens, created a unique Open storyline as the golf world headed to the sandhills of North Carolina. A typical Open setup includes thick collars of rough hard against the putting surfaces. But at Pinehurst, with its inverted cereal-bowl greens and steep, shaved slopes falling away on all sides, competitors became preoccupied with inventing recovery shots from the bottoms of those slopes.

It was clear that Pinehurst would call for imagination and extra doses of patience and concentration. The latter had been a hurdle in recent years for Payne, diagnosed and treated for a minor case of attention deficit disorder. That became a topic of discussion for Payne in the weeks approaching the Open.

"What people don't realize is that God gave him tempo, rhythm, and feel, but he's had to work very hard on his concentration," said Dick Coop, Payne's golf psychologist. "However, under the right conditions, like many ADD sufferers, he could hyperfocus. That's why he did better in majors than in the John Deere Classics." Also because Payne never played in a John Deere Classic; but Coop's point was made.

Payne revealed that he had stopped taking the medicine that had been prescribed for the condition many months earlier. He said the symptoms had disappeared and, on the eve of the Open at Pinehurst, he declared himself ready to make a run at the title he had let slip away the previous summer at Olympic.

"Most people never get a second chance," he said. "You live for the chance and pray you can get in the same situation again, but it usually doesn't happen. That's just the reality of it. But I'm here to play out that chance. I've waited a year. I want to take the trophy back *home*."

The 1999 season had opened with a hint that Dame Fortune was into a payback mode for Payne, whose career, to that point, included twenty-three second-place finishes but just nine official wins. Number ten would come quickly, at Pebble Beach, where the weather-plagued AT&T was declared official after fifty-four holes with Payne sitting on the overnight lead. That came as a long-overdue reversal of fortune after the several tournaments in which he was in serious contention after three rounds, only to have final-round rain-outs hand titles to the guy he was chasing.

Understandably, Payne made no apologies when Clint Eastwood handed him the AT&T trophy. Instead, he spoke about the continued changes in his perspective on life. "I'm a lot older and I'm a lot wiser, too," said Payne, then just a week past his forty-second birthday. "I'm more mature. I know that I want to watch my family grow up, and then I'm going to focus on my golfing. After I get done here, I'm going to the airport and going home. I'm looking forward to about six-thirty tomorrow morning, when my son is going to come walking in there saying, 'Knock, knock, you awake?' So it will be great. I will get up, make breakfast, and take him to school."

Significantly, the AT&T was the first tournament in which Payne used the odd SeeMore putter, a device that features a red dot atop the heel of its thick blade. The theory is if you hide the red dot from view with the putter shaft, you wind up with the club in the same position each time. The instant success Payne enjoyed with the SeeMore putter carried over to a solid season. He virtually eliminated the inconsistency on short-to-medium putts that had often caused his downfall.

"Payne was always a tremendous player," Tour official Mark Russell said a few months later. "Striking the ball was never a problem. That was easy. The only problem was putting inside of ten feet. But he has gone to this SeeMore putter and straightened out his putting. I'm really looking for him in the next year or two to win a bunch of tournaments."

Russell's words were still warm when Payne used that SeeMore to sink the three consecutive crucial putts on the closing holes at Pinehurst, finally and forever sealing an indisputable legacy as an unflinching champion of the highest order.

PAYNE HAD COME TO PINEHURST with more arrows in his quiver than the SeeMore and nagging memories of the loss at Olympic. ("I could either build on what happened last year or let it beat me up, never to return. I could have crawled away and hid.") He also was armed with a healthy attitude toward a tournament where crafting patient pars is rewarded, his new spiritual calm, and the soothing wonders of lamb's wool.

While many of the competitors were bemoaning the unique challenges that Donald Ross and the USGA-shaved, greenside slopes were presenting in practice rounds, Payne smiled knowingly. As a younger player, Payne had also joined the locker-room chorus of grumbling that erupted each year when the pampered stars of the PGA Tour were thrown onto some USGA bed of nails.

"I've had to learn to accept Open situations," Payne said on the eve of the tournament. "I came to realize that complaining about it gets you nowhere, and it doesn't change anything. So I just accept that 280 [even par] is going to be a good number at the end of the week and try to figure out a way to make pars."

The lamb's wool was a discovery he had made as a way to combat "hot feet," a condition caused by walking long distances in golf spikes during summer tournaments. Each day before play, Payne plopped down on a bench, spread a towel beneath his bare feet, and performed a ritual. He'd pull swatches from a large ball of lamb's wool and meticulously wrap the strands around and between his toes. Once satisfied with the application, he'd douse it with a heavy coat of foot powder, then pull on his long knickers socks.

He noticed a nosy columnist blinking in curiosity at the scene before one round and broke into his distinctive smile. "Makes my feet feel *grrrrrreat!*" he explained.

Through two rounds, Payne found himself in the halfway lead with young lion David Duval and expectant father Phil Mickelson, who was vowing to leave—no matter what his position in the tournament—the moment wife, Amy, went into labor back home in Arizona. Late in the second round, Payne provided a preview of what was to come, clinging to his three-under-par status by getting up-and-down from 102 yards on the brutally long sixteenth, then willing in an eight-footer at the eighteenth to save par.

At Payne's request, his golf coach, Chuck Cook, hung around for most of the tournament.

"Normally, I work with my guys Monday through the first round," Cook explained. "I usually leave on Thursday night or Friday morning. The year before at Olympic, I had stayed through Friday's round and caught the red-eye home that night. I had decided to do that in Pinehurst, too. But here he was, in contention again and said, 'Can you stay for the whole tournament?' I reminded him that Sunday was Father's Day and I needed to get back, but that I would wait until Saturday night to leave."

So before Saturday's round, there was Cook encouraging his man on the practice tee, where he overheard an attempt by Tiger Woods to apply a bit of gamesmanship.

"Tiger comes up to him and says, 'Payne, when I build a golf course it's gonna be eight thousand yards long.' He obviously was trying to let Payne know he could outhit him. Payne came right back and said, 'Yeah, but if it's a U.S. Open, you'll still have to drive it in the fairway.' He wasn't going to let Tiger get the best of him, or intimidate him at all."

Notably, Woods pulled his opening drive into the heavy rough and started the round with a double-bogey. Touché.

Cook tried words of his own to help his knickered client on the practice tee that day: "You know, Payne, the pressure's on these other guys. You've won this tournament before and these guys haven't. You know how to do this."

Cook paused and the two men looked at each other and started laughing.

Cook: "Okay, that's all the clichés I can think of."

Payne *(chuckling):* "Yeah, I just gotta deal with it."

He dealt with it in brave fashion. Three straight bogeys in the middle of that third round tested his resolve to remain at the top of the leaderboard. He answered the test with a crucial, par-saving putt on the eleventh, then capped off the day with a rare birdie at the taxing eighteenth to reclaim a one-shot lead over Mickelson. The closing birdie, he said, "leaves a very, very good taste in my mouth. I was hoping to have this opportunity again. Now I've got to go out tomorrow and deal with it."

He would share the tournament's final pairing with Mickelson, who was still insisting he would drop everything, race to the airport, and whoosh home in his private jet the instant his due-any-minute wife called the beeper carried by his caddie. Payne and Tracey had discussed the matter the previous evening. "That's a real tough call, especially if he's leading," said Payne. "But I would have kicked myself if I wasn't there when our first child was born. The birth of a child is pretty special. I cut the umbilical cord on both of our children. It's an unbelievable experience."

The prospect of Mickelson winning the Open *and* becoming a dad on Father's Day seemed a script too good to be true. But Payne had his own Father's Day angle. Just before departing for the course he watched as NBC aired a segment about him and his father, Bill. Payne stood in front of the television, tears welling in his eyes as he watched images of his late father. In that moment, he said, he found some inner strength.

Oddly, Payne didn't cry at his father's funeral in 1985. But then, on a visit to the grave a few years later, the tears came in torrents. Daughter Chelsea, then a preschooler, looked up and asked, "Daddy, why are you crying?"

"Because," he said, "I loved my father very much."

Months after the Pinehurst triumph, Mike Hicks, the caddie, would marvel at the way Payne handled himself during that final round. "He really stayed on an even keel that day and didn't really get overemotional or get too low," Hicks said during a Golf Channel interview. "And I tried to stay on that same wavelength with him that whole day. And then there was the exuberance and the adrenaline of the moment on the eighteenth green when he made the winning putt. My gosh, it still sends chills up my spine."

That putt was the third in a run of courageous moments over the closing holes. The first, a twenty-five-footer to save par at the sixteenth, erased Mickelson's brief, one-stroke lead. Then came a dead-center four-footer for birdie at seventeen—after Mickelson had missed from five feet—to seize the lead. Payne pushed his tee shot at the last into heavy rough on the right side, slashed out into the fairway, then lofted a lob-wedge approach to within fifteen feet of the pin.

Mickelson two-putted for par, leaving the stage, dramatically, for Payne to either win the tournament or two-putt to fall into a Monday play-off. With a chilly mist coming down, a light breeze blowing, and history and tens of thousands poised breathless, Payne stroked the ball on a line aimed just inside the right corner of the cup. An instant before it curled into the center, he chased it home with a joyous whoop and a clenched fist, then leaped for the heavens. "It felt so good," he would say. "I don't know how high I jumped. It felt like it was sky-high. It felt like I was way up there. It felt so good to accomplish what I did."

Hicks deliriously wrapped himself around the new champ, Yogi Berra style. Then Payne grabbed Mickelson's face in a two-handed grip, as if holding a cantaloupe, and congratulated him on his impending fatherhood. "And you're going to be a *great* father!" Payne shouted in summation, his nose just inches from Mickelson's.

"To be honest, I can't tell you now what he said, verbatim," Mickelson would reflect months later. "He said something like, 'You're about to become a father and it's the greatest joy you could imagine. And I am so happy for you.' And I just thought for him to have just won, arguably, the biggest tournament in the game, for him to be thinking about someone else other than himself, well, that said a lot about who Payne Stewart was."

Or had become.

Afterward, in the pressroom, Payne said, "Last year, everybody said, 'Great try.' Well, I didn't want to hear that. I didn't want to hear that when

I go back home to Orlando and all my friends come up and say, 'Boy, you sure tried.' That motivated me."

If there remained a single media critic not ready to buy into Payne's metamorphosis from ungracious competitor to a competitor of generous spirit and remarkable skill, that stubborn holdover would have been drowned out by the accolades now validating Payne the person and Payne the champion. "Seldom does an athlete's entire career come down to one crisis that he knows in his heart will define the way he is remembered in sport forever," wrote the *Washington Post*'s Tom Boswell. "It's even rarer for that athlete to rise to the occasion . . . and erase all the doubts that have dogged him."

Joe Concannon, a veteran golf writer for the *Boston Globe,* called it "the most gutsy performance seen in the nation's major tournament." Bill Plaschke, a *Los Angeles Times* columnist, wrote that Payne and Mickelson "took a situation that often brings out our worst, and gracefully showed us how it can be used to reveal a man's best."

MANY HOURS AFTER THE ROAR at the eighteenth startled sleeping tree frogs for miles around, Chuck Cook's phone jangled at his home in Austin. He wondered who'd be calling him so close to midnight. When he answered, a familiar voice danced in his ear.

"You'll never guess where I am!" Payne Stewart playfully challenged.

"Well, no, I don't know where you are," Cook chuckled. "But I'll bet you're sipping champagne."

"Nope," Payne corrected. "I'm in Hicksie's truck and we're driving to Mebane, North Carolina, where I'm doing a charity outing for a children's hospital in the morning. And I'm sitting in the back with a six-pack of Bud Light!"

ALTHOUGH RELIGIOUS LEADERS may rank beer somewhat down their list of preferred celebratory elixirs, they were nonetheless pleased to have a U.S. Open champion expressing interest in things spiritual. Payne's curiosity about these matters was set off by those visits with Paul Azinger when Azinger was off the Tour in 1994 battling lymphoma.

The curiosity grew gradually by osmosis, through his children, who began to bring home precepts they were learning at their school. It gained depth when, in 1997, major-league pitcher Orel Hershiser invited him to attend a series of Sunday school lessons that Hershiser was conducting as a fill-in teacher at First Baptist. Hershiser's theme dealt with being "real" in everyday life, as opposed to playing expected roles. He gave each member of the class two small books of Scripture, organized by Kenneth Boa: *Handbook to Prayer* and *Handbook to Renewal*.

Brian Bowen, the volunteer golf coach at The First Academy, had been around "both" Paynes. A medical-supplies salesman, Bowen had been an assistant pro at Orlando's Grand Cypress Resort during the early 1980s, when Payne had first moved to Orlando and often worked on his game at Grand Cypress. In the last two years, Bowen had embraced the new and improved Payne as a new member of his informal men's fellowship group.

"He'd come play in our game in the afternoons down at Grand Cypress with the bag-room guys," Bowen remembers. "He was definitely full of himself then. So I saw the transition he made to the great humility he had at the end. There was a definite and dramatic change. The thing that inspired me so much is, despite the fact he was gone so much, his kids absolutely adored him. He was a great father, and that was because he had such great respect for his own father."

Any time Payne was in the presence of his golf team, Bowen would "make them go over and pick his brain. He would encourage those kids. He loved kids, I guess because he was such a big kid himself. I think he did better with kids than adults."

Former Tour player Wally Armstrong, who helped launch the Tour's weekly Bible-study group, sensed the sincerity of Payne's growing faith when he encountered the champion at a charity pro-am in March 1999 at Orlando's Lake Nona Club. During and after his career, Armstrong had been involved in faith-based clinics and with newsletters and books aimed at golfers—including the 1997 book *In His Grip: Insights on God and Golf*, coauthored with Jim Sheard, a Ph.D. in organizational behavior.

After the plane carrying Payne and five others disintegrated in a South Dakota field in October 1999, that copy of Wally's book—Payne's copy—was found thirty yards away from his mangled but still-fastened briefcase. An indication he may have been strengthening his faith right up to the moment when something went terribly wrong with the little chartered jet.

In an instant, the world of golf and the world in general had lost one of its most compelling and multifaceted souls.

William Payne Stewart.

Devoted husband. Avid cook. Harmoni-cat. Doting father. Treacherous fly-caster. Loving son. Showoff. Faithful friend. Prankster. Angel. Devil. Philanthropist. Rowdy spectator. Champion.

William Payne Stewart, 1957–1999.

And not a single minute of it dull or wasted.

part four

PAYNE'S LEGACY

chapter   1 2

A Lasting
Gift

R andall James, Tracey Stewart, and First Baptist Church pastors Jim
Henry and J. B. Collinsgworth sensed that Payne's far-reaching
popularity, the mesmerizing jolt of his bizarre and sudden death,
and the memorial service beamed worldwide had combined to ensnare an
astounding number of hearts. Just how many, they couldn't have fathomed,
though the staggering numbers and the intensity of the impact began to
overwhelm them in the first few days following the memorial.

There was a garrison charge down the aisles of churches all over the
globe that Sunday by souls moved to profess their faith. The two pastors
and Tracey were quickly buried under an avalanche of phone calls, letters,
and E-mails—an emotional outpouring that had been unleashed by that
golfer in knickers.

"The emotional impact was not only tremendous, but the amazing
thing was that it cut across all levels of people—Christian, non-Christian,
secular, sports fans, nonsports fans," said Henry. "From the letters and
E-mails that I've received alone—several hundred in the first few weeks—
they were from all walks of life. They were women, they were young
people, they were older people, people who golfed, people who didn't golf.
It was just a blanket kind of thing."

Most of the worldwide contact was funneled toward Collingsworth,
who, it became obvious on the telecast, was the church official closest to
the Stewart family, and to James's foundation, to which Tracey had urged
that people send donations in Payne's name in lieu of flowers or other
courtesies.

Within days, Collingsworth was deluged with calls from cleric friends
around the world anxious to pass along reports of those who had been

inspired by Payne Stewart's story. Within a month, James's office had processed more than three thousand letters, many with donations in Payne's honor, many requesting a copy of the video, many just extending their hearts and sympathies to Tracey and the children. James and his small staff waded through the letters, extracting checks and the information needed to fill requests for the tapes and/or WWJD bracelets, then delivered them in large bundles to Tracey—including the donations and other gifts earmarked for the Stewarts' own charitable family foundation instead of the church's charitable outreach arm.

The $500,000 that Payne had quietly pledged in August to the foundation had been specifically pegged for The First Academy's developing athletic complex, where he anticipated Chelsea and Aaron would continue to blossom as athletes. The money was first to be spent on the two softball fields on the drawing boards, and the school had intended to name that part of the multifaceted complex in Payne's honor. The plans had changed, however, when his magnanimous gift began to multiply. Payne had privately announced the grant at a barbecue at his house and nudged several affluent friends in attendance to chip in another several thousand dollars.

By the time the flood of donations cascaded in after the memorial, the foundation was close to funding the entire $3 million project. Before the end of the year, plans were being shifted to name the whole state-of-the-art athletic complex after Payne. Fortunately, some of the donations were for general use by the foundation, which undergirds The First Academy on the FBC campus, as well as nondenominational outreach programs.

But the postmemorial impact was far more than fiscal.

Especially as it affected Stewart's peers, the Tour golf pros who had suddenly gleaned from him something much more important than swing tempo or jaunty fashion.

"I think that since his passing, he has had a direct impact on a lot of people—not just in their daily lives but in their spiritual lives, as well," Open runner-up Phil Mickelson said a week after attending the service. "A number of players on Tour have talked about how this has really made them think, and it pushes you one way or another. It either drives you away from God or pushes you closer."

"It's a reality check that things like this can happen," he added later. "I think what it has done for me is that it has made me cherish each day and each opportunity that I have, not just with my wife and baby but also my parents, my brothers and sister, my grandparents and cousins. A lot of time, distant relatives get overlooked, taken for granted. It's been a great inspiration to me to strengthen my relationship with those relatives."

Said pro David Peoples: "I'm wearing the bracelet they gave out in the service and probably will always wear it from now on. It made me think about speaking out about my faith more because of what Payne did in his last years."

One Tour regular who was jolted to look inward was Mike Hicks, Stewart's caddie for the past decade. If not for the happenstance of the 1999 tour schedule, Hicks could have been on that doomed flight with his boss. Hicks frequently hopped a ride with Payne, but because the previous tournament was at Disney World, he had driven his family down from North Carolina to enjoy the Magic Kingdom. So he had to drive them back home after the event and then fly out of Raleigh-Durham that Monday morning to rejoin Payne in Houston for the Tour Championship.

Hicks was on the ninth hole of Champions Golf Club, stepping off yardages, when he received a cell-phone call from his wife with the stunning news.

In a later appearance on The Golf Channel, Hicks described the effects the emotional ordeal had on his life. "Well, the first week was really tough. Coming down to attend the memorial services and just seeing all the presence of God at that service . . ." Hicks paused to compose himself. "I know my life changed."

Hal Sutton saw it as a bonding of his colleagues. "After all that was said at the Ryder Cup about us being individuals who didn't really care about one another, I hoped the whole world could see that we truly are a family," he said. "We all found out how much of a family we were that day. And there's not a day that goes by now that I don't think about Payne. He has made me ask every day how I can be a better person, a better husband, a better father."

A few seats over on the same pew, pro Andrew Magee was being moved to do something in response to the sights and sounds that were battering his heart. He came up with a plan he would propose to his madcap partner in charity back home in Arizona, Senior Tour player and television commentator Gary McCord. Together, they had formed what they call the Santa Claus Foundation, which had reaped more than $1 million over five years from their annual pro-am tournament to benefit various children's charities.

Two weeks afterward, Magee sent a check for $25,000 out of that pot to The First Orlando Foundation in Payne's honor. Fittingly, in January Magee became the first recipient of the Tour's Payne Stewart Award for excellence in charitable activities and general professionalism.

Peter Jacobsen said there have been two deaths that have had an extreme impact on his life. First was the passing of his younger brother Paul, in 1988. A homosexual, Paul had died of AIDS, and Peter had struggled for the longest time trying to accept that one of his siblings was gay. "I just couldn't make any sense of it, but I finally accepted it," he said.

The other was that of the happy-go-lucky fun-mate that Jacobsen and the other pros had gathered there on a sunny Friday morning to memorialize. Payne had been such a dear friend and, for Jacobsen, the fact he was gone at the age of forty-two served as a parallel to his brother's death.

"But there was so much good that Payne did in his death and the events surrounding it," Jacobson reasoned. "He brought people together around the world. It's been incredible. I'm so proud of Payne because of the circumstances leading up to his death. And I can actually sit back now, after talking to Tracey and spending time with her after the memorial service, just kinda hanging and thinking, and accept it.

"And you know what? This guy was all right. We laughed, we had fun together, we played music together, we drank beer together, we played golf together. We beat each other. And it all comes down to the fact he was a good guy and he helped people. And that's the way you want to be remembered."

THE IMPACT OF PAYNE'S DEATH was magnified by the fact he had been so pleasingly embraced by the masses, far beyond the scope of the Tour, beyond the scope of sport, and even across international boundaries. That is part of the reason CNN decided at the last minute to telecast the memorial globally. The Golf Channel already had assured penetration beyond the oceans, but the CNN decision pushed the message beyond golf.

Noting that many of the letter writers from different countries said they had watched the service on CNN, James wrote an appreciative message to the cable company's flamboyant icon, Ted Turner. He responded with what James described as a "very nice" letter.

Henry said missionaries had E-mailed him from Tanzania, saying they watched the service.

"We were hearing from Mexico and Canada and England and Saudi Arabia. All over," gushed Henry, still energized by it all. "In terms of my own little world, I went to the airport two or three weeks after the memorial service and three different Delta gate agents came up to me—'Thank y'all for that service' . . . 'It was awesome' . . . 'It just touched me so much.' Everywhere I go there has been that same kind of response, people saying how Payne's life and what happened had an impact on them."

Dallas Cowboys star running back Emmitt Smith penned a tender letter to the foundation, enclosed a generous donation in Payne's name, and asked for nothing in return. He had already received plenty, Smith noted, while glued to his TV set during the memorial.

A New Hampshire police officer, an avid Payne Stewart fan who said he had not been a believer, sat misty-eyed through the memorial telecast and decided to hasten a planned trip to Orlando. After rearranging his work schedule, he drove to Florida the next day, inexplicably drawn to visit the church he had seen on the televised service.

When he arose that Sunday morning in a hotel room in Orlando's International Drive tourist corridor, he quashed the urge that he had felt so strongly and decided not to go. He clicked on the TV set, scanned the channels, and stopped on a local station carrying a taped service from the previous week at that very same First Baptist Church. He dressed quickly and asked a front-desk clerk for directions. Within minutes, he sat in the very sanctuary he had seen on television and listened intently to Henry's sermon, which included several references to Payne's memorial just two days earlier.

During the invitation at the end of the service, the cop started down the aisle toward Henry, "then spotted the other pastor [Collingsworth] I had seen on Payne's memorial service and made a beeline for him."

After professing his faith, the cop still had tears in his eyes as he reviewed the events with Henry a half hour later. "I'm not usually like this, but I came all the way down here and became a Christian," he said. "You won't believe this, but my boss, the police chief, has been talking to me about this. I'm going to go back and tell him that all this time I didn't want to have anything to do with what he was talking about, and now I'm a believer, too! All because of Payne Stewart."

Henry related a letter received from a fourteen-year-old golfer in California who had sought Payne's autograph at a recent Bob Hope Desert Classic. Although Payne had just missed the cut, he not only granted the lad's request but also lingered long enough to answer the boy's questions about the knickers and give him several golf-swing tips. "Here he was having missed the cut and didn't know me from Adam. He stood there with me and told me all this," the youngster wrote. "When I finish this letter, I'm going to the closet and get out my knickers and my tam-o'-shanter cap and I'm going to be the next Payne Stewart. . . ."

Yet another young man, Darin Hoff, a twenty-something aspiring golf pro from South Bend, Indiana, said Stewart had been such an idol of his in high school that he wanted to wear knickers while competing on the Clay High golf team. The coach refused. So Hoff, the number four man on the team at the time, declined to play.

"That's how much respect and admiration I had for Payne," said Hoff, who moved to Orlando to work at a golf club and had been discussing his faith with Collingsworth. "I know something happened to Payne in his life and I want the same thing to happen to me."

The day after Payne died, Hoff received word that his high school coach had tried to call, to apologize for barring the knickers.

Some of those who were moved to pick up pen and paper were poignant in their brevity. Early in the week after the memorial, a letter to the foundation arrived from an elderly woman who said she is "on Social Security, so I can't do much. But I loved Payne Stewart. And I thought the memorial service was wonderful. I wanted to help, so here's a dollar."

Touched by the gesture, James sent the woman a tape of the service even though she hadn't asked for one.

By Christmas, orders for almost two thousand videotapes of the Payne Stewart memorial had been filled. Many were given away free, but the bulk were sold at a price church officials said was to cover the cost of producing the tapes and the moderate outlay the church made for extra connecting devices to provide the video feed of the service to the eighteen television trucks out in Parking Lot B.

At least one skeptic wasn't convinced it was all a break-even proposition.

Payne's mother, Bee Payne-Stewart, said she returned home to Springfield the day after the service, seething at her perceptions of what had just taken place: She felt the church had hitched its coffers up to her son's tragedy and massaged the international media into reporting that Payne had only discovered religion in the previous few months.

In truth, Payne hadn't gone from zero to sixty in his faith under the influence of the FBC, his kids' church school, and the church members of his informal fellowship. It was more like forty-five to sixty.

"The one thing that has made me just a little bitter about all this God thing," Bee would say, "is that we've always been a Christian family. The way they made it sound, it was like he had never been a Christian. Payne was raised a Christian, our children were christened in the Methodist Church and baptized in the Methodist Church. But from what I read, all of this was like he just discovered God and had just become a Christian."

She emphatically noted that meal blessings and prayer had been commonplace in her home and that she and Bill Stewart had routinely escorted their three children to Sunday morning church service at Grace Methodist unless Bill or Payne was playing in a golf tournament.

"Payne's son is going to that Baptist school. He brought home that wristband that Payne wore to please his son. I became bitter about the press or the church or something. I thought they were commercializing my son's tragedy," she said six weeks after the service. "But I'm about to get over that part. I'm a lot better than I was at first. I was just mad that it happened and it shouldn't have. But what can I do? We can't bring him back. I loved what all the fellas [eulogy speakers] and Tracey had to say. And here were all the golfers. I loved that. But what went out over radio and TV, no, I didn't like it."

Bee Payne-Stewart, her immediate family now down to only her two married daughters, said she remains a member of Grace Methodist. "I loved my son dearly," she said. "His life was very special."

T he first definitive sign I saw of Payne Stewart's personal metamorphosis from clown prince to just plain *prince* came during the 1994
British Open at Turnberry, Scotland. For the other three major
tournaments, the *Orlando Sentinel* typically assigned both me and our golf
beat writer. Leaving the nuts and bolts of the broader tournament to our
beat writer allowed me the liberty of crafting a column on a particular
player or angle. I wandered aimlessly about the course or swapped yarns
with other loitering journalists in the press lounge.

However, due to the extra expense involved, I was the *Sentinel's* only
man at my nine British Opens. This meant I actually had to work. Of the
two dozen or so PGA Tour players based in Orlando, about half would
make the annual crossing in pursuit of the "auld claret jug." That meant
lots of "local angles" to protect. I scurried about the grounds to check with
as many of them as possible each day to see which might have saved a baby
from drowning that morning or battled the heather and gorse to a quintu-
ple bogey on some craggy hole. Whatever might make a story or notes
item.

Payne Stewart had a midmorning tee time the first day and I found
him afterward having a late lunch in the clubhouse grill with his coach,
Chuck Cook. I cruised by the table and asked Payne if he had a moment.

He jerked his head around, his face contorted in irritation. "Larry!" he
snapped. "Can't you see I'm eating?!" He turned his back to me, without
another word, leaving me standing there feeling as foolish and embarrassed
as I probably deserved to. I tried not to notice the several snickering pros
at nearby tables.

Three hours later, the phone at my press seat jangled. It was Payne,
calling from the Turnberry Hotel manager's house he had rented for the
week, just across the road from Turnberry's first hole.

"Scoop? This is Payne," he said softly, using the nickname he'd
assigned me years ago. "I just wanted to call and apologize for being so

rude to you today. That wasn't very good of me and I'm sorry. If you still need me, I'll be glad to walk back over there."

Suddenly, I felt like the nickname fit. Indeed I had a scoop: "Superstar Athlete Apologizes for Abusing Lowlife Sportswriter." I can count the times on one hand. This was "Man Bites Dog," with oak-leaf clusters.

I said his walking back to the club wasn't necessary, explaining that I was merely checking the Orlando guys for anything newsworthy. He assured me that my intrusion wasn't the reason for his ill temper. Instead, it was the triple-bogey 7 that spoiled his round when he dunked a shot into Wilson's Burn—so named for the caddie discovered one morning long ago, face-down and dead in the little creek fronting Turnberry's sixteenth green.

We chatted easily for a moment and hung up. I remember sitting back and smiling, savoring the moment. I was proud of him. Here was a star athlete who was making a distinct step toward becoming a *person*. A rare event in today's celebrity-obsessed sports world. In the intervening years, I watched those steps grow larger and more frequent until Payne had completely reversed the flippant, shallow, self-absorbed dance he did during his first dozen years on golf's grand stage.

Steadily he became kinder and gentler, even to the lower forms of life behind the gallery ropes and in the press tent. On the eve of the 1996 U.S. Open, he declared himself a new man, one who wouldn't be snarling and disrespectful to others just because the putts didn't fall that day. Skeptical scribes familiar with Payne's mercurial moods gathered at the clubhouse door to check out his new demeanor after he had shot himself out of the thirty-six-hole lead with a horrendous Saturday round. He passed astonishingly, plopping down on a stair step and yukking his way through his misadventures until the last notepad was filled.

"I just discovered that snapping at reporters or walking away from them in the parking lot just because I played bad that day doesn't help anybody," he said, adding with his familiar chuckle, "I'm thirty-nine years old. Maybe it's time I grew up."

He would develop a genuine affinity for people without pedigrees or Roman numerals. In an era when so many of our sports heroes are reluctant to tolerate their adoring public, here was a major champion who

increasingly seemed to prefer mixing with John and Jane Doe to hobnob-
bing with jet-setters. He was a member of one of the world's most fash-
ionable clubs: Isleworth, the gated Orlando enclave famous for its roster of
athletic superstars that included Tiger, Shaq, O'Meara, and Griffey Jr. But
during his last couple of years he was drawn to my nearby Orange Tree
Golf Club, many rungs down the social ladder, where he relished interacting with just plain folk.

One of his first stops with the Open trophy in the summer of 1999 was
the bar at Orange Tree, where he shared the famous cup with working
stiffs, plying them for hours with tales of Pinehurst and pitchers of beer.
He truly had become, as his friend Pastor J. B. Collingsworth noted, a regular guy who was also a great golfer.

The bittersweet consolation I clutched amid the searing sorrow after
the tragedy was that, ten days before his death, at a dinner held in his honor,
I had summoned the candor to embrace Payne and Tracey. I told them how
much I loved what he had become and what sheer joy it had been to watch
it unfold from my ringside seat.

Perhaps that was the key ingredient in the emotional stew tasted by so
many worldwide with Payne's passing. He was much more than the
beknickered golfer who happened to be the reigning U.S. Open champion
and who happened to die bizarrely as millions watched on live TV. He was
a man who had done a one-eighty to become a unique major celebrity you
wanted to *hug*, not just applaud.

Katie Couric. Bill Cosby. Barbara Bush. Payne Stewart. That just
about exhausts *my* list.

The dinner was an annual affair at which the First Orlando Foundation presents its Legacy Award—a crystal eagle lighted from within—to
someone who has exhibited spiritual and personal growth. Payne had been
selected for his Christian witness immediately after winning the Open at
Pinehurst, as millions around the globe watched.

But the more inspirational event of the banquet was the thunderclap
news that Payne and Tracey had decided to donate half a million dollars to
the foundation. Among the many blown away by the magnanimous gesture
that night were me and my wife, Mary. Payne attempted to explain the
reasons for the donation the next day at his lakefront manse.

"Tracey and I and our kids have more than we deserve. That's just the way it is," he said. "So it's not hard to give something back. We decided we wanted to give where it would make an impact, mostly in the lives of children. It excites me almost as much as winning a golf tournament to help people and see their faces."

At the banquet, Payne and I had talked again about doing a book on his life. He was beginning to warm to the idea. But, exercising that new-found humility, he once again scoffed that he couldn't imagine why anyone would want to read a whole book about him. (Those of you who've made it this far, raise your hands for Payne to see.) "Legacy?" he challenged, breaking into yet another toothy smile. "What possible legacy would I leave?"

Of the many, here's one to consider: Payne's undeniable sincerity about his evolving faith helped swing the pendulum on the way sports journalists quote athletic believers. The skeptical press has, for decades, patently ignored comments by athletes tying their performance to faith, any faith. Reporters typically rolled their eyes and waited for something more germane, like the length of the chip on the third hole or the yardage to carry the water hazard at the eighteenth. Suddenly, with people like Payne and Super Bowl Most Valuable Player Kurt Warner leading the discussion, their words on spirituality actually were making it into sports sections.

Making the front page may take longer. At many papers, the main news section is in the hands of enlightened guardians who think nothing of bannering stories about alternative lifestyles or indiscriminate causes but break into a cold sweat at the first sighting of "God" or "Allah." I was asked to write a column for page A1 the day after Payne perished. No, the prose and metaphor will not threaten Shakespeare, but I began it thusly:

The atmosphere around the Heavenly Golf Club just got a lot lighter. Grumpy angels will be hard-pressed to keep up their grousing about unraked bunkers or missed putts in the company of their newest member, that grinning guy over there trying to pull knickers over his robe and fit a jaunty cap under his halo.

With his glib presence and infectious personality, Payne Stewart always had a habit of wiping away all the scowls around him during the forty-two years he was down here amongst us mortals. No doubt he will have the same effect on St. Peter and the boys, smoothing out a lot of backswings *and* attitudes . . ."

Heavenly Golf Club? St. Peter?

The way I hear it, three editors had to be revived after the column had been jettisoned (thankfully) back to the sports section.

In the days that followed, I received an outpouring of missives from readers, some wanting to define the impact Payne had on their lives, some wanting to relate a gentle personal story of thoughtfulness by Payne, others offering some raucous tale of the fun-loving Payne.

The Reverend Gloria E. Wheeler of Altamonte Springs, Florida, pointed me to a Ralph Waldo Emerson poem she suggested might fit the moment:

To live a good life
To laugh often and much;
To win the respect of intelligent people
    and the affection of children;
To earn the appreciation of honest critics
    and endure the betrayal of false friends;
To appreciate beauty;
To leave the world a bit better,
    whether by a healthy child,
    a garden patch or
    a redeemed social condition;
To know even one life has breathed easier
    because you have lived;
This is to have succeeded.

And to think I wasn't aware that Mr. Emerson even knew Payne. Much less, so precisely.

Appendix 1

Payne Stewart's Tournaments, Scores, and Winnings

1981

KEY:

P:	PLAY-OFF
DNS:	DID NOT SIGN
DSQ:	DISQUALIFIED
DNQ:	DID NOT QUALIFY
CUT:	CUT FROM FIELD
WD:	WITHDRAWN

PAYNE STEWART

DATE	TOURNAMENT NAME	POS	ROUNDS 1ST	2ND	3RD	4TH	5TH	TOTAL SCORE	YEAR TO DATE SCORING AVG	PGA TOUR AVG	OFFICIAL MONEY	TOTAL MONEY
6/28	Danny Thomas Memphis Classic	DNQ										
7/05	Western Open	DNQ										
8/02	Canadian Open	CUT	75	74				149	74.50	74.500		
8/16	Sammy Davis Jr. Hartford	T51	71	68	67	69		275	70.67	70.667	716	716
8/23	Buick Open	CUT	74	71				145	71.13	71.125		
9/06	B.C. Open	T34	71	71	68	74		284	71.08	71.083	1,333	1,333
9/13	Pleasant Valley	T15	70	70	71	69		280	70.81	70.813	4,500	4,500
9/20	Lajet Classic	T35	72	73	72	77		294	71.35	71.350	1,652	1,652
9/27	Hall Of Fame	CUT	74	77				151	71.73	71.727		
10/04	Texas Open	CUT	69	72				141	71.63	71.625		
10/11	Southern Open	T9	67	65	70	73		275	71.21	71.214	5,200	5,200
10/18	Pensacola Open	CUT	70	75				145	71.30	71.300		
10/25*	Walt Disney World National	CUT	64	67	65			196				9

	NUMBER OF TIMES 1ST	2ND	3RD	TOP TEN	TOP 25	CUTS MADE	NUMBER OF TIMES CUT	DNQ	WD	DSQ	NO. OF EVENTS ENTERED
				1	2	5	5	2			10

	RANK	OFFICIAL MONEY	TOTAL MONEY
CAREER MONEY	160	13,401	13,410
13,400			

* Unofficial Money/Partial Round

PAYNE STEWART

DATE	TOURNAMENT NAME	POS	ROUNDS					TOTAL SCORE	YEAR TO DATE		OFFICIAL MONEY	TOTAL MONEY
			1ST	2ND	3RD	4TH	5TH		SCORING AVG	PGA TOUR AVG		
1/24	Phoenix Open	DNQ										
1/31	Wicks/Andy Wms San Diego	DNQ										
2/07	Bing Crosby National	DNQ										
2/14	Hawaiian Open	DNQ										
2/28	Doral–Eastern Open	CUT	73	78				151	75.50	75.500		
3/06	Honda Inverrary Classic	T42	69	74	70	71		284	72.50	72.500	1,322	1,322
4/04	Greater Greensboro	CUT	73	77				150	73.13	73.125		
4/11	Magnolia Classic	1	65	67	71	67		270			13,500	13,543
4/18	Tallahassee Open	CUT	67	77				144	72.90	72.900		
4/25	USF&G Classic	DNQ										
5/02	Byron Nelson Golf Classic	CUT	74	70				144	72.75	72.750		
5/09	Michelob–Houston Open	T18	73	71	71	68		283	72.25	72.250	4,260	4,673
5/23	Georgia–Pacific Atlanta	T16	70	71	72	67		280	71.80	71.800	4,800	4,800
5/30	Memorial Tournament	T67	71	75	80	72		298	72.25	72.250	1,525	1,525
6/06	Kemper Open	T42	76	73	71	74		294	72.43	72.429	1,322	1,322
6/13	Danny Thomas Memphis Clas	T9	75	72	67	69		283	72.22	72.219	10,400	10,400
6/27	Manufacturers Hanover	T67	69	71	69	76		285	72.11	72.111	816	816
7/04	Western Open	T62	74	73	68	80		295	72.28	72.275	742	742
7/11	Greater Milwaukee Open	WD	76					76	72.37	72.366		
7/18	Miller High Life QCO	1	66	71	68	63		268	71.89	71.889	36,000	36,000
7/25	Anheuser–Busch Golf	T18	69	68	74			211	71.79	71.792	4,410	4,410
8/01	Canadian Open	T69	70	72	80	74		296	71.96	71.962	854	854
8/08	PGA Championship	CUT	76	72				148	72.04	72.037		650
8/22	Buick Open	T3	68	69	67	72		276	71.83	71.828	18,200	18,200

| DATE | TOURNAMENT NAME | POS | ROUNDS | | | | | TOTAL SCORE | YEAR TO DATE | | OFFICIAL MONEY | TOTAL MONEY |
			1ST	2ND	3RD	4TH	5TH		SCORING AVG	PGA TOUR AVG		
9/05	B.C. Open	CUT	72	74				146	71.87	71.867		
9/12	Bank of Boston Classic	CUT	74	73				147	71.92	71.919	535	535
9/19	Hall of Fame	T60	71	73	77	74		295	72.03	72.030		
9/26	Southern Open	CUT	72	76				148	72.09	72.088		
10/10	LaJet Classic	CUT	71	76				147	72.13	72.129		

| | NUMBER OF TIMES | | | | | | | NUMBER OF TIMES | | | | NO. OF EVENTS ENTERED | RANK | OFFICIAL MONEY | TOTAL MONEY |
	1ST	2ND	3RD	TOP	TOP TEN	CUTS MADE	CUT	DNQ	WD	DSQ					
CAREER MONEY	1	1	1	4	7	14	9	5	1		24	39	98,686	99,792
112,086														

* Unofficial Money/Partial Round

PAYNE STEWART

DATE	TOURNAMENT NAME	POS	ROUNDS					TOTAL SCORE	YEAR TO DATE		OFFICIAL MONEY	TOTAL MONEY
			1ST	2ND	3RD	4TH	5TH		SCORING AVG	PGA TOUR AVG		
1/09	Joe Garagiola–Tucson Open	T9	69	68	69	68		274 -6	68.50	68.500	8,100	8,100
1/16	Glen Campbell–Los Angeles	T42	66	69	73	73		281 -3	69.38	69.375	992	1,329
1/23	Bob Hope Desert Classic	T13	66	70	71	70	69	346 -14	69.31	69.308	7,250	7,325
1/30	Phoenix Open	CUT	72	72				144 +2	69.67	69.667		
2/06	Bing Crosby National	T14	72	68	72	72		284 -4	69.95	69.947	5,379	6,399
2/13	Hawaiian Open	T24	71	71	68	69		279 -9	69.91	69.913	2,702	2,702
3/06	Honda Inverrary Classic	T10	65	72	73	73		283 -5	70.04	70.037	8,044	8,457
3/13	Bay Hill Classic	T57	70	80	77	73		300 +16	70.68	70.677	774	1,029
3/20	USF&G Classic	WD	80					80 +8	70.97	70.969		175
3/27	Tournament Players Champ	CUT	78	78				156 +12	71.38	71.382		500
4/11	Masters Tournament	T32	70	76	78	71		295 +7	71.63	71.632	2,900	2,900
4/17	Sea Pines Heritage	CUT	73	73				146 +4	71.70	71.700		
4/24	MONY T of C	28	75	79	74	74		302 +14	72.05	72.045	4,700	4,879
5/01	Byron Nelson Golf Classic	CUT	74	72				146 +4	72.09	72.087		
5/08	Houston Coca-Cola Open	CUT	77	74				151 +9	72.23	72.229		
5/29	Memorial Tournament	T14	70	74	71	72		287 -1	72.19	72.192	7,200	7,275
6/05	Kemper Open	T56	72	72	73	80		297 +9	72.34	72.339	884	1,184
6/12	Manufacturers Hanover	T56	71	74	73	73		291 +7	72.37	72.367	990	1,478
6/26	Danny Thomas Memphis Classic	CUT	72	78				150 +6	72.45	72.452		443
7/03	Western Open	T6	73	70	72	74		289 +1	72.44	72.439	13,900	14,221
7/10	Greater Milwaukee Open	T3	70	69	70	67		276 -12	72.24	72.243	13,000	13,000
7/17	Miller High Life QCO	T7	65	68	66	70		269 -11	71.97	71.973	6,450	7,096
7/24	Anheuser-Busch Golf	T16	71	70	66	76		283 -1	71.91	71.910	5,075	5,528
8/07	PGA Championship	CUT	78	71				149 +7	71.98	71.975		1,000

PAYNE STEWART

1983

DATE	TOURNAMENT NAME	POS	ROUNDS					TOTAL SCORE	YEAR TO DATE		OFFICIAL MONEY	TOTAL MONEY
			1ST	2ND	3RD	4TH	5TH		SCORING AVG	PGA TOUR AVG		
8/14	Buick Open	T32	72	71	65	75		283 -5	71.92	71.917	1,778	1,778
8/21	Sammy Davis Jr. Greater	T43	64	69	74	72		279 -5	71.82	71.818	877	1,337
9/18	Panasonic Las Vegas Pro	T42	70	72	69	67	75	353 -5	71.75	71.753	2,700	3,833
9/25	LaJet Coors Classic	CUT	77	75				152 +8	71.84	71.842		
10/02	Texas Open	T39	69	66	71	72		278 -2	71.75	71.747	1,140	1,198
10/09	Southern Open	T4	65	72	68	70		275 -5	71.63	71.631	11,000	11,000
10/23	Walt Disney World Classic	1	69	64	69	67		269 -19	71.47	71.467	72,000	72,517
10/30	Pensacola Open	T39	73	70	72	67		282 -2	71.43	71.432	975	1,444
12/11*	J.C. Penney Classic	T32	74	69	67	73		283				2,225
12/18*	Chrysler Team Championship	T17	65	64	69			198				2,264

	NUMBER OF TIMES						NUMBER OF TIMES				NO. OF EVENTS ENTERED
	1ST	2ND	3RD	TOP TEN	TOP 25	CUTS MADE	CUT	DNQ	WD	DSQ	
	1	1	1	7	12	23	8		1		32

	RANK	YEAR TO DATE	
		OFFICIAL MONEY	TOTAL MONEY
CAREER MONEY	25	178,809	192,615
290,895			

* Unofficial Money/Partial Round

PAYNE STEWART

DATE	TOURNAMENT NAME	POS	1ST	2ND	3RD	4TH	5TH	TOTAL SCORE	YEAR TO DATE SCORING AVG	YEAR TO DATE PGA TOUR AVG	OFFICIAL MONEY	TOTAL MONEY
1/08	Seiko/Tucson Match Play	T17	73	68	73	71	67	352 -8			10,000	10,000
1/15	Bob Hope Classic	T30	70	71	70	71		282 -2	70.40	70.400	2,228	2,228
1/22	Phoenix Open	T51	68	65	68	78		279 -9	70.44	70.444	947	991
1/29	Isuzu/Andy Williams San	T23	72	69	75	70		286 -2	70.23	70.231	3,002	3,489
2/05	Bing Crosby National	T17	68	72	69	73		282 -6	70.53	70.529	4,720	5,840
2/12	Hawaiian Open	T39	70	71	70	70		281 -7	70.52	70.524	1,950	2,125
3/04	Honda Classic	CUT	78	72				150 +6	70.91	70.913		675
3/11	Doral-Eastern Open	CUT	73	74				147 +3	71.12	71.120		
3/18	Bay Hill Classic	CUT	74	72				146 +4	71.26	71.259		300
4/01	Tournament Players Championship	T64	79	70	75	76		300 +12	71.74	71.742	1,688	1,688
4/08	Greater Greensboro	T41	72	75	71	74		292 +4	71.89	71.886	1,400	1,547
4/15	Masters Tournament	T21	76	69	68	74		287 -1	71.87	71.872	6,475	6,475
4/22	Sea Pines Heritage	T48	76	71	70	71		288 +4	71.88	71.884	1,005	1,493
5/06	MONY T of C	T14	70	72	69	76		287 -1	71.87	71.872	8,000	8,217
5/13	Byron Nelson Golf Classic	T9	75	70	68	69		282 -2	71.76	71.765	12,500	12,500
5/20	Colonial National Invitational	2	68	66	64	72		270 -10	71.45	71.455	54,000	54,000
5/27	Memorial Tournament	T3	67	75	72	69		283 -5	71.41	71.407	26,000	26,000
6/03	Kemper Open	T15	73	76	70	70		289 +1	71.46	71.460	7,000	7,000
6/17	U.S. Open Championship	CUT	75	78				153 +13	71.62	71.615		600
6/24	Georgia-Pacific Atlanta	T15	70	68	69	73		280 -8	71.52	71.522	6,000	6,815
7/01	Canadian Open	T20	77	70	68	75		290 +2	71.58	71.575	5,000	6,201
7/08	Western Open	WD	76					76 +4	71.64	71.635		
8/05	Danny Thomas Memphis Classic	T14	73	73	69	72		287 -1	71.64	71.641	8,750	9,238
8/12	Buick Open	2	69	65	69	69		272 -16	71.46	71.463	43,200	43,344

PAYNE STEWART

1984

| DATE | TOURNAMENT NAME | POS | ROUNDS | | | | | TOTAL SCORE | | YEAR TO DATE | | OFFICIAL MONEY | TOTAL MONEY |
			1ST	2ND	3RD	4TH	5TH			SCORING AVG	PGA TOUR AVG		
8/19	PGA Championship	CUT	80	73				153	+9	71.58	71.583		1,000
8/26	NEC World Series of Golf	T24	74	72	71	69		286	+6	71.58	71.580	8,000	8,000
9/16	Greater Milwaukee Open	T13	68	72	71	71		282	-6	71.53	71.533	5,300	6,650
9/23	Panasonic Las Vegas Invitational	T3	67	73	67	64	72	343	-13	71.38	71.381	52,200	53,100
10/14	Southern Open	T15	71	68	70	66		275	-5	71.28	71.277	4,800	4,800
10/21	Walt Disney World Classic	T6	70	64	68	69		271	-17	71.14	71.143	13,400	13,986
10/28	Pensacola Open	T39	70	73	67	73		283	-1	71.13	71.128	1,230	1,580

| | NUMBER OF TIMES | | | | | CUTS MADE | NUMBER OF TIMES | | | | NO. OF EVENTS ENTERED |
	1ST	2ND	3RD	TOP TEN	TOP 25		CUT	DNQ	WD	DSQ	
		2	2	6	18	25	5		1		31

	RANK	OFFICIAL MONEY	TOTAL MONEY
CAREER MONEY	11	288,795	299,882
579,691			

* Unofficial Money/Partial Round

PAYNE STEWART

DATE	TOURNAMENT NAME	POS	ROUNDS					TOTAL SCORE	YEAR TO DATE		OFFICIAL MONEY	TOTAL MONEY
			1ST	2ND	3RD	4TH	5TH		SCORING AVG	PGA TOUR AVG		
1/27	Los Angeles Open	T25	70	67	72	72		281 -3	70.25	70.250	3,267	3,267
2/03	Bing Crosby National	T5	72	73	74	66		285 -3	70.75	70.750	19,000	19,000
2/10	Hawaiian Open	T55	71	68	68	77		284 -4	70.83	70.833	1,125	1,125
2/17	Isuzu/Andy Williams San	T26	69	70	69	69		277 -11	70.44	70.438	3,080	3,080
3/03	Honda Classic	T48	72	71	73	71		287 -1	70.70	70.700	1,310	1,560
3/10	Hertz Bay Hill Classic	T12	71	70	70	72		283 -1	70.71	70.708	9,500	9,500
3/31	Tournament Players Championship	T13	73	70	69	75		287 -1	70.86	70.857	16,875	16,875
4/07	Greater Greensboro	T22	71	77	72	73		293 +5	71.16	71.156	3,713	3,713
4/14	Masters Tournament	T25	69	71	76	76		292	71.36	71.361	5,670	5,670
4/28	Houston Open	T4	66	72	70	71		279 -9	71.20	71.200	19,688	20,318
5/12	Byron Nelson Golf Classic	2	67	71	66	68		272 -12	70.91	70.909	54,000	54,000
5/19	Colonial National Invitational	T19	71	71	66	71		279 -1	70.81	70.813	5,643	5,643
5/26	Memorial Tournament	T18	71	70	75	75		291 +3	70.96	70.962	7,390	7,682
6/02	Kemper Open	T56	71	73	78	72		294 +6	71.14	71.143	1,115	1,803
6/16	U.S. Open Championship	T5	70	70	71	70		281	71.08	71.083	18,459	18,459
6/23	Georgia-Pacific Atlanta	CUT	75	73				148 +4	71.18	71.177		75
6/30	St. Jude Memphis Classic	T29	72	72	72	71		287 -1	71.21	71.212	3,179	3,179
7/28	Canon–Sammy Davis Jr.	T37	68	71	74	66		279 -5	71.13	71.129	2,580	2,580
8/04	Western Open	DSQ										
8/11	PGA Championship	T12	72	72	73	68		285	71.14	71.135	9,017	9,017
8/18	Buick Open	T62	70	71	75	71		287 -1	71.17	71.167	954	1,829
9/08	Bank of Boston Classic	CUT	72	77				149 +7	71.25	71.250		
9/15	Greater Milwaukee Open	T11	68	72	71	70		281 -7	71.20	71.202	6,600	6,600
10/06	Southern Open	T6	68	68	69	67		272 -8	71.06	71.057	11,725	11,725

PAYNE STEWART

| DATE | TOURNAMENT NAME | POS | ROUNDS | | | | | TOTAL SCORE | | | YEAR TO DATE | | OFFICIAL MONEY | TOTAL MONEY |
			1ST	2ND	3RD	4TH	5TH				SCORING AVG	PGA TOUR AVG		
10/13	Walt Disney World/Olds.	T4	69	69	65	66		269 -19			70.89	70.891	17,600	17,600
10/20	Pensacola Open	T31	69	70	69	69		277 -7			70.82	70.823	1,740	1,740
10/27	Seiko/Tucson Match Play	T33												3,610
12/08*	J.C. Penney Classic	T31	73	71	67	71		282					2,500	1,980
12/15*	Chrysler Team Championship	27	67	66	67	68		268						1,550

| CAREER MONEY | NUMBER OF TIMES | | | | | | NUMBER OF TIMES | | | | | NO. OF EVENTS ENTERED | RANK | OFFICIAL MONEY | TOTAL MONEY |
	1ST	2ND	3RD	TOP TEN	TOP 25	CUTS MADE	CUT	DNQ	WD	DSQ					
805,420		1		6	15	24	2			1		27	19	225,729	233,178

* Unofficial Money/Partial Round

PAYNE STEWART

DATE	TOURNAMENT NAME	POS	ROUNDS					TOTAL SCORE	YEAR TO DATE		OFFICIAL MONEY	TOTAL MONEY
			1ST	2ND	3RD	4TH	5TH		SCORING AVG	PGA TOUR AVG		
1/19	Bob Hope Chrysler Classic	T5	72	67	71	64	65	339 -21	67.80	67.800	21,900	22,450
2/02	AT&T Pebble Beach	2	71	69	70			210 -6	68.63	68.625	64,800	66,960
2/09	Shearson Lehman—Andy Wms	T41	73	70	69			212 -4	69.18	69.182	1,492	1,980
2/23	Los Angeles Open	CUT	77	75				152 +10	70.23	70.231		
3/02	Honda Classic	T8	69	74	73	75		291 +3	70.82	70.824	15,000	15,000
3/09	Doral-Eastern Open	CUT	71	73				144 E	70.95	70.947		
3/16	Hertz Bay Hill Classic	T43	74	71	69			214 +1	71.00	71.000	1,650	1,650
3/30	Tournament Players Championship	T10	71	67	75	70		283 -5	70.96	70.962	21,600	21,920
4/06	Greater Greensboro	T6	70	70	74	67		281 -7	70.87	70.867	15,125	15,125
4/13	Masters Tournament	T8	75	71	69	69		284 -4	70.88	70.882	23,200	23,200
4/27	Houston Open	T7	69	73	71	67		280 -8	70.79	70.789	16,125	16,125
5/04	Panasonic Las Vegas Invitational	T28	69	72	70	68	69	348 -12	70.65	70.651	7,822	7,822
5/11	Byron Nelson Golf Classic	T4	70	66	67	71		274 -6	70.47	70.468	23,625	23,625
5/18	Colonial National Invitational	2	72	67	66			205 -5	70.34	70.340	64,800	65,550
5/25	Memorial Tournament	T7	72	69	69	68		278 -10	70.28	70.278	17,313	17,895
6/15	U.S. Open Championship	T6	76	68	69	70		283	70.31	70.310	19,009	19,009
6/29	Canadian Open	CUT	79	75				154 +10	70.53	70.533		
7/06	Canon—Sammy Davis Jr.	T75	69	70	71	80		290 +6	70.66	70.656	1,323	1,548
7/13	Anheuser-Busch Golf	CUT	71	73				144 +2	70.70	70.697		350
7/27	Buick Open	CUT	75	72				147 +3	70.78	70.779		750
8/10	PGA Chamionship	T5	70	67	72	72		281 -3	70.75	70.750	32,500	32,500
8/17	The International	CUT									700	
8/31	Federal Express St. Jude	3	71	70	71	70		282 -6	70.74	70.737	41,202	41,346
9/07	B.C. Open	T16	71	69	68	71		279 -5	70.69	70.688	5,611	5,611

PAYNE STEWART

1986

DATE	TOURNAMENT NAME	POS	ROUNDS					TOTAL SCORE	YEAR TO DATE			OFFICIAL MONEY	TOTAL MONEY
			1ST	2ND	3RD	4TH	5TH		SCORING AVG	PGA TOUR AVG			
9/21	Greater Milwaukee Open	CUT	75	71				146 +2					563
10/05	Southern Open	T6	66	67	68	71		272 -8	70.74	70.744		11,725	11,725
10/12	Pensacola Open	T37	69	69				138 -4	70.62	70.616		900	900
10/19	Walt Disney World/Olds.	T4	65	66	71	74		276 -12	70.58	70.580		20,667	21,602
10/26	Vantage Championship	2	67	65	65			197 -13	70.51	70.511		108,000	108,728
11/09*	Nissan Cup WCOG	4							70.36	70.358			16,114
11/16*	Isuzu Kapalua Int'l.	T11	76	68	73	71		288				15,000	9,667

* Unofficial Money/Partial Round

	NUMBER OF TIMES					NUMBER OF TIMES				NO. OF EVENTS ENTERED	
	1ST	2ND	3RD	TOP TEN	TOP 25	CUTS MADE	CUT	DNQ	WD	DSQ	
		3	1	16	17	22	7				29

	RANK	OFFICIAL MONEY	TOTAL MONEY
CAREER MONEY	3	535,389	570,415
1,340,809			

PAYNE STEWART

DATE	TOURNAMENT NAME	POS	ROUNDS					TOTAL SCORE		YEAR TO DATE		OFFICIAL MONEY	TOTAL MONEY
			1ST	2ND	3RD	4TH	5TH			SCORING AVG	PGA TOUR AVG		
1/18	Bob Hope Chrysler Classic	T30	68	71	74	70	74	357	-3	71.40	71.400	5,468	5,468
1/25	Phoenix Open	T9	69	71	70	64		274	-10	70.11	70.111	15,000	16,854
2/01	AT&T Pebble Beach	2	69	69	69	72		279	-9	70.00	70.000	64,800	65,920
2/08	Hawaiian Open	CUT	72	73				145	+1	70.33	70.333		500
3/01	Doral-Ryder Open	CUT	75	71				146	+2	70.65	70.647		
3/08	Honda Classic	T2	75	68	68	71		282	-6	70.62	70.619	52,800	53,963
3/15	Hertz Bay Hill Classic	1	69	67	63	65		264	-20	69.88	69.880	108,000	108,000
3/29	Tournament Players Championship	CUT	77	68				145	+1	70.07	70.074		1,200
4/05	Greater Greensboro	T3	74	71	70	70		285	-3	70.23	70.226	31,200	33,500
4/12	Masters Tournament	T42	71	75	74	78		298	+10	70.71	70.714	3,333	3,333
4/26	Big "I" Houston Open	3	70	68	72	67		277	-11	70.56	70.564	40,800	41,450
5/03	Panasonic Las Vegas Invitational	T6	67	71	69	68	72	275	-13	70.40	70.395	43,438	43,763
5/10	Byron Nelson Golf Classic	T19	64	71	66	72		273	-7	70.21	70.213	6,313	9,313
5/17	Colonial National Invitational	T64	71	70				141	+1	70.22	70.224	1,236	1,761
5/31	Memorial Tournament	T30	74	69	70	71		284	-4	70.28	70.283	5,769	5,769
6/05	Kemper Open	T21	66	75	73	70		284	E	70.33	70.333	7,280	8,336
6/21	U.S. Open Championship	CUT	74	74				148		70.46	70.458		600
7/26	Buick Open	T18	66	72	68	69		275	-13	70.35	70.349	8,100	9,813
8/02	Federal Express St. Jude	T15	68	73	72	68		281	-7	70.34	70.343	10,185	10,185
8/09	PGA Championship	T24	72	75	75	74		296	+8	70.55	70.549	5,975	5,975
8/23	Beatrice Western Open	T13	72	68	71			211	-5	70.54	70.541	14,133	14,133
8/30	NEC World Series of Golf	T13	72	71	71	70		284		70.56	70.564	14,500	15,100
9/06	B.C. Open	T18	69	73	69	69		280	-4	70.54	70.537	5,216	5,216

PAYNE STEWART

1987

DATE	TOURNAMENT NAME	POS	ROUNDS					TOTAL SCORE	YEAR TO DATE		OFFICIAL MONEY	TOTAL MONEY
			1ST	2ND	3RD	4TH	5TH		SCORING AVG	PGA TOUR AVG		
10/04	Southern Open	T30	74	68	72	70		284 +14	70.56	70.558	2,377	3,102
10/18	Walt Disney World/Olds.	CUT	74	69	70			213 -3	70.57	70.573		1,613
10/25	Seiko Tucson Open	T19	70	63	72	72		277 -11	70.52	70.516	7,303	7,503
11/01	Nabisco Championship	T21	72	69	68	72		281	70.51	70.505	36,800	37,092
11/01	Nabisco Individual	17									21,000	21,000
11/08*	Kirin Cup											69,333
11/14*	Isuzu Kapalua Intl.	T17	67	69	77	68		281				6,750
12/13*	Chrysler Team Championship	T12	64	64	66	65		259				6,700

	NUMBER OF TIMES						NUMBER OF TIMES				NO. OF EVENTS ENTERED		
	1ST	2ND	3RD	TOP TEN	TOP 25	CUTS MADE	CUT	DNQ	WD	DSQ			
	1	2	2	7	17	22	5				27		

CAREER MONEY										RANK	OFFICIAL MONEY	TOTAL MONEY
1,851,835										12	511,026	613,245

* Unofficial Money/Partial Round

PAYNE STEWART

DATE	TOURNAMENT NAME	POS	ROUNDS					TOTAL SCORE	YEAR TO DATE		OFFICIAL MONEY	TOTAL MONEY
			1ST	2ND	3RD	4TH	5TH		SCORING AVG	PGA TOUR AVG		
1/17	MONY T of C	T7	68	71	71			210 -6	70.00	71.036	15,063	15,163
1/24	Bob Hope Chrysler Classic	T4	72	71	67	67	65	342 -18	69.00	70.271	44,000	44,350
1/31	Phoenix Open	T26	70	67	70	74		281 -3	69.42	70.129	4,615	4,615
2/07	AT&T Pebble Beach	CUT	74	77	74			225 +9	70.53	70.660		700
2/28	Los Angeles Open	T41	71	71	69	72		283 -1	70.58	70.597	3,000	3,900
3/13	Honda Classic	T2	73	71	67	67		278 -10	70.39	70.272	52,267	54,167
3/20	Hertz Bay Hill Classic	T6	68	72	70	72		282 -2	70.41	70.029	23,475	23,475
3/27	The Players Championship	T8	71	65	71	73		280 -8	70.35	69.912	36,250	39,250
4/10	Masters Tournament	T25	75	76	71	72		294 +6	70.71	70.050	7,975	7,975
5/01	Independent Insurance Age	T28	69	67	74	73		283 -5	70.72	70.122	4,555	4,810
5/08	Panasonic Las Vegas Invitational	T9	70	72	66	69		277 -11	70.58	70.084	38,889	39,589
5/15	GTE Byron Nelson Golf Classic	T24	66	71	68	73		278 -2	70.49	69.938	6,075	9,219
5/22	Colonial National Invitational	T22	75	65	68	72		280 E	70.45	69.849	6,417	7,167
5/29	Memorial Tournament	T6	72	69	67	75		283 -5	70.47	69.823	26,881	26,881
6/12	Manuf. Hanover Westchester	T18	73	68	69	73		283 -1	70.49	69.771	9,128	9,128
6/19	U.S. Open Championship	T10	73	73	70	67		283	70.51	69.679	17,871	17,871
7/17*	British Open Championship	T27	69	70	69	75		283 +3	70.52	69.731	6,772	8,197
8/07	Federal Express St. Jude	T9	70	69	70	73		282	70.52	69.662	21,500	21,500
8/14	PGA Championship	CUT										
8/21	The International											
8/28	Provident Classic	2	65	67	67	65		264 -16	70.28	69.488	48,600	48,875
9/11	Greater Milwaukee Open	T19	73	69	68	70		280 -8	70.27	69.554	6,949	7,949
10/02	Southern Open	T21	73	65	68	70		276 -4	70.20	69.500	3,653	4,463
10/09	Gatlin Southwest	T18	71	70	67	69		277 -11	70.16	69.538	4,869	5,575

PAYNE STEWART

DATE	TOURNAMENT NAME	POS	ROUNDS					TOTAL SCORE			YEAR TO DATE		OFFICIAL MONEY	TOTAL MONEY
			1ST	2ND	3RD	4TH	5TH				SCORING AVG	PGA TOUR AVG		
10/16	Texas Open	T5	69	65	68	68		270 -10			70.04	69.446	20,340	20,340
10/28	Nabisco Individual Comp.	14											24,000	24,000
10/30	Walt Disney World/Olds.	T35	69	69	72	67		277 -11			70.01	69.521	3,162	4,162
11/06	Northern Telecom Tucson	T12	66	73	70	66		275 -13			69.96	69.510	12,600	13,500
11/13	Nabisco Championship	T3	73	70	64	73		280 -8			69.96	69.539	104,667	104,667

	NUMBER OF TIMES							NUMBER OF TIMES				NO. OF EVENTS ENTERED	RANK	OFFICIAL MONEY	TOTAL MONEY
	1ST	2ND	3RD	TOP TEN	TOP 25	CUTS MADE	CUT	DNQ	WD	DSQ					
CAREER MONEY		2	1	12	20	25	2					27	14	553,571	571,486
2,405,406															

* Unofficial Money/Partial Round

PAYNE STEWART

DATE	TOURNAMENT NAME	POS	1ST	2ND	3RD	4TH	5TH	TOTAL SCORE	YEAR TO DATE SCORING AVG	YEAR TO DATE PGA TOUR AVG	OFFICIAL MONEY	TOTAL MONEY
1/15	Bob Hope Chrysler Classic	T30	70	72	68	72	68	350 -10	70.00	71.108	6,650	6,670
1/22	Phoenix Open	CUT	70	77				147 +5	71.00	71.623		338
1/29	AT&T Pebble Beach	WD	74					74 +2	71.38	71.901		900
2/05	Nissan Los Angeles Open	WD	76	74				150 +8	72.10	72.195		
3/05	Honda Classic	2	68	65	70	67		270 -18	70.79	71.109	86,400	86,681
3/12	Nestlé Invitational	T4	76	69	65	70		280 -4	70.61	70.470	33,067	33,648
3/19	The Players Championship	CUT	70	78				148 +4	70.95	70.698		1,000
3/26	USF&G Classic	T5	70	69	69	71		279 -9	70.75	70.463	26,344	27,508
4/09	Masters Tournament	T24	73	75	74	70		292 +4	71.07	70.517	10,250	10,250
4/16	MCI Heritage Golf Classic	1	65	67	67	69		268 -16	70.56	69.934	144,000	146,175
4/23	Kmart Greater Greensboro	T11	71	69	76	71		287 -1	70.69	69.949	22,000	22,150
5/07	GTE Byron Nelson Golf Classic	T8	64	70	68	67		269 -11	70.35	69.732	29,000	29,444
5/14	Memorial Tournament	3	70	73	73	65		281 -7	70.34	69.627	60,440	60,440
5/21	Southwestern Bell Colonial	T8	70	70	70	68		278 -2	70.27	69.487	28,000	28,144
5/28	BellSouth Atlanta Golf Classic	T19	69	73	71	71		284 -4	70.33	69.548	10,157	10,157
6/11	Manuf. Hanover Westchester	WD	74					74 +3	70.40	69.623		
6/18	U.S. Open Championship	T13	66	75	72	71		284 +4	70.44	69.483	15,634	15,634
7/02	Beatrice Western Open	T27	66	74	73	71		284 -4	70.48	69.555	6,380	6,380
7/23*	British Open Championship	DQ	74					74				
7/30	Buick Open	T2	71	67	64	72		274 -14	70.35	69.542	74,667	74,667
8/06	Federal Express St. Jude	T53	67	69	75	76		287 +3	70.43	69.590	2,304	3,417
8/13	PGA Championship	1	74	66	69	67		276 -12	70.36	69.516	200,000	200,000
8/27	NEC World Series of Golf	3	72	67	68	71		278 -2	70.31	69.386	68,000	68,040
10/21	Walt Disney World/Olds.	T47	67	70	76	71		284 -4	70.35	69.510	2,009	2,026

PAYNE STEWART

1989

| DATE | TOURNAMENT NAME | POS | ROUNDS | | | | | TOTAL SCORE | YEAR TO DATE | | OFFICIAL MONEY | TOTAL MONEY |
			1ST	2ND	3RD	4TH	5TH		SCORING AVG	PGA TOUR AVG		
10/28	Nabisco Individual Comp.	2									106,000	106,000
10/29	Nabisco Championship	2	69	70	71	66		276 -8	70.28	69.485	270,000	271,100

| | NUMBER OF TIMES | | | | CUTS MADE | NUMBER OF TIMES | | | | NO. OF EVENTS ENTERED | RANK | OFFICIAL MONEY | TOTAL MONEY |
	1ST	2ND	3RD	TOP TEN	TOP 25		CUT	DNQ	WD	DSQ				
				11	15	19	2		3		24	2	1,201,301	1,210,769

| CAREER MONEY | NUMBER OF TIMES | | | | |
	1ST	2ND	3RD	TOP TEN	TOP 25
3,606,707	2	3	2	11	15

* Unofficial Money/Partial Round

PAYNE STEWART

1990

DATE	TOURNAMENT NAME	POS	1ST	2ND	3RD	4TH	5TH	TOTAL SCORE	SCORING AVG	PGA TOUR AVG	OFFICIAL MONEY	TOTAL MONEY
1/07	MONY T of C	T10	67	75	69	73		284 -4	71.00	71.440	19,625	19,855
1/28	Phoenix Open	T60	75	68	74	71		288 +4	71.50	71.303	1,953	2,338
2/04	AT&T Pebble Beach	T3	66	71	74	73		284 -4	71.33	70.173	58,000	62,133
2/18	Shearson Lehman Hutton	T37	70	71	70	75		286 -2	71.38	70.421	3,340	3,752
3/04	Doral-Ryder Open	T23	70	73	72	68		283 -5	71.25	70.528	11,515	11,553
3/11	Honda Classic	T63	75	75	70	78		298 +10	71.79	70.816	2,100	2,513
3/18	The Players Championship	T11	71	73	71	73		288 E	71.82	70.740	31,800	32,500
3/25	Nestlé Invitational	T55	77	69	72	72		290 +2	71.91	70.938	2,025	2,025
4/08	Masters Tournament	T36	71	73	77	74		295 +7	72.11	71.077	6,133	6,133
4/15	MCI Heritage Golf Classic	1	70	69	66	71		276 -8	71.80	70.738	180,000	180,500
4/22	Kmart Greater Greensboro	CUT	75	73				148 +4	71.90	70.792		800
5/06	GTE Byron Nelson Golf Classic	1	67	68	67			202 -8	71.60	70.403	180,000	181,050
5/13	Memorial Tournament	2	74	74	69			217 +1	71.65	70.262	108,000	108,000
5/20	Southwestern Bell Colonial	T7	70	72	68	67		277 -3	71.46	70.065	30,125	30,125
6/10	Centel Western Open	2	68	67	72	72		279 -9	71.34	69.926	108,000	108,143
6/17	U.S. Open Championship	CUT	73	75				148	71.43	70.010		1,000
7/08	Anheuser-Busch Golf	T23	70	67	72	69		278 -6	71.31	69.989	7,673	10,373
7/22*	British Open Championship	T2	68	68	68	71		275 -13				
7/29	Buick Open	T16	74	68	66	70		278 -10	71.20	69.998	15,000	15,000
8/12	PGA Championship	T8	71	72	70	79		292	71.30	69.963	34,375	34,375
8/26	NEC World Series of Golf	T11	65	73	73	72		283 +3	71.27	69.912	26,400	26,400
9/01	Greater Milwaukee Open	CUT	74	68				142 -2	71.26	69.960		365
9/09	Hardee's Golf Classic	CUT	70	72				142 +2	71.26	69.988		
10/07	H.E.B. Texas Open	T37	68	69	66	71		274 -6	71.12	69.952	3,680	3,680

PAYNE STEWART

DATE	TOURNAMENT NAME	POS	ROUNDS 1ST	2ND	3RD	4TH	5TH	TOTAL SCORE	YEAR TO DATE SCORING AVG	PGA TOUR AVG	OFFICIAL MONEY	TOTAL MONEY
10/14	Las Vegas Invitational	T11	71	73	66	66	65	341 -19	70.95	69.970	26,650	26,750
10/20	Walt Disney World/Olds.	T21	68	70	61	76		275 -13	70.86	70.018	9,388	10,410
10/28	Nabisco Individual Comp.	3										68,000
10/28	Nabisco Championship	T25	77	71	73	70		291 +7	70.94	70.124	68,000	68,000
11/08*	Asahi Glass 4 Tours	DNS									42,500	44,225
												37,350

	NUMBER OF TIMES 1ST	2ND	3RD	TOP TEN	TOP 25	CUTS MADE	NUMBER OF TIMES CUT	DNQ	WD	DSQ	NO. OF EVENTS ENTERED	RANK	OFFICIAL MONEY	TOTAL MONEY
CAREER MONEY	2	2	1	8	16	22	4				26	3	976,282	1,029,348
4,582,988														

* Unofficial Money/Partial Round

DATE	TOURNAMENT NAME	POS	1ST	2ND	3RD	4TH	5TH	TOTAL SCORE	SCORING AVG	PGA TOUR AVG	OFFICIAL MONEY	TOTAL MONEY
1/06	Infiniti T of C	21	74	70	75	71		290 +2	72.50	73.032	14,000	14,135
1/10	Northern Telecom Open	CUT	78	72				150 +6	73.33	73.867		15,671
2/03	AT&T Pebble Beach	T20	69	71	74	71		285 -3	72.50	72.273	11,471	7,786
2/10	Bob Hope Chrysler Classic	T26	68	69	72	66	67	342 -18	71.13	71.876	7,486	42,133
4/21	MCI Heritage Golf Classic	T4	68	68	70	69		275 -9	70.63	71.074	41,333	17,500
4/28	Kmart Greater Greensboro	T17	69	69	70	73		281 -7	70.57	70.964	17,500	8,600
5/05	GTE Byron Nelson Golf Classic	T30	70	70	65	75		280 E	70.48	70.606	7,150	6,030
5/19	Memorial Tournament	T36	79	68	72	69		288 E	70.68	70.701	6,030	6,030
5/26	Southwestern Bell Colonial	CUT	72	71				143 +3	70.73	70.741		83
6/02	Kemper Open	T24	71	66	67	69		273 -11	70.46	70.596	7,567	7,567
6/09	Buick Classic	T17	72	71	69	69		281 -3	70.44	70.463	13,533	13,533
6/16	U.S. Open Championship	1	67	70	73	72		282 -6	70.44	70.212	235,000	235,000
7/22*	British Open Championship	T32	72	72	71	68		283	70.49	70.306		9,295
8/04	Buick Open	CUT	74	69				143 -1				
8/11	PGA Championship	T13	74	70	71	70		285 -3	70.55	70.256	24,000	24,000
8/25	NEC World Series of Golf	T16	73	77	68	67		285 +5	70.60	70.193	18,600	18,600
9/08	Canadian Open	T14	73	68	68	72		281 -7	70.58	70.180	16,500	16,500
10/16	Walt Disney World	T37	70	68	69	72		279 -9	70.52	70.252	4,400	4,400
10/27	Indep. Ins. Agent	T12	69	67	70	71		277 -11	70.45	70.251	15,200	15,300
11/03	The Tour Championship	T21	69	76	75	71		291 +7	70.58	70.324	37,200	38,447
12/01*	Skins Game	1										208,000

		NUMBER OF TIMES								NUMBER OF TIMES			
		1ST	2ND	3RD	TOP TEN	TOP 25			CUTS MADE	CUT	DNQ	WD	DSQ
CAREER MONEY		1			2	12			16	3			1
5,059,959													

	NO. OF EVENTS ENTERED	RANK	OFFICIAL MONEY	TOTAL MONEY
	19	31	476,971	702,580

* Unofficial Money/Partial Round

PAYNE STEWART

DATE	TOURNAMENT NAME	POS	ROUNDS					TOTAL SCORE	YEAR TO DATE		OFFICIAL MONEY	TOTAL MONEY
			1ST	2ND	3RD	4TH	5TH		SCORING AVG	PGA TOUR AVG		
1/26	Phoenix Open	T52	70	71	67	72		280 -4	70.00	70.929	2,265	2,265
2/02	AT&T Pebble Beach	T25	73	66	70	74		283 -5	70.38	70.783	8,044	8,044
3/08	Doral-Ryder Open	T37	71	69	73	70		283 -5	70.50	70.990	6,020	6,020
3/15	Honda Classic	CUT	69	75				144 E	70.71	71.160		675
3/22	Nestlé Invitational	CUT	75	75				150 +6	71.25	71.442		
3/29	The Players Championship	T13	69	70	72	70		281 -7	71.05	71.104	33,750	33,750
4/12	Masters Tournament	CUT	74	75				149 +5	71.36	71.424		1,500
4/19	MCI Heritage Golf Classic	T22	70	67	71	72		280 -4	71.15	71.151	10,000	11,005
4/26	Kmart Greater Greensboro	T36	70	73	73	70		286 -2	71.20	71.132	5,887	5,887
5/03	Shell Houston Open	CUT	73	72				145 +1	71.28	71.219		988
5/17	GTE Byron Nelson Golf Classic	T47	71	67	69			207 -3	71.09	71.051	2,791	4,041
5/24	Southwestern Bell	T34	70	68	71	68		277 -3	70.90	70.872	6,565	6,565
5/31	Kemper Open	T6	70	68	70	70		278 -6	70.77	70.624	34,430	34,685
6/07	Memorial Tournament	T3	72	70	66	66		274 -14	70.57	70.515	75,400	75,400
6/14	Federal Express St. Jude	T13	70	64	67	70		271 -13	70.35	70.406	18,288	18,663
6/21	U.S. Open Championship	T51	73	70	72	83		298 +10	70.65	70.476	6,370	6,370
7/05	Centel Western Open	T38	75	69	72	70		286 -2	70.71	70.522	4,400	4,400
7/19*	British Open Championship	T34	70	73	71	72		286 -2				11,520
8/16	PGA Championship	T69	76	69	79	72		296 +12	70.92	70.566	2,488	2,488
9/06	Greater Milwaukee Open	T6	68	72	67	67		274 -14	70.78	70.503	33,500	34,250
9/27	B.C. Open	T20	69	72	68	70		279 -5	70.72	70.428	9,653	9,653
10/04	Buick Southern Open	T39	72	73	71			216 E	70.77	70.450	2,523	2,631
10/18	Walt Disney World/Olds.	4	64	67	67	70		268 -20	70.58	70.394	48,000	49,050
10/25	H.E.B. Texas Open	T7	68	66	72	63		269 -15	70.41	70.297	24,364	24,473

PAYNE STEWART

1992

| DATE | TOURNAMENT NAME | POS | ROUNDS |||||| TOTAL SCORE | | YEAR TO DATE ||| OFFICIAL MONEY | TOTAL MONEY |
			1ST	2ND	3RD	4TH	5TH			SCORING AVG	PGA TOUR AVG			
11/15*	Franklin Funds Shark Shoot	T13												35,250
11/29*	Skins Game	1												176,000

| CAREER MONEY | NUMBER OF TIMES |||| CUTS MADE | NUMBER OF TIMES |||| NO. OF EVENTS ENTERED | RANK | OFFICIAL MONEY | TOTAL MONEY |
	1ST	2ND	3RD	TOP TEN	TOP 25		CUT	DNQ	WD	DSQ				
5,394,698			1	5	10	19	4				23	44	334,738	565,573

* Unofficial Money/Partial Round

PAYNE STEWART

DATE	TOURNAMENT NAME	POS	1ST	2ND	3RD	4TH	5TH	TOTAL SCORE	SCORING AVG	PGA TOUR AVG	OFFICIAL MONEY	TOTAL MONEY
1/17	United Airlines Hawaiian	CUT	74	71				145 +1	72.50	72.319		20,770
1/24	Northern Telecom Open	T13	71	70	68	68		277 -11	70.33	70.798	20,020	20,770
2/07	AT&T Pebble Beach	T9	72	70	71	70		283 -5	70.50	70.447	27,969	34,969
2/14	Bob Hope Chrysler Classic	T12	70	66	64	67	72	339 -21	69.60	70.458	20,271	20,596
2/21	Buick Invitational of California	3	72	66	75	70		283 -5	69.84	70.105	68,000	68,000
2/28	Nissan L.A. Open	T2	72	66	71			209 -4	69.82	69.842	66,000	66,700
3/07	Doral-Ryder Open	T16	74	67	69	68		278 -10	69.77	69.914	19,005	19,005
3/21	Nestlé Invitational	T35	75	70	76	71		292 +4	70.20	70.083	5,038	5,121
3/28	The Players Championship	T11	70	70	66	74		280 -8	70.18	70.081	53,000	54,250
4/04	Freeport-McMoRan Golf Classic	T2	70	70	73	69		282 -6	70.21	69.867	88,000	89,069
4/11	Masters Tournament	T9	74	70	72	69		285 -3	70.31	69.873	47,600	47,600
4/18	MCI Heritage Golf Classic	T33	65	70	72	77		284 E	70.37	69.870	6,216	8,016
5/02	Shell Houston Open	T3	66	68	66			200 -16	70.14	69.777	67,600	67,600
5/09	BellSouth Classic	T32	69	71	72	70		282 -6	70.17	69.858	6,640	6,734
5/16	GTE Byron Nelson Golf Classic	T5	70	66	68	68		272 -8	70.02	69.699	43,800	43,800
5/30	Southwestern Bell Colonial	DSQ	69	78*				147 +7	70.14	69.814		225
6/06	Memorial Tournament	3	69	66	67	74		276 -12	70.06	69.752	95,200	95,200
6/13	Buick Classic	T7	74	72	68	69		283 -1	70.10	69.660	31,167	31,917
6/20	U.S. Open	2	70	66	68	70		274 -6	70.01	69.481	145,000	145,000
7/04	Sprint Western Open	CUT	71	74				145 +1	70.08	69.550		
7/18*	British Open Championship	12	71	72	70	63		276				33,110
8/01	Federal Express St. Jude	T63	70	71	70	75		286 +2	70.16	69.656	2,343	2,343
8/08	Buick Open	T9	66	71	71	70		278 -10	70.12	69.657	27,000	27,017
8/15	PGA Championship	T44	71	70	70	73		284 E	70.16	69.686	4,607	4,607

PAYNE STEWART

| DATE | TOURNAMENT NAME | POS | ROUNDS | | | | | TOTAL SCORE | | YEAR TO DATE | | OFFICIAL MONEY | TOTAL MONEY |
			1ST	2ND	3RD	4TH	5TH			SCORING AVG	PGA TOUR AVG		
9/19	Hardee's Golf Classic	T2	66	68	67	65		266 -14		70.00	69.565	88,000	88,000
10/10	Walt Disney World/Oldsmobile	CUT	70	70	74			214 -2		70.04	69.695		528
10/31	The Tour Championship	26	74	72	73	73		292 +8		70.17	69.821	50,400	50,400
11/21*	Franklin Funds Shark Shoot	T9	66	68	64			198 -18					32,000
11/28*	Skins Game	1											280,000

| | NUMBER OF TIMES | | | | CUTS MADE | NUMBER OF TIMES | | | | NO. OF EVENTS ENTERED | RANK | OFFICIAL MONEY | TOTAL MONEY |
	1ST	2ND	3RD	TOP TEN	TOP 25		CUT	DNQ	WD	DSQ				
CAREER MONEY	4	3	12	16	22		3			1	26	6	982,875	1,342,577
6,377,573														

* Unofficial Money/Partial Round

PAYNE STEWART

DATE	TOURNAMENT NAME	POS	ROUNDS					TOTAL SCORE		YEAR TO DATE		OFFICIAL MONEY	TOTAL MONEY
			1ST	2ND	3RD	4TH	5TH			SCORING AVG	PGA TOUR AVG		
1/23	Northern Telecom Open	T42	70	67	71	72		281	-7	70.28	71.320	3,960	4,823
2/06	AT&T Pebble Beach	T57	68	73	73	77		291	+3	71.50	71.156	2,800	6,800
2/13	Nissan L.A. Open	T66	70	74	74	75		293	+9	72.08	71.320	2,070	2,070
2/20	Bob Hope Chrysler Classic	5	67	69	71	68	63	338	-22	70.76	70.770	44,000	44,133
2/27	Buick Invitational of California	T19	70	66	68	74		278	-10	70.52	70.691	13,332	13,332
3/20	Nestlé Invitational	T62	73	71	73	74		291	+3	70.88	70.973	2,592	2,592
3/27	The Players Championship	CUT	72	73				145	+1	71.00	71.091		
4/03	Freeport-McMoRan Classic	72	72	70	77	81		300	+12	71.52	71.497	2,352	2,420
4/10	Masters Tournament	CUT	78	78				156	+12	71.91	71.759		
5/15	GTE Byron Nelson Golf Classic	CUT	70	71				141	E	71.83	71.682		913
5/22	Memorial Tournament	CUT	78	74				152	+8	72.05	71.839		
6/05	Kemper Open	T57	73	68	72	75		288	+4	72.05	71.725	2,860	2,860
6/12	Buick Classic	T65	72	72	72	74		290	+6	72.09	71.730	2,508	2,508
6/19	U.S. Open Chanpionship	CUT	74	75				149	+7	72.19	71.707		1,000
6/26	Canon Greater Hartford	CUT	72	71				143	+3	72.16	71.649		
7/24	New England Classic	T64	70	70	75	70		285	+1	72.09	71.631	2,060	2,060
7/31	Federal Express St. Jude	T15	66	68	69	69		272	-12	71.81	71.441	20,625	20,625
8/14	PGA Championship	T66	72	73	72	74		291	+11	71.87	71.372	2,600	2,600
8/21	Sprint International	WD											
9/11	Bell Canadian Open	T10	68	72	72	69		281	-7	71.77	71.259	32,500	32,500
10/09	Walt Disney World/Oldsmobile	T24	69	70	69	70		278	-10	71.64	71.243	8,323	8,323
10/16	Texas Open	CUT	74	68				142	E	70.62	71.261		
10/23	Las Vegas Invitational	T65	70	69	69	71	73	352	-7	71.54	71.331	3,105	3,605
11/27*	Skins Game	T3											80,000

	NUMBER OF TIMES					NUMBER OF TIMES					NO. OF EVENTS ENTERED		RANK	OFFICIAL MONEY	TOTAL MONEY
	1ST	2ND	3RD	TOP TEN	TOP 25	CUTS MADE	CUT	DNQ	WD	DSQ					
CAREER MONEY				2	5	15	7		1		23		123	145,687	233,164
6,523,260															

* Unofficial Money/Partial Round

PAYNE STEWART

DATE	TOURNAMENT NAME	POS	1ST	2ND	3RD	4TH	5TH	TOTAL SCORE	SCORING AVG	PGA TOUR AVG	OFFICIAL MONEY	TOTAL MONEY
					ROUNDS				YEAR TO DATE			
1/22	Northern Telecom Open	CUT	73	73				146 +3	73.00	72.809		263
1/29	Phoenix Open	T4	71	68	67	66		272 -12	69.67	69.926	53,733	53,733
2/05	AT&T Pebble Beach	5	71	67	69	70		277 -11	69.50	69.686	56,000	56,000
2/12	Buick Invitational of Califronia	T16	66	73	67	72		278 -10	69.50	69.862	15,240	16,140
3/05	Doral-Ryder Open	76	68	74	76	74		292 +4	70.28	70.669	2,820	3,345
3/12	Honda Classic	CUT	72	74				146 +4	70.55	70.778		144
3/19	Nestlé Invitational	T31	69	70	73	72		284 -4	70.63	70.808	6,960	7,628
3/26	The Players Championship	T3	69	73	71	72		285 -3	70.71	70.535	156,000	156,000
4/09	Masters Tournament	T41	71	72	72	78		293 +5	71.03	70.808	8,567	8,567
4/16	MCI Classic	T24	70	66	70	74		280 -4	70.92	70.700	9,837	12,837
4/23	Kmart GGO	CUT	72	72				144 E	70.97	70.766		
4/30	Shell Houston Open	P1	73	65	70	68		276 -12	70.79	70.561	252,000	252,000
5/14	GTE Byron Nelson Golf Classic	T32	68	66	71	69		274 -6	70.59	70.418	6,746	7,846
5/28	Colonial National	T52	66	72	74	73		285 +5	70.64	70.393	3,248	3,248
6/04	Memorial Tournament	T59	70	75	71	71		287 -1	70.72	70.542	3,740	3,740
6/11	Kemper Open	T9	69	69	65	73		276 -8	70.60	70.420	35,000	35,000
6/18	U.S. Open Championship	T21	74	71	71	69		287 +7	70.68	70.284	20,085	20,085
7/02	FedEx St. Jude Classic	CUT	70	71				141 -1	70.67	70.318		
7/16	Anheuser-Busch Golf	T11	70	68	71	69		278 -6	70.60	70.247	21,843	22,476
7/23	British Open Championship	T11	72	68	75	71		286 -2	70.65	70.224	41,470	41,470
8/06	Buick Open	8	65	65	73	71		274 -14	70.54	70.201	37,200	37,200
8/13	PGA Championship	T13	69	70	69	67		275 -9	70.45	70.135	33,750	33,750
8/27	NEC World Series of Golf	T25	67	74	75	72		288 +8	70.52	70.125	17,100	17,100
9/10	Bell Canadian Open	CUT	73	76				149 +5	70.62	70.184		

PAYNE STEWART

| DATE | TOURNAMENT NAME | POS | ROUNDS | | | | | TOTAL SCORE | | YEAR TO DATE | | OFFICIAL MONEY | TOTAL MONEY |
			1ST	2ND	3RD	4TH	5TH			SCORING AVG	PGA TOUR AVG		
10/08	Walt Disney World/Oldsmobile	T28	70	64	71			205 -11		70.54	70.220	7,480	7,543
10/22	La Cantera Texas Open	T15	69	71	78	68		286 -2		70.58	70.215	16,500	16,850
10/29	The Tour Championship	T16	69	75	74	75		293 +13		70.69	70.230	60,900	61,314
12/10*	Diners Club Matches	T5											15,550

| | NUMBER OF TIMES | | | | | | NUMBER OF TIMES | | | | NO. OF EVENTS ENTERED | RANK | OFFICIAL MONEY | TOTAL MONEY |
	1ST	2ND	3RD	TOP TEN	TOP 25	CUTS MADE	CUT	DNQ	WD	DSQ				
CAREER MONEY	1		1	6	15	22	5				27	12	866,219	889,829
7,389,479														

PAYNE STEWART

DATE	TOURNAMENT NAME	POS	1ST	2ND	3RD	4TH	5TH	TOTAL SCORE	SCORING AVG	PGA TOUR AVG	OFFICIAL MONEY	TOTAL MONEY
1/07	Mercedes Championships	T12	74	69	71	68		282 -6	70.50	71.525	24,750	24,990
1/21	Bob Hope Chrysler Classic	T4	71	65	71	63	70	340 -20	69.11	70.644	53,733	54,483
1/27	Phoenix Open	T35	68	71	71	68		278 -6	69.23	70.487	6,273	6,273
2/04	AT&T Pebble Beach	CUT	72	72				144 E				5,000
2/11	Buick Invitational	T35	68	68	71	73		280 -8	69.41	70.644	5,298	5,298
3/10	Honda Classic	T3	70	70	68	68		276 -12	69.33	70.211	67,600	67,600
3/17	Bay Hill Invitational	CUT	73	77				150 +6	69.83	70.565		462
3/24	Freeport-McDermott Classic	T4	74	71	67	71		283 -5	69.96	70.377	43,500	46,583
3/31	The Players Championship	T41	73	70	68	71		282 -6	70.03	70.495	12,950	12,950
4/14	Masters Tournament	CUT	74	76				150 +6	70.33	70.651		
4/21	MCI Classic	CUT	72	73				145 +3	70.46	70.774		
5/05	Shell Houston Open	T9	72	70	69	70		281 -7	70.44	70.670	37,500	42,500
5/12	GTE Byron Nelson Golf Classic	CUT	72	69				141 +1	70.44	70.639		
5/19	MasterCard Colonial	T6	69	69	72	68		278 -2	70.36	70.382	48,563	49,525
5/26	Kemper Open	T10	70	67	68	72		277 -7	70.27	70.237	37,500	38,250
6/02	Memorial Tournament	T21	68	70	75	72		285 -3	70.34	70.280	18,720	18,720
6/16	U.S. Open Championship	T27	67	71	76	73		287 +7	70.44	70.164	17,809	17,809
7/07	Motorola Western Open	T26	70	70	68	75		283 -5	70.46	70.205	13,611	14,442
7/21	British Open Championship	T44	70	73	71	71		285 +1	70.51	70.221	9,920	9,920
8/04	Buick Open	CUT	75	68				143 -1	70.54	70.286		275
8/11	PGA Championship	T69	73	70	73	76		292 +4	70.68	70.411	3,813	3,813
9/01	Greater Milwaukee Open	76	67	72	70	72		281 -3	70.65	70.490	2,256	2,481
9/08	Bell Canadian Open	WD	78					78 +6	70.75	70.592		
9/29	Buick Challenge	CUT	75	70				145 +1	70.79	70.650		88

PAYNE STEWART

DATE	TOURNAMENT NAME	POS	ROUNDS					TOTAL SCORE
			1ST	2ND	3RD	4TH	5TH	
10/06	Las Vegas Invitational	T50	63	68	73	74	67	345 -14
10/20	Walt Disney World/Oldsmobile	2	68	63	70	67		268 -20
11/03*	Sarazen World Open Championship	T3	69	68	71	70		278 -10

	YEAR TO DATE		OFFICIAL MONEY	TOTAL MONEY
	SCORING AVG	PGA TOUR AVG		
	70.69	70.699	3,898	4,098
	70.52	70.640	129,600	130,000
			99,000	99,775

	NUMBER OF TIMES					NUMBER OF TIMES				NO. OF EVENTS ENTERED			OFFICIAL MONEY	TOTAL MONEY
	1ST	2ND	3RD	TOP TEN	TOP 25	CUTS MADE	CUT	DNQ	WD	DSQ		RANK		
		1	1	7	9	18	6		1		25		537,293	655,335

CAREER MONEY							
7,926,773							

* Unofficial Money/Partial Round

PAYNE STEWART

1997

DATE	TOURNAMENT NAME	POS	ROUNDS 1ST	2ND	3RD	4TH	5TH	TOTAL SCORE	YEAR TO DATE SCORING AVG	PGA TOUR AVG	OFFICIAL MONEY	TOTAL MONEY
2/23	Tucson Chrysler Classic	T35	74	70	70	70		284 -4	71.00	71.060	6,409	6,409
3/02	Nissan Open	T9	65	72	72	70		279 -5	70.38	70.072	31,325	33,908
3/16	Honda Classic	T2	68	68	68	71		275 -13	69.83	68.651	132,000	133,025
3/23	Bay Hill Invitational	T3	69	70	70	67		276 -12	69.63	69.561	78,000	78,000
3/30	The Players Championship	CUT	69	78				147 +3	70.06	69.880		
4/06	Freeport-McDermott Classic	T48	69	73	69	76		287 -1	70.36	70.186	3,870	6,120
4/20	MCI Classic	T30	71	72	72	71		286 +2	70.54	70.224	8,013	8,031
5/04	Shell Houston Open	62	74	72	76	72		294 +6	70.93	70.513	3,456	7,456
5/11	BellSouth Classic	T34	75	66	72	73		286 -2	71.00	70.562	7,256	7,256
5/18	GTE Byron Nelson Golf Classic	T30	69	68	65	70		273 -7	70.71	70.354	11,700	12,281
5/25	MasterCard Colonial	T48	68	66	68	77		279 -1	70.62	70.322	4,021	4,646
6/01	Memorial Tournament	CUT	76	72				148 +4	70.77	70.481		
6/15	U.S. Open Championship	T28	71	73	73	71		288 +8	70.88	70.307	17,443	17,443
6/29	FedEx St. Jude Classic	T36	73	63	73	69		278 -6	70.77	70.375	7,375	7,375
7/06	Motorola Western Open	CUT	76	74				150 +6	70.93	70.421		33
7/20	British Open Championship	59	73	74	71	74		292 +8	71.07	70.469	9,718	9,718
8/11	Buick Open	T11	72	65	72	70		279 -9	70.98	70.432	33,000	33,000
8/17	PGA Championship	T29	70	70	72	74		286 +6	71.02	70.318	13,625	13,625
8/24	Greater Vancouver Open	T6	64	68	68	71		271 -13	70.83	70.217	45,375	45,375
9/07	Bell Canadian Open	T8	66	72	72	70		280 E	70.78	70.066	43,500	43,500
10/12	Michelob Championship	T9	68	70	70	69		277 -7	70.71	69.997	43,400	43,400
10/19	Walt Disney World/Oldsmobile	T10	64	67	70	75		276 -12	70.62	70.010	32,143	33,710
10/26	Las Vegas Invitational	T40	70	66	75	74	71	356 -4	70.66	70.072	6,660	6,660
11/09*	Sarazen World Open Championship	55	74	73	76	78		301 +13			5,800	5,940

		NUMBER OF TIMES					NUMBER OF TIMES					NO. OF EVENTS ENTERED
		1ST	2ND	3RD	TOP TEN	TOP 25	CUTS MADE	CUT	DNQ	WD	DSQ	
CAREER MONEY			1	1	7	8	20	3				23
8,465,062												

	RANK	OFFICIAL MONEY	TOTAL MONEY
	40	538,289	556,911

* Unofficial Money/Partial Round

PAYNE STEWART

DATE	TOURNAMENT NAME	POS	ROUNDS					TOTAL SCORE	YEAR TO DATE		OFFICIAL MONEY	TOTAL MONEY
			1ST	2ND	3RD	4TH	5TH		SCORING AVG	PGA TOUR AVG		
2/01	AT&T Pebble Beach	T19	71	70	67			208 -8	69.33	69.917	32,500	32,500
2/08	Buick Invitational	T22	66	72	71			209 -7	69.50	70.112	20,160	20,160
2/22	Tucson Chrysler Classic	T18	69	70	70	70		279 -9	69.60	70.225	27,000	27,000
3/01	Nissan Open	T4	70	67	69	70		276 -8	69.43	69.533	92,400	92,400
3/15	Honda Classic	T52	76	66	71	72		285 -3	69.83	70.044	4,198	4,198
3/22	Bay Hill Invitational	T65	71	75				146 +2	70.15	70.270	4,000	4,000
3/29	The Players Championship	T8	72	71	75	65		283 -5	70.25	70.126	116,000	116,000
4/19	MCI Classic	T3	69	71	64	72		276 -8	70.07	69.848	110,200	112,807
5/03	Shell Houston Open	T53	71	74	74	71		290 +2	70.38	70.094	4,587	8,658
5/17	GTE Byron Nelson Golf Classic	T19	68	67	68	71		274 -6	70.17	69.934	29,250	31,750
5/24	MasterCard Colonial	T18	68	72	66	70		276 -4	70.05	69.820	24,485	24,485
5/31	Memorial Tournament	71	67	72	74	83		296 +8	70.41	70.228	4,356	4,356
6/21	U.S. Open Championship	2	66	71	70	74		281 +1	70.40	69.870	315,000	315,000
6/28	Motorola Western Open	T57	72	74	69	76		291 +3	70.58	70.038	4,840	5,125
7/19	British Open Championship	T44	71	71	78	75		295 +15	70.80	69.995	12,471	12,471
8/16	PGA Championship	CUT	76	74				150 +10	70.95	70.058		
8/30	Greater Vancouver Open	2	64	69	65	70		268 -16	70.69	69.876	216,000	216,000
10/04	Buick Challenge	T14	70	71	71	67		275 -13	70.58	69.889	24,750	24,750
10/11	Michelob Championship	T4	70	70	67	69		273 -11	70.44	69.758	83,600	83,600
10/25	National Car at Disney	CUT	76	70				146 +2	70.51	69.842		
11/01	The Tour Championship	T24	69	72	76	74		291 +11	70.63	69.931	68,200	68,200
11/08*	Sarazen World Open Championship	T37	71	75	74	74		294				9,750

	NUMBER OF TIMES					CUTS MADE	NUMBER OF TIMES			
	1ST	2ND	3RD	TOP TEN	TOP 25		CUT	DNQ	WD	DSQ
		2	1	6	13	19	2			

CAREER MONEY	NO. OF EVENTS ENTERED	RANK	OFFICIAL MONEY	TOTAL MONEY
9,659,058	21	19	1,193,996	1,213,210

* Unofficial Money/Partial Round

PAYNE STEWART

1999

DATE	TOURNAMENT NAME	POS	ROUNDS 1ST	2ND	3RD	4TH	5TH	TOTAL SCORE	YEAR TO DATE SCORING AVG	PGA TOUR AVG	OFFICIAL MONEY	TOTAL MONEY
1/24	Bob Hope Chrysler Classic	T18	71	70	66	71	67	345 -15	69.00	70.116	42,000	44,383
1/31	Phoenix Open	T18	69	73	75	68		285 +1	70.00	69.719	40,500	40,500
2/07	AT&T Pebble Beach	1	69	64	73			206 -10	69.67	68.987	504,000	507,033
2/21	Nissan Open	CUT	72	73				145 +3	70.07	69.457		2,000
2/28	WGC Andersen Consulting	T33									25,000	25,000
3/14	Honda Classic	2	70	67	72	70		279 -9	70.00	69.368	280,800	280,800
3/21	Bay Hill Invitational	T13	75	65	68	74		282 -6	70.09	69.507	48,333	48,333
3/28	The Players Championship	T23	72	70	74	78		294 +6	70.62	69.673	40,167	40,167
4/11	Masters Tournament	T52	73	75	77	75		300 +12	71.20	70.138	9,980	9,980
4/18	MCI Classic	P2	68	64	72	70		274 -10	70.88	69.881	220,000	222,625
5/02	Shell Houston Open	T60	74	70	72	76		292 +4	71.11	70.092	5,425	5,425
5/09	Compaq Classic of New Orleans	CUT	74	70				144 E	71.15	70.228		
6/06	Memorial Tournament	T24	75	65	73	72		285 -3	71.16	70.271	20,181	20,181
6/13	FedEx St. Jude Classic	CUT	73	69				142 E	71.15	70.361		4,500
6/20	U.S. Open Championship	1	68	69	72	70		279 -1	71.04	69.928	625,000	625,000
7/18	British Open Championship	T30	79	73	74	74		300 +16			18,056	18,056
8/15	PGA Championship	T57	75	71	75	74		295 +7	71.50	70.064	7,175	7,175
8/29	WGC NEC Invitational	T15	70	67	69	75		281 +1	71.42	70.030	88,000	88,000
9/05	Air Canada Championship	T4	68	67	69	68		272 -12	71.21	69.898	103,333	103,333
10/24	National Car at Disney	CUT	71	71				142 -2	71.21	69.982		667
10/31	The Tour Championship	DNS									80,000	80,000
11/07	WGC American Express	DNS										25,000

CAREER MONEY	NUMBER OF TIMES 1ST	2ND	3RD	TOP TEN	TOP 25	CUTS MADE	NUMBER OF TIMES CUT	DNQ	WD	DSQ	NO. OF EVENTS ENTERED
11,737,008	2	2		5	11	16	4				20

RANK	OFFICIAL MONEY	TOTAL MONEY
7	2,077,950	2,198,158

* Unofficial Money/Partial Round

Payne Stewart's Ryder Cup Record

1987 — Europe 15, USA 13

Muirfield Village Golf Club, Dublin, Ohio

Foursomes: Seve Ballesteros/José María Olazábal def.
Payne Stewart/Larry Nelson, 1 up

Foursomes: Seve Ballesteros/José María Olazábal def.
Payne Stewart/Ben Crenshaw, 1 up

Four-ball: Payne Stewart/Andy Bean def.
Eamonn Darcy/Gordon Brand Jr., 3 and 2

Singles: Payne Stewart def. José María Olazábal, 2 up

1989 — Europe 14, USA 14 (Europe retains Cup)

The Belfry, Sutton Coldfield, England

Foursomes: Payne Stewart/Lanny Wadkins def.
Howard Clark/Mark James, 1 up

Foursomes: Ian Woosnam/Nick Faldo def.
Payne Stewart/Larry Wadkins, 3 and 2

Four-ball: Howard Clark/Mark James def.
Payne Stewart/Curtis Strange, 1 up

Singles: José María Olazábal def. Payne Stewart, 1 up

1991 — USA 14½, Europe 13½

The Ocean Course, Kiawah Island, South Carolina

Foursomes: Payne Stewart/Mark Calcavecchia def.
Nick Faldo/Ian Woosnam, 1 up

Foursomes: Payne Stewart/Mark Calcavecchia def.
Mark James/Steven Richardson, 1 up

Four-ball: Payne Stewart/Fred Couples vs.
Seve Ballesteros/José María Olazábal, halved

Singles: David Feherty def. Payne Stewart, 2 and 1

1993 — USA 15, Europe 13
The Belfry, Sutton Coldfield, England

Foursomes: Ian Woosnam/Bernhard Langer def.
Payne Stewart/Fred Couples, 7 and 5

Foursomes: Payne Stewart/Ray Floyd def.
Peter Baker/Barry Lane, 3 and 2

Four-ball: Payne Stewart/Ray Floyd def.
José María Olazábal/Joakim Haeggman, 2 and 1

Singles: Payne Stewart def. Mark James, 3 and 2

1999 — USA 14½, Europe 13½
The Country Club, Brookline, Massachusetts

Four-ball: Payne Stewart/Davis Love III vs.
Miguel Angel Jimenez/Padraig Harrington, halved

Four-ball: Sergio Garcia/Jesper Parnevik def.
Payne Stewart/Justin Leonard, 3 and 2

Singles: Colin Montgomerie def. Payne Stewart, 1 up

**Stewart's cumulative Ryder record:
5 years, 19 matches, 8-9-2 overall, 2-3 singles**